The Zero-Waste Lifestyle

THE
ZERO-WASTE
LIFESTYLE

Live Well by
Throwing Away Less

AMY KORST

TEN SPEED PRESS
Berkeley

To my husband, Adam, for walking alongside me on the beach, in the mountains, and through this journey we call life.

Library of Congress Cataloging-in-Publication Data
Korst, Amy, 1984-
   The zero-waste lifestyle : live well by throwing away less / Amy Korst. — First edition.
      pages cm
1. Sustainable living. 2. Green movement. 3. Consumer education. I. Title.
   GE196.K67 2012
   640.28'6—dc23

                       2012027296

ISBN 978-1-60774-348-4
eISBN 978-1-60774-349-1

Printed in the United States of America using vegetable-based inks on 100 percent post-consumer fiber. The use of this recycled paper has saved 64 trees, more than 62,000 gallons of water, nearly 8,000 pounds of waste, more than 20,000 pounds of carbon dioxide (emissions of 3 cars for a year), 100 MMBTU (nearly 500,000 light bulbs for an hour), and 61 pounds of nitrogen oxides (emissions of a truck for 86 days).

Design by Chloe Rawlins

10 9 8 7 6 5 4 3 2 1

First Edition

Contents

Acknowledgments   vii

Foreword by Bill McKibben   ix

Introduction: Trash, Trash, Everywhere   1

PART 1: GETTING STARTED   13

1   A Trashed Planet   14

2   Planning to Go Waste Free   21

3   Reduce and Reuse   46

4   Recycle   64

5   Organic Waste   89

PART 2: TRASH-FREE CHALLENGES   105

6   The Zero-Waste Kitchen   106

7   The Zero-Waste Bathroom   132

8   The Zero-Waste Bedroom   155

9   Zero-Waste Cleaning   162

10   Zero-Waste Kids   171

11   Zero-Waste Travel   183

12   The Zero-Waste Workplace   201

13   Zero-Waste Holidays and Special Occasions   207

PART 3: NEXT STEPS   229

14   The Global Zero-Waste Movement   230

Epilogue   241

An A-to-Z Guide to Recycling (Just About) Anything   248

Further Reading   253

Bibliography   255

About the Author   257

Index   258

Acknowledgments

Truly, it takes a village to raise a book from infancy to the grown-up product you're holding today. I'd like to thank my personal village for believing in this project, including:

My agent, Jeff Kleinman—who saw potential in this book and who helped my writing more than anyone ever has—as well as the entire team at Folio Literary Agency.

My editor, Julie Bennett, for taking a chance on a project about trash, and all the talented folks at Ten Speed Press, including the hard-working publicity and marketing team: Patricia Kelly, Michele Crim, Kara Van de Water, and Ashley Matuszak. Your work to spread the zero-waste message never ceases to amaze me; I appreciate you.

The Salem-Keizer Master Recycler Program, for teaching me the ins and outs of recycling.

Zero-waste contributors and their families—April Luebbert, Rose Brown, Chris Burger, Joe Barnes, Desira Fuqua, and Robert Haley—for opening up your lives to me and dealing with lots of phone calls, emails, and paperwork.

My readers at www.greengarbageproject.com and my Facebook fans, for a network of support.

The Korst, Bowden, and Fiala families, for wrapping our Christmas gifts in, variously, towels, fabric, newspaper, aviation maps, comic strips, and baskets, just so you didn't add to our garbage tally.

Taylor and Hunter, for spending a week with Aunt Amy and Uncle Adam and dealing with us while we were still getting this whole zero-waste thing figured out.

Mom and Dad, for telling me I can do anything.

Steve and Carol, Joey and Ashley, for support and laughter.

And finally, my husband, Adam, without whom none of this would have happened.

Foreword

Once a year I volunteer to run the biweekly trash and recycling day in our small Vermont town. For three hours on Saturday morning, people show up in station wagons and pickups, all groaning with sacks of garbage, and with cans, bottles, papers, all carefully separated out. My main thought, every time, is: how does this tiny town (500 people) manage to generate quite so much trash? Because, man, there's a lot—last time, by the end of the three hours, I was stomping the recycling bin like a vintner in the grape vat, just trying to make room for the last few carloads.

I'm, of course, as guilty as most. I may not generate as much trash as some Americans, but compared to parts of the poor world where I've spent lots of time, I'm a wastrel of the first order. And compared to Amy Korst, author of this book—well, there's no comparison. She's pared down her waste to the vanishing point, which is an admirable act, and she's willing to share her secrets, which is even more admirable. There's no way to read this book without absorbing lots of good ideas about how you might change your life.

If you follow this advice, you'll be helping the planet. But I'd be remiss if I didn't add that we also need you to do more. The fight against scourges like climate change must be fought on the local front, as Korst advises, and also nationally and internationally, by building the movements that can change some of the structures that lead to waste and carelessness. In the end, we need Exxon and Chevron to be zero waste too.

This book is a great gift. Don't feel guilty reading it, and don't obsess about the truly tiny things (the foil cap under the plastic lid on the ketchup bottle); feel grateful for all the good advice, and take as much of it as you possibly can!

—Bill McKibben

Introduction:
Trash, Trash, Everywhere

Everybody has a trash can. In fact, it's a safe bet that we all have multiple trash cans crowding our lives—in the bathroom, in the car, under the kitchen sink, and in the garage.

Before I started living trash free with my husband, Adam, we had all of the above in our house, for a total of five trash cans at our instant disposal. One day, while out running errands I counted how many trash cans I came in contact with in public restrooms, restaurants, movie theaters, and stores: thirty-two! I couldn't believe it. Then I heard a statistic that still troubles me: the average American produces three pounds of landfill-bound garbage each day. I started seeing trash everywhere, especially in places it doesn't belong, like littering the sides of the road and all over the wilderness where we went hiking and camping. I watched the trash pile up in our five garbage cans, and I hauled a full 32-gallon can to the curb each week. We tried hard to be green, so I didn't understand how we could be responsible for creating so much trash. Where did it all come from?

I decided to take a closer look at our country's trash habits, and the more I dug, the dirtier things appeared to be. Although these piles of trash we each produce every year are stinky and unsightly, the problem is much worse than that—for our environment and our health. Trash is intimately connected to every environmental problem we face today, from climate change and habitat destruction to water pollution and chemical exposure. It's also intensely personal and impacts every decision in our daily lives, including everything from how much money we spend to how much weight we gain.

Facing My Trash Addiction

When I first faced these facts, I couldn't believe how something as innocuous as our garbage could be negatively connected to so many of my personal and political concerns, but the facts were undeniable—if I wanted to change the country's trash addiction, I had to address my own trash problem first. But how?

I had heard about people in other parts of the world living "trash free," which basically means sending nothing to the landfill—ever. I wondered if the same could be done here in the United States, in a country where people produce more trash than anywhere else in the world.

One night, after scraping dinner leftovers into the trash can, something inside me snapped. I had spent all week agonizing over every item I threw away, from tiny metal paper clips to empty deodorant containers.

Tentatively I broached the subject with Adam.

"Remember last weekend when my parents were here?"

"Yeah." He was looking at his computer, distracted.

"We were joking about living trash free for a whole year? I think I want to do it."

This got his attention. He looked at me, eyebrows raised. He studied my face to see whether I was serious. I was afraid I had gone too far around the environmental bend even for my liberal husband.

"Okay," he said. And he went back to work.

"Okay? That's the whole conversation? Just 'okay'?"

He turned back to me. "Look, I've been thinking about it all week, too. It feels like it's time we do something big for the environment, put our money where our mouths are. If you want to do it, I'm on board."

With that, we decided to attempt trash-free living. The Green Garbage Project was born.

Getting to Zero Waste

Ten years ago, if you'd told me that I would dedicate most of my free time to garbage, I would have called you crazy. Like everyone else, I find garbage to be stinky, smelly, and generally disgusting. Unlike most people, I also find it fascinating.

Today, whereas most Americans produce about three pounds of landfill-bound trash each day, over the course of our entire Green Garbage Project *year*, Adam and I managed to produce less than three pounds of such trash between us. We found that, although to most people this seems to be an incredible feat, garbage-free living isn't hard at all. After that first trash-free year, we decided to make our zero-waste lifestyle a permanent way of life.

Today I spend most of my spare time thinking about trash, reading about trash, writing about trash, or sorting through my own trash. I now know more about trash than I ever really wanted to know. (For instance, did you know that bubble wrap, which was originally designed to be wallpaper, can be recycled if all the bubbles are popped?)

Mostly I'm passionate about trash because it can help anyone get involved in saving the planet. Trash is something we all make, and it's downright easy to start reducing what goes into your garbage can.

So What Exactly Does "Trash Free" Mean?

Trash-free living means different things to different people, as you'll see throughout this book. For some families, a trash-less life might mean moving from filling a giant, 64-gallon garbage can a week to filling a 32-gallon garbage can once a month. To others, it might mean a small grocery sack of garbage a week. To still others, going trash free means sending absolutely nothing to the landfill at all.

I fall into this last category. For the year of our Green Garbage Project, Adam and I tried to make absolutely no garbage. We came awfully close to our goal—by the end of the year, all our trash fit inside a regular shoebox. Surprisingly, we found that once we had a system in place for purchasing goods and recycling packaging, trash-free living became second nature.

So, whether you're interested in moderate or extreme trash reduction, whether you want to simply pare down your army of trash cans or try to produce zero garbage in a year, I can show you how to do it.

Benefits of a Trash-free Life

Although the obvious benefits of producing no garbage are environmental, they don't stop there. In addition to reducing your impact on the planet, here are some other benefits of your new zero-waste lifestyle:

Your life just got a whole lot simpler: We all wish we had a little more time in the day. Trash-free living helps streamline many areas of your life, from grocery shopping to cleaning the house. You'll learn to repurpose everyday products like baking soda and lemon juice to do double duty, in the kitchen and in the cleaning bucket. You'll spend less time at the store and more time at home with family and friends.

You will spend less money and be happier with your purchases: When I started paying attention to my purchases, I realized I was buying a lot of things I wanted but didn't need. Going trash-free means becoming much more conscientious about your purchases. You'll deliberately buy items that can serve dual purposes, and you'll look for durable goods that last a long time before breaking.

ONE YEAR OF TRASH

During the first twelve months of our zero-waste lifestyle, this is the trash the two of us created:

- Broken dog squeaky toy, run over by lawn mower
- Severed bungee cords
- One lightbulb
- Broken Christmas ornament
- Ear plugs
- Two pens and a highlighter
- Eight razor blades for a Gillette Sensor Excel razor
- Two toothbrush heads for battery-powered toothbrush
- Birth control pill packaging: twelve plastic wrappers, twelve plastic cases, and twelve plastic-foil pill packs
- Flea medicine packaging
- One hospital bracelet
- Two Theraflu pouches
- One insect-sting relief pad
- Seals from contact lens blister packs
- Various pill blister packs
- One Styrofoam cup from Teacher Appreciation Week, given to me as a gift
- Popped balloons, given to us as a gift
- Two pieces of wrapping paper
- Cut-flower preservative powder
- Plastic tag
- Two pairs of latex gloves
- Two Crackerjack liners
- Fourteen seals from medicine jars or condiment bottles
- Big ball of plastic and tape
- Plastic mailer
- Flat packing foam
- Odds and ends—tags from clothing, a plastic tag from a bundle of radishes, two suction cups from the bottom of our bath mat

You will support local businesses: Shopping locally benefits the environment, because goods are not trucked all over the country for consumption. Equally important is the impact you can have on your local community when you support family-owned establishments instead of big corporations. Studies show that "three times as much money stays in the local economy when you buy goods and services from locally owned businesses instead of large chain stores," according to the Institute for Local Self-Reliance.

You will eat healthier: And if you pair that with some good exercise, you'll lose weight and feel better. Cutting out garbage means eating more whole foods that don't come overpackaged in plastic. You'll shop the periphery of the grocery store and frequent local farmers' markets, buying good-for-you foods like fruits and veggies and locally sourced meat, dairy, and eggs.

You'll be doing your part to preserve the planet for future generations: It's no secret the earth is in trouble. Landfills are overflowing, our water systems are becoming polluted, animal species are becoming endangered and going extinct at an alarming rate, and we are finding toxic chemicals in our food and beauty products. This book will show you how trash is connected to each of these environmental problems and more. Every time you choose sustainable over throwaway, you're doing your part to eliminate these problems.

Your efforts will help beautify natural areas and decrease littering: Have you ever been hiking in the wilderness or making a sandcastle at the beach, only to have a piece of garbage flutter across your path? Seen someone toss a cigarette butt out the car window? The less garbage we make collectively, the less litter there will be to spoil nature's beauty.

You will reduce your exposure to toxic chemicals and artificial colors and sweeteners: A garbage-free life means you'll choose healthier options than the prepackaged, processed foods that line the grocery store shelves. We know food-like substances like Pop-Tarts and Cheetos aren't good for us—avoiding the garbage is just one more reason to look for healthier alternatives.

You'll become more self-sufficient: One of the most enjoyable parts of a garbage-free life is learning some skills our culture has all but forgotten. Pretty much anything store-bought can be made at home, if you have the time and interest. This book includes simple recipes for everyday products like English muffins and all-purpose cleaning spray as well as advanced recipes for ricotta cheese and bagels, among others.

For these reasons and more, people across the country—and around the world—are already living trash free. All of us are devoted to the lifestyle because we've found it to be easy and rewarding. As with any new experience, Adam and I encountered some pitfalls along the way, but we have learned from our mistakes and are here to offer our stories to help you transition into this wonderful lifestyle more easily.

One thing you'll discover is that living trash free has its regional variations and challenges, because each part of the country has different programs established for recycling, composting, and bulk food shopping. You'll discover, too, that each family circumstance presents its own set of unique challenges when working toward a trash-free lifestyle. This book gives you strategies for finding and using the systems established in your area. Whatever your particular circumstances or challenges are, you will find that adopting a zero-waste lifestyle is doable—and infinitely rewarding.

Introducing the Zero-Waste Contributors

As I was writing this book, I enlisted the advice of my fellow trash-free citizens, several of whom I connected with during my first trash-free year. The zero-waste lifestyle is still new enough that it's nice to have a community of friends with whom to share tips and troubleshoot common problems. You'll hear their stories throughout; look for the sidebars in each chapter labeled "Trash-Free Tip" for advice from the trenches. Together we represent an array of different lifestyles. Compiled here together, we demonstrate that garbage-free living is an attainable goal no matter who you are, where you live, how much money you make, or how much (or little) effort you'd like to expend to adopt this lifestyle.

Allow me to introduce you to the book's zero-waste contributors. Included in each bio is a list of the trashy items each family struggles to eliminate from their lives completely.

April Luebbert, Bellevue, Washington: April lives with her husband and their two young children in an upscale suburb of Seattle. April is a stay-at-home mom while her husband works for Microsoft. The Luebbert family became trash free in May 2011 after April was inspired by another trash-free family featured on an Earth Day TV news segment. She says, "I saw a video on a zero-waste home and loved the way the home looked and how healthy they were." The Luebberts live in a small apartment, which poses a number of trash-related obstacles, including setting up a composting system that works in a confined space.

April set up the blog www.trashfreeliving.blogspot.com to chronicle her family's challenges and discoveries as they adopted this new lifestyle. Several months into their new lifestyle, the four members of the Luebbert family were producing about one 32-gallon bag of trash every two weeks, whereas previously they produced about double that amount.

A self-described shopping fanatic, April recalls that before making the garbage-free switch, she used to buy something on eBay every day. She also created a lot of trash. "I was probably the worst. I didn't donate or recycle. I just tossed it," she says. Now she's saving money by cutting back on groceries and online shopping, and she's proud of the way she's decluttered her family's life, allowing them to focus less on material things and more on each other.

Trash she can't avoid: Baby diapers and pull-ups, especially for her oldest child; meat bones/scraps and packaging for other protein items that are part of her current diet.

Rose Brown, Charlottesville, Virginia: Rose Brown lives in a rented house with a dog and two cats. She works as the program manager for a nonprofit organization called Stream Watch. Rose's interest in living without creating trash grew from her work to protect the environment, particularly the river and stream systems flowing through her own town. She made the decision to give up garbage in January 2009, and so far she has produced one small plastic bag of trash each year—an impressive feat.

"On the personal-life level, I can't say enough about how it's improved my life," she says, explaining how her life has changed since she stopped making garbage. "I'm a happier person now. It's hard to explain to someone who hasn't tried it. I want everyone to feel this free and weightless and simple."

Rose also writes a blog at zerogarbagechallenge.info, where she posts an array of tips anyone can use to reduce their trash output. Unlike April Luebbert, Rose relies on online shopping as a way to reduce her garbage, shopping in particular at Etsy.com, an online craft site, because she is able to request that crafters package their homemade, natural products in recyclable materials. She also buys used products at Craigslist.org.

Her advice to beginners: "I focus a lot on keeping it fun, like an adventure. 'Oh, I want that, but I can't recycle it—how do I avoid the garbage?'"

Trash she can't avoid: Packaging for pet food and treats; little pieces of plastic.

Robert Haley, San Francisco, California: Serving as San Francisco's Zero Waste Manager, Robert lives by himself on a sailboat in Sausalito. His interest in the zero-waste movement started as a child, when he collected cans for money. Hooked on recycling at an early age, he later helped college friends establish a recycling nonprofit. Over time, he found himself pursuing careers in the waste reduction field and wasting less and less in his personal life until he reached the level of producing virtually no waste at all. After years of practicing this lifestyle, he creates only a literal handful of garbage a week and a small paper bag filled with recyclables.

Robert's job focuses on the bigger picture of waste reduction, so although he's achieved zero waste in his own life, he also advocates for waste reduction at a corporate or producer level. The ultimate goal is to get manufacturers to make products that, when they are no longer needed, can be deconstructed and either reused or completely recycled.

Trash he can't avoid: Dental floss, occasional food packaging. "Sometimes I have a spike in trash," he says, "mostly when I have to do some work on the sailboat."

Desira Fuqua, Rutherford, Tennessee: Desira Fuqua is married with no children. She and her husband own their home in the suburbs and live with two indoor dogs and some fish. She produces roughly one curbside bin of garbage every six months. She describes herself as a hippie and says that as such, "Recycling is a no-brainer. It becomes like a game; it's fun to get better and better." The hardest part about living zero waste, she says, is just getting started. And she adds, "You have to be willing to be a little weird sometimes."

Trash she can't avoid: Deodorant containers, occasional junk food wrappers, toothpaste tubes, safety seals, and medicine foil packets.

Chris Burger, Whitney Point, New York: Chris Burger and his wife are empty-nesters at just over sixty years old. Chris has two grown children, and he lives with his wife in a house in the country, about eighteen miles from the nearest metro area. He started deliberately reducing his trash on Earth

Day in 1970. Since then, this family of four waste-busters has so drastically reduced their trash that it took them fifteen years to fill a paper bag with garbage. Today Chris writes computer software and is cochair of the Sierra Club's Zero Waste Task Force. He is living proof of the permanence of this lifestyle and the viability of raising kids in a zero-waste household.

When his concern for the environment first began, Chris says he and his wife asked themselves, "What's our role here? What can we do as individuals? It seemed pretty evident to us that our biggest impact on the environment is the waste that we produce and the energy we use."

Today Chris is approaching his twentieth anniversary of the last time he visited the dump. His biggest piece of advice for those new to the lifestyle? "You make it convenient for yourself, otherwise you're spending all your time doing this."

Trash he can't avoid: Medicine blister packs and broken items made from mixed materials, such as a toilet bowl brush.

Amy Korst, Pacific City, Oregon: Yours truly! My husband, Adam, and I started our garbage-free journey in Oregon's Willamette Valley three years ago, producing only a shoebox's volume of trash in a year. We then moved to the picturesque Oregon Coast, where we found ourselves without access to the state-of-the-art recycling facilities we had grown used to. This means we've had to find new, creative solutions to our garbage conundrums. Currently we produce about a plastic grocery bag's worth of garbage a month. We rent a house on the beach, where we live with our pets but no children.

Trash we can't avoid: Dry pet food and pet treat bags, toothpaste tubes, cheese wrappers, and the occasional bag of chips.

This team of contributors is living proof that you can lead a happy, full life and produce little to no waste. The no-garbage lifestyle is for anyone, whether you are single, married, own or rent your home, have no kids, or have young kids, teenagers, or pets. This way of life can be tweaked to fit your own circumstances—whatever they may be—by following the guidelines laid out in this book.

How to Use This Book

This book is organized into three distinct parts: "Getting Started," "Trash-Free Challenges," and "Next Steps." The chapters are designed to be read in order, but feel free to skim over sections that don't apply to you. Here's what you'll find in each section:

Getting Started

The first five chapters of the book tell you how to reorganize your life around the concept of trash-free living. These chapters contain the basics—what you need to know to successfully pull off a zero-waste lifestyle. You'll first do a home-waste audit to find out what's in your trash. Then you'll learn about the 3 Rs: reduce, reuse, and recycle. A fourth R—rot—will help you navigate the world of composting (it won't be stinky, I promise!), even if you live in an apartment or don't have a garden. You'll learn how to determine what's recyclable in your area, why the Rs always come in that order, and how recycling really works. The basic steps of your day-to-day life are also covered, from grocery shopping to meal planning to remembering your reusable totes.

This section of the book is designed for all readers, no matter your circumstances. These chapters will help you build a foundation for your waste reduction. You'll learn a little about trash production in our country today as well as the damaging environmental impact trash can have on our planet. After your home-waste audit, you'll set a waste-reduction goal and bring the rest of your family on board. Then you'll set up efficient systems for sorting your recyclables and organic wastes from your trash. You'll learn to love the Depression-era mantra, "Use it up, wear it out, make do, or do without" as you embrace the "forgotten Rs" of reduce and reuse.

Trash-Free Challenges

Part 2 is designed to cover specialized topics in an in-depth fashion. Here you may want to read the chapters that specifically relate to your lifestyle. This section focuses on tricky trash-free areas, like navigating holidays without creating trash (it can be done, even at Christmas), raising kids without garbage, and eating out in restaurants without creating waste. The goal of garbage-free living is to maintain as normal a lifestyle as possible; that includes going to movies, shopping at the mall, eating out in restaurants, and taking family vacations. These activities make life more enjoyable, so part 2 aims to help you tread lightly on the planet without depriving yourself of these pleasures.

Next Steps

The final part of the book provides a big-picture look at the world's trash problem and looks at global initiatives to curb our wastefulness. In addition to lightening the load we haul to the curb each week, there are larger political movements afoot that are working to make companies and governments more aware of the blight of trash and their contribution to it. Raising awareness for these initiatives helps more people go trash free and makes the whole process even easier.

This book is designed for anybody, whether you are interested in beginning, moderate, or advanced trash reduction. Throughout the book, you'll also find tips targeted toward your comfort level. The most important thing is to be aware of your trash and work to reduce it—every little bit helps.

What if I told you that you could go from an overflowing can perched on the curb each week to making less than five pounds of trash in a year? That taking the trash-free plunge would simplify your life, ease the strain on your pocketbook, and help the planet, all at the same time?

All this is not only possible, it's downright easy. And this book will teach you how to do it. Let's get started.

PART 1

Getting Started

Whether you are diving into this lifestyle headfirst or simply testing the waters to moderately reduce your trash, you are bound to have lots of questions: What happens to my trash after it's picked up at the curb? Is trash really all that bad for the environment? What will my friends and neighbors think? What if I break something?

Part 1 answers all these questions and more, in order to put you at ease. Your goal at this point is probably the same as mine was—to reduce your trash as much as possible with as little effort as possible. You want the contents of your garbage can to change, not your whole life to change. Never fear—these first five chapters are designed to help you do exactly that.

Chapter 1

A Trashed Planet

Most of us have a general sense that three pounds of landfill-bound trash a day times three hundred million Americans isn't a good thing—but how, exactly, is our trash bad for public health and the environment? This chapter explores the dirty inner workings of today's landfills, which are filled with environmental hazards threatening our air and water quality. You'll also learn the truth about several landfill misconceptions. Think your apple core biodegrades inside the dump? Think again. And what about plastic—that insidious and disturbingly permanent hallmark of modern society? Guess what—it's not truly recyclable. You'll also get a look inside the average American's trash can. If you want to dive right into your own waste bin first and come back later to read about where your trash goes, feel free to skip ahead to chapter 2.

America's Trash Addiction

To understand why trash is such a problem in the United States, it's necessary to understand a little about the inner workings of a landfill. After our household trash (called municipal solid waste or MSW by those in the garbage-hauling industry) is picked up at the curb, it is generally hauled to a local landfill and dumped. A landfill is basically a pit (a very, very large pit) in the ground covered with a plastic liner—essentially a giant ground cloth designed to protect the land underneath from being polluted by the contents of the landfill.

Leachate

Here we reach the first major problem with all landfills. Over time, landfills produce a nasty, stinky liquid that trickles through all the trash and pools at the bottom. This liquid is called *leachate*, and it's a disgusting slurry of many things, including rain, liquefied food, and household chemicals that have escaped from their containers. This leachate is a particular environmental hazard because it contains a mixture of household chemicals and, potentially, improperly-disposed-of hazardous waste (such as battery acid from batteries carelessly tossed into the trash). A sophisticated system involving the liner, a filtration system, and pumps is designed to keep landfill leachate from seeping into the ground at all costs. The problem is, no matter how new or how state-of-the-art the plastic liner material is, eventually all landfill liners age, become brittle, and ultimately leak. A study conducted by Leak Location Services in 2000 found that 82 percent of surveyed landfills had leaks. The danger is that once a liner leaks, leachate seeps into the ground or runs off into waterways, polluting both soil and water.

Methane Gas

Another problem with today's landfills involves a different kind of emission—the release of methane gas into the air. Methane is a greenhouse gas that traps heat in our atmosphere and contributes to global warming. According to the Environmental Protection Agency (EPA), landfills are the third largest source of methane emissions in the country. Some, but by no means all, landfills employ methane gas collection and venting systems. Methane is produced when items inside a landfill biodegrade in an anaerobic (oxygen-less) environment. The decomposition of organic materials like food scraps, paper, and yard clippings does not have to release methane; in fact, an active, aerobic (oxygen-rich) compost pile breaks down more quickly and releases carbon dioxide, a much less harmful gas.

The Landfill Reality

Not only do landfills pollute the earth and the air, they do not work as we assume they do. The idea behind landfills isn't so bad—send all our trash to one place, where its stink and unsightliness will be contained while it biodegrades. The problem is, landfills do not function like this in practice. We send all sorts of materials to landfills, from the innocuous—orange peels and paper—to the hazardous. Once our trash is dumped on top of the big pile, it is covered with more and more waste until it no longer sees the light of day. This lack of exposure to sunlight and oxygen is precisely the issue.

The myth that landfills are essentially giant compost piles was dispelled by William Rathje's Garbage Project. Rathje and his team of anthropologists started the Garbage Project in 1972, based on the idea that studying the refuse of a modern household could shed light on whether the United States is in the midst of a "garbage crisis." What Rathje's team found is surprising, and it helps shed light on the way we should be addressing our garbage concerns.

One of garbology's most significant findings (yes, *garbology* is the study of garbage) is that things like food and paper don't always biodegrade in a landfill. The garbology team found that, even after twenty years buried in a landfill, one-third to one-half of food and yard waste was in recognizable condition. The Garbage Project reports finding still-readable newspaper clippings about the Apollo moon landings or the Truman election. This means that one of society's most powerful assumptions about landfills—that trash will slowly break down and disappear—is largely false. This is not to say that no biodegradation occurs within a landfill. After all, leachate and methane gas are two byproducts of decomposition. It does mean that easily compostable things like paper or food scraps are going to waste inside a landfill where they are entombed rather than broken down into valuable nutrients that could reenter the earth's life cycle.

Nor is it to say that biodegradation is necessarily desirable inside a landfill. Today our dumps are filled with many hazardous or toxic materials. This is a very serious issue, as we worry that toxic materials may seep into the ground or be released into the air. It may seem hard to believe that these hazardous substances come from the average American household, but if you look through your cupboards, under your sink, and in your garage, you may notice a number of chemicals and cleaners you don't want added to your drinking water. This can include things like paint thinner, nail polish, oven cleaner, and insecticides. When these materials are dumped in a landfill, their containers are often broken, and they mix together into a potentially toxic goo that creeps through the contents of the landfill. This is an ever-increasing danger, as modern society is far more dependent on chemicals in general and hazardous chemicals in particular than ever before. So although decomposition in a landfill might be good in theory, the presence of toxic chemicals gives us a reason to want landfills to stay inert and inactive to keep these hazards out of our environment.

Of course, the solution to these problems lies in decreasing our dependency on toxic chemicals, which is the focus of chapter 9, "Zero-Waste Cleaning," and chapter 5, "Organic Waste."

Plastic Trash

Our trash problem doesn't stop inside the boundaries of the landfill either. Although we've seen that landfills pollute the air and water and waste valuable organic scraps, trash is insidiously harmful outside the local dump, too. It is unsightly in the form of litter, where it can pollute the environment, pose a problem to our health, and reenter our food chain, and it is deadly to the animals we share our planet with.

We all know that littering is a common problem—after all, how often do you see a driver flick a cigarette butt out of the car window? Litter has become so pervasive we see it everywhere, even if a trash can is in the immediate vicinity. Litter is absorbed by the environment, often winding up tangled in a tree or being swept away into a storm drain or a creek or river. Eventually the garbage starts to break down in the elements. Something organic like an apple core will decompose, but the majority of litter is made from materials that will never biodegrade. Plastic, which constitutes some 90 percent of all marine litter, falls into this category. (Read more about the issues associated with disposing of plastic in chapter 4, "Recycle.") Instead, plastic photodegrades, meaning the elements break it down into smaller and smaller particles until eventually these tiny particles become known as *microplastics*. These microplastics, when floating around in the ocean, can absorb what are known as persistent organic pollutants (POPs) such as DDT. Plastics absorb POPs at up to one hundred thousand to a million times the levels found in seawater. When microplastics are ingested by marine species like fish, they enter our food chain. The danger to us is called *bioaccumulation*, which means that we are absorbing a toxic chemical at a more rapid rate than our bodies can expel it.

Plastic trash is a particular problem in our oceans, an issue that has been well publicized in recent years. A great floating mass of trash, located roughly between the continents of Asia and North America and estimated to be twice the size of Texas, has been called variously the Great Pacific Garbage Patch, the Pacific Garbage Gyre, and the Trash Vortex. Although exaggerated claims have been made that the patch is visible from space (the materials are too dispersed to form that kind of visible mass), this concentration of trash is a real concern. It consists mostly of plastic, especially those microscopic particles, as well as debris from fishing ships.

Tragically trash is deadly to countless animals each year. The EPA estimates that one hundred thousand marine mammals are killed annually through encounters with marine litter. On top of that, between seven hundred thousand and one million annual sea bird deaths are attributed to trash. Land animals are at risk, too; raccoons, for example, have been found with their paws stuck in pop cans. Trash poses two major risks to animals—ingestion and entanglement. Animals, particularly marine mammals and birds, frequently mistake floating plastic for food. They eat the plastic and either choke to death or slowly starve as their stomachs feel full but their bodies are deprived of nutrients. A well-publicized example is the sperm whale Inky, who was discovered with three cubic feet of plastic in her stomach. Inky survived, but the gray whale that washed ashore in Seattle in 2010 did not. This otherwise-healthy whale had ingested a huge amount of trash, including twenty plastic bags, a golf ball, and a pair of sweatpants. The saddest story by far comes from photographer Chris Jordan, who photographed the corpses of baby albatrosses stuffed with plastic on the Midway Atoll. The babies were fed small bits of plastic by their mothers, who mistook the colorful plastic pieces for food. In Jordan's images, pieces of human trash are easily identified inside the birds, including lighters and bottle caps. On his website, Jordan writes, "These birds reflect back an appallingly emblematic result of the collective trance of our consumerism and runaway industrial growth. Like the albatross, we first-world humans find ourselves lacking the ability to discern anymore what is nourishing from what is toxic to our lives and our spirits."

What's in Your Trash?

Before you can start reducing your trash, you need to take a look at what's in it. Every two years the EPA releases a report titled *Municipal Solid Waste Generation, Recycling, and Disposal in the United States* that tells us just that. The most recent available figures are from 2010.

The statistic cited most often—that Americans each produce on average about four pounds of trash a day—comes from this report. As of 2010, Americans were producing 4.43 pounds of waste a day and recycling or composting 1.51 pounds of this a day. Collectively Americans generated 250 million pounds of trash in 2010 and recycled 34.1 percent of this waste. Although 4.43 pounds of trash a day is pretty high, we are starting to slowly reduce our trash. In 2000, this figure was 4.72, and in 2005, it was 4.67 pounds a day. It would be encouraging to see this trend continue until it matched that of 1960, when Americans generated only 2.68 pounds of trash a day.

Municipal solid waste, or MSW, includes household waste, institutional waste, and commercial waste. Household waste, which includes trash from apartment buildings, is about 55 percent of all MSW. In addition to MSW, our country also produces large amounts of industrial, manufacturing, and demolition waste, though these latter categories don't fall within the scope of this book.

The EPA also takes a look at what's in our MSW. The single largest category of trash we produce is paper, followed by food scraps; yard trimmings; plastics; metals; rubber, leather, and textiles; wood; glass; and other. Although a lot of this heads directly to the landfill, remember that 34 percent of it is recycled. This number is an average and varies from material to material; for example, 71.6 percent of paper is recycled, whereas only 35.5 percent of tires are recycled. As the "What's in Your Trash?" chart demonstrates, there is plenty of room for improvement when our recycling rates for aluminum cans, glass bottles, and plastic bottles, all of which are easily recyclable, are all under 50 percent.

The MSW report also breaks down our trash by weight (see the sidebar on page 20). Here it is clear why a zero-waste lifestyle is so beneficial. The majority of our trash by weight is from packaging, with food scraps and yard trimmings each adding about 13 percent in weight to the garbage can; these are three categories where it is dead easy to drastically reduce the trash we create. The tips you'll find in this book will teach you to target these areas, which together make up more than 57 percent of the trash in your garbage can.

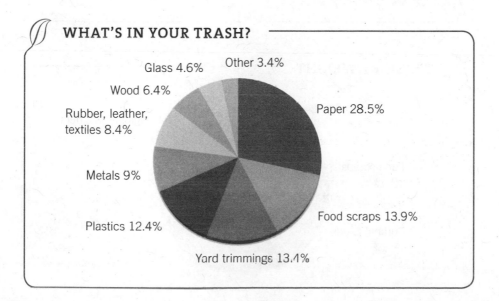

WHAT'S IN YOUR TRASH?

Glass 4.6%
Other 3.4%
Wood 6.4%
Rubber, leather, textiles 8.4%
Paper 28.5%
Metals 9%
Food scraps 13.9%
Plastics 12.4%
Yard trimmings 13.4%

The bad news is that America's trash situation is pretty dire—leachate filled with hazardous waste, methane emissions, eternal plastics, and low recycling rates combine to paint an ugly picture. The good news is that now that you see how the system works—or rather, doesn't work—you can start tackling what's in your garbage cans at home. Clearly we all make trash—an average 4.43 pounds a day of it!—but much of this trash is packaging and a lot of it is recyclable. Turn to the next chapter for lots of different strategies to start reducing your trash right now.

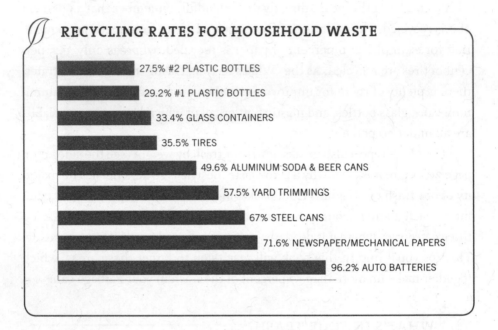

RECYCLING RATES FOR HOUSEHOLD WASTE

27.5% #2 PLASTIC BOTTLES
29.2% #1 PLASTIC BOTTLES
33.4% GLASS CONTAINERS
35.5% TIRES
49.6% ALUMINUM SODA & BEER CANS
57.5% YARD TRIMMINGS
67% STEEL CANS
71.6% NEWSPAPER/MECHANICAL PAPERS
96.2% AUTO BATTERIES

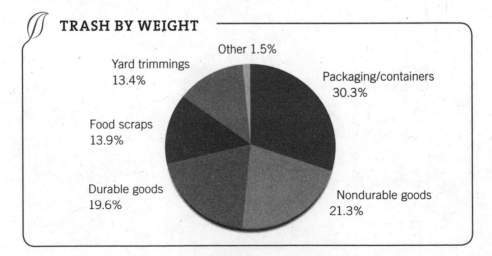

TRASH BY WEIGHT

Other 1.5%
Yard trimmings 13.4%
Packaging/containers 30.3%
Food scraps 13.9%
Durable goods 19.6%
Nondurable goods 21.3%

Chapter 2

Planning to Go Waste Free

It is time to take your first zero-waste steps! This chapter helps you establish a foundation for your new garbage-free lifestyle. With tips throughout from our team of zero-waste contributors, I'll guide you through the process of getting your family members on board with this lifestyle, because you're bound to meet up with some skepticism. Once everyone is enthused about your goals, you'll gather your family together to do a home-waste audit, finding out what's in your trash so you can start reducing it. Don't skip the audit! The rest of the book uses the info you gather in this chapter to help you remove waste from all areas of your life. Finally, we'll take a look at the first month of your zero-waste lifestyle, giving you strategies to deal with any challenges that may crop up.

Rallying the Troops

All of our contributors agree—if your spouse, roommate, or family isn't on board with a zero-waste lifestyle, your good intentions will never get off the ground. Before you take the zero-waste plunge, it's important to sit down and talk about this lifestyle change with your significant others and family members. Here are some tips for getting everyone excited about this new adventure.

Explain Your Passion

Explaining why a zero-waste lifestyle is important should be a key part of your conversation with family members. If you need a starting point, you'll find a number of the reasons explained in this book's introduction. Briefly, trash is unsightly and can be toxic and dangerous to humans and animals. Remember, only seventy-five years ago, most Americans lived a virtually trash-free lifestyle—it wasn't until the advent of single-use disposables that we became so attached to our garbage.

In addition to listing the environmental reasons behind a zero-waste lifestyle, be sure to stress the other benefits outlined in the introduction; for example, you will save money and time, and you will simplify your life and learn to be more self-sufficient. All this, and it's easy, too.

Understand Family Concerns

Zero-waster April Leubbert says her husband was a bit apprehensive at first about the zero-waste switch. "I try to dive in headfirst," she says. "I have to remind myself it's not just me changing, it's my family." If your family members have concerns, listen to those concerns and take them seriously. Their worries might include a lack of time, a worry about extra household chores, concern about being perceived as weird by other people, their attachment to favorite packaged food items, or the belief that a zero-waste lifestyle is impossible.

Get Everyone Involved

A zero-waste lifestyle is a family effort, not an individual one. A single person shouldn't have to bear the brunt of making this lifestyle work, as this will just lead to resentment and frustration. Instead, involve other members of the family in living without waste. Get everyone involved in the waste audit; brainstorm creative solutions to your garbage conundrums together. Experiment in the kitchen—if your son's favorite packaged food is Oreo cookies, find a homemade substitute recipe and try it out.

Avoid Fanaticism

It's easy to become obsessed with making no trash, to the point where trash becomes the deciding factor in most of your decisions. A zero-waste lifestyle should not take over your life; instead, your life should dictate how far you're willing to go. Remember, every little bit of trash reduction helps the planet, so there's no wrong way to implement these changes.

Conducting Your Home-Waste Audit

Once everyone in your household is on board with your zero-waste plan, it's time to get dirty (don't worry, only a little). You are going to spend the next week surveying your trash output in order to perform a home-waste audit. I'll walk you through this process room by room. Your goal is to get a better idea of what kind of trash you are producing in each room of your home. Then you'll sort and measure this trash so you know where you are starting from. Knowing what's in your trash will enable you to set a realistic waste-reduction goal and enable you to track your progress.

Now, I promise this is the only part of the whole project that forces a close encounter with your own trash. You can modify the auditing procedure to your level of comfort, but remember that the ultimate goal is to see how much trash you are generating each day. This gives you a baseline to work from when you set your own personal waste-reduction goal later in the chapter.

To help you in your home-waste audit, I've put together a waste-tracking sheet (see pages 24–30) for you to record how much trash is produced by your family each week. Feel free to make a copy for each member of your household or just write in the book in the spaces provided in each section that follows. You will tackle one room per day, recording the trash produced there. Basically you need two main pieces of information from each room: *How much trash is produced there in a day?* and *How much does this trash weigh?* On the weekend, you'll compile all your results and perform the actual audit.

One final note: For the purpose of the home-waste audit, you are tracking *all* waste that you make during a single day—this includes items you would normally compost or recycle. You'll do this in order to see how you stack up against the EPA statistic that each American produces 4.43 pounds of trash a day. Just over three pounds of this goes into the landfill, but the rest is recycled or composted. The home-waste audit helps you do a comparison so you can see how your trash measures up against the rest of the country.

Monday: The Bathroom

Most of us have a trash can in our bathrooms that fills up with the remnants of our morning and evening hygiene routines, meaning the trash produced in the bathroom is easy to track, since it doesn't really change day-to-day. Record on the Waste Tracker information about trash produced during your daily hair, teeth, and skin care routines. Once you've collected and recorded this information, you have two options:

1. Weigh your day's trash output from the bathroom, record this information on the Waste Tracker, and dispose of it as usual.

2. Label your bag of trash and keep until the weekend, when you will compile waste info from all rooms of your house.

Most of the trash produced in the bathroom is going to be of the single-use disposable variety (cotton balls, floss, and the like), although you will occasionally add some packaging to the mix, too (empty shampoo bottle, deodorant container, and so on). Although you might expect most bathroom trash to be "icky," this is really not the case, with only a few exceptions (such as used feminine hygiene products and used tissues). For items in the latter category, I'm certainly not suggesting you hang onto them—record them on your waste audit and get rid of them in a sanitary fashion.

The following is a list of items commonly used in the bathroom.

STEP 1: Check all items that you disposed of today:

- ☐ Facial tissues
- ☐ Floss
- ☐ Empty floss containers
- ☐ Toothbrushes
- ☐ Toothbrush packaging
- ☐ Toothpaste tubes
- ☐ Toothpaste tube packaging
- ☐ Deodorant tubes/canisters
- ☐ Disposable razors
- ☐ Disposable razor blades
- ☐ Mouthwash containers
- ☐ Makeup containers
- ☐ Shampoo or conditioner bottles
- ☐ Q-tips
- ☐ Cotton balls
- ☐ Tampons (plus packaging)

- ☐ Sanitary pads (plus packaging)
- ☐ Medicine packaging (pill blister packs, safety seals, and so on)
- ☐ Hairspray or other hair product containers
- ☐ Skin care containers
- ☐ Contact lenses (plus packaging)
- ☐ Contact lens solution containers
- ☐ Hair
- ☐ Body wash containers
- ☐ Broken hair elastics
- ☐ Other: _____
- ☐ Other: _____
- ☐ Other: _____
- ☐ Other: _____
- ☐ Other: _____

Total pieces of trash in bag: _____

Total weight of day's trash: _____

STEP 2: Place all of the day's trash from the bathroom in a small paper sack. Label the bag clearly with the following information:

- The room the trash came from
- How many people contributed trash to the bag

STEP 3: Save the bag for Sunday's waste audit. Alternatively, if the thought of saving your trash isn't appealing, you can weigh the trash now and throw it all away.

Tuesday: The Bedroom

Trash produced in the bedroom tends to be minimal, in my experience. The type of trash produced in a bedroom will depend on who is occupying said bedroom. Teens, for instance, tend to live in their rooms and so will throw away garbage ranging from food wrappers to discarded homework. Young children might throw away broken toys or remnants of craft projects. Mom and Dad, meanwhile, might be discarding anything from old, holey socks to condom wrappers.

The Waste Tracker provides general categories of bedroom waste and leaves lots of space for you to write in the trash from your lifestyle. Include trash from all household bedrooms on the the Waste Tracker.

STEP 1: Check all items that you disposed of today:

☐ Old clothes	☐ Diapers
☐ Condoms and condom wrappers	☐ Wet wipes
☐ Facial tissues	☐ Empty containers
☐ Clothing tags	☐ Other: _____
☐ Food packaging	☐ Other: _____
☐ Food	☐ Other: _____
☐ Paper	☐ Other: _____
☐ Art/craft supplies	☐ Other: _____
☐ Magazines	☐ Other: _____
☐ Discarded electronics (cords, cell phones, and the like)	☐ Other: _____
	☐ Other: _____
☐ Pens/pencils	☐ Other: _____

Total pieces of trash in bag: _____

Total weight of day's trash: _____

STEP 2: Place all of the day's trash from the bedroom in a small paper sack. Label the bag clearly with the following information:

- The room the trash came from
- How many people contributed trash to the bag

STEP 3: Save the bag for Sunday's waste audit. Alternatively, if the thought of saving your trash isn't appealing, you can weigh the trash now and throw it all away.

Wednesday: The Kitchen

The kitchen is the room that yields the most trash on a daily basis. The good news is that this trash is the easiest to eliminate; first, however, you need to see what kind of trash is coming from your kitchen. Mostly your trash will come from three different categories: food scraps, food preparation, and food packaging.

Food scraps: All food scraps need to be tallied for the home-waste audit to be accurate, so even if you normally compost, you should still calculate how much waste in food weight you produce each day.

Food preparation: Many families use disposable products for preparing and storing their food and washing dishes. You are on the lookout for things like paper towels, sponges, foil, plastic wrap, and waxed paper.

Food packaging: The convenience of frozen, canned, and microwaveable food comes at a price—tons of packaging. This broad category will include items such as chips bags, ice cream cartons, granola bar wrappers, pudding cups, and the plastic bags from produce like carrots, potatoes, and apples.

STEP 1: Check all items that you disposed of today:

- ☐ Sponge
- ☐ Foil
- ☐ Plastic wrap
- ☐ Waxed paper
- ☐ Food storage containers
- ☐ Paper towels

- ☐ Paper napkins
- ☐ Paper plates, bowls, cups
- ☐ Plastic cutlery
- ☐ Plastic bags
- ☐ Paper bags
- ☐ Cleaning wipes

- ☐ Food scraps

  Meat: _____

  Fruits and veggies: _____

  Grains: _____

  Dairy and eggs: _____

  Sweets: _____

- ☐ Empty food bags (chips, cookies)
- ☐ Plastic trays
- ☐ Styrofoam trays
- ☐ Single-serve wrappers (fruit snacks, granola bars)
- ☐ Empty plastic bottles
- ☐ Empty glass jars

- ☐ Empty cans (soup, beverage, beans, olives, and so on)
- ☐ Boxes
- ☐ Liner bags (cereal, crackers)
- ☐ Plastic baggies
- ☐ Twist-ties
- ☐ Other: _____
- ☐ Other: _____
- ☐ Other: _____
- ☐ Other: _____
- ☐ Other: _____
- ☐ Other: _____

Total pieces of trash in bag: _____

Total weight of day's trash: _____

STEP 2: Place all of the day's trash from the kitchen in a small paper sack. Label the bag clearly with the following information:

- The room the trash came from
- How many people contributed trash to the bag

STEP 3: Save the bag for Sunday's waste audit, or if you have messy food scraps, you can weigh the trash now and throw it all away.

Thursday: The Living Spaces

Today you will look at waste produced in what I'm calling the "living spaces" of your home—places like the family room, living room, office, or den. After yesterday's slog through the kitchen trash, today will be a breeze. Very little trash is produced in these living areas. Most people I know don't even have a trash can in the family room. Everything needed for entertainment is brought in from a different room, so the trash stays there. For this section of the house, you'll be looking for things like broken toys and other objects, used-up office supplies, art supplies, junk mail, old magazines and books, and wrappers from DVDs or video games.

STEP 1: Check all items that you disposed of today:

- ☐ Junk mail
- ☐ Phone books
- ☐ Magazines
- ☐ Books
- ☐ Wrappers from CDs, DVDs, video games
- ☐ Greeting cards
- ☐ Used-up pens/pencils
- ☐ Receipts
- ☐ Price tags/stickers
- ☐ Paper or plastic grocery bags
- ☐ Broken toys

- ☐ Used-up art supplies
- ☐ Gift wrap (tissue paper, wrapping paper, gift bags)
- ☐ Food packaging
- ☐ Other: _____
- ☐ Other: _____
- ☐ Other: _____
- ☐ Other: _____
- ☐ Other: _____
- ☐ Other: _____
- ☐ Other: _____
- ☐ Other: _____

Total pieces of trash in bag: _____

Total weight of day's trash: _____

STEP 2: Place all of the day's trash from the living spaces in a small paper sack. Label the bag clearly with the following information:

- The room the trash came from
- How many people contributed trash to the bag

STEP 3: Save the bag for Sunday's waste audit. Alternatively, if the thought of saving your trash isn't appealing, you can weigh the trash now and throw it all away.

Friday: The Outdoor Spaces

Not everyone has an outdoor living space (garage, shed, studio), and those who do don't always use it weekly (like in the middle of winter). If, however, you have a yard and weather conditions are conducive to spending time in it, you should take into account any trash produced in this easy-to-overlook area of the home. If you are a gardener, your supplies might yield trash like plastic plant pots, empty fertilizer containers, seed packets, or broken hoses. The garage, on the other hand, might produce used oil from an at-home oil change, car parts, or insecticides.

STEP 1: Check all items that you disposed of today:

☐ Charcoal	☐ Lightbulbs
☐ Lighter fluid container	☐ Broken hoses and other
☐ Charcoal bag	watering hardware
☐ Birdseed packaging	☐ Other: _____
☐ Broken tools	☐ Other: _____
☐ Motor oil	☐ Other: _____
☐ Pesticide, herbicide, or	☐ Other: _____
insecticide container*	☐ Other: _____
☐ Paint*	☐ Other: _____
☐ Batteries*	☐ Other: _____

Items often classified as hazardous waste. Please do not dispose of these in regular trash without consulting local solid waste department.

Total pieces of trash in bag: _____

Total weight of day's trash: _____

STEP 2: Place all of the day's trash from the outdoor spaces in a paper sack or plastic garbage bag. Label the bag clearly with the following information:

- The room the trash came from
- How many people contributed trash to the bag

STEP 3: Save the bag for Sunday's waste audit. Alternatively, if the thought of saving your trash isn't appealing, you can weigh the trash now and throw it all away.

Saturday: The Laundry Room

The laundry room, a room in the house not used daily, still generates a small amount of trash that should be included in your home-waste audit. In a given week, you might throw away dryer lint, dryer sheets, empty detergent or fabric softener containers, or worn-out clothes.

STEP 1: Check all items that you disposed of today:

☐ Dryer lint	☐ Other: _____
☐ Dryer sheets	☐ Other: _____
☐ Dryer sheet box	☐ Other: _____
☐ Plastic containers: Detergent or	☐ Other: _____
fabric softener	☐ Other: _____
☐ Empty bottles of stain remover	☐ Other: _____
☐ Worn-out clothes	☐ Other: _____

Total pieces of trash in bag: _____

Total weight of day's trash: _____

STEP 2: Place all of the day's trash from the laundry room in a small paper sack. Label the bag clearly with the following information:

- The room the trash came from
- How many people contributed trash to the bag

STEP 3: Save the bag for Sunday's waste audit. Alternatively, if the thought of saving your trash isn't appealing, you can weigh the trash now and throw it all away.

Sunday: The Home-Waste Audit

Now that you have your room-by-room tally completed, it's time to see how you measure up to the average American.

At the end of the week, sort your waste into piles on newspaper according to the following categories: food scraps, recyclables, and landfill bound. Weigh each pile separately, then add the numbers together, and divide by the number of people in your household to see how you compare with the EPA's statistic of 4.43 pounds of trash per person per day. If you're lower than 4.43 pounds a day, good for you! There's still plenty of room for improvement. If you produce more than the average, that's okay—you'll see immediate and drastic changes in your trash output as soon as you start using the principles outlined in this book.

Before scooping up the whole mess and carting it off to the trash, spend a minute reflecting on the contents of your trash. You'll notice some patterns emerging. If you have a lot of recyclables in your pile and you don't yet recycle, this is a good place to start. Ditto with food scraps and compost-ing. You might notice, as I did, that the majority of your trash comes from food packaging and containers. Or you might find that your family threw away something that could be reused or repurposed, like a twisty tie or a piece of string. This immediately gives you a category to keep in mind as you start to decrease your trash. Save that Waste Tracker list, because you'll refer to it throughout the process of getting to zero waste.

Once you're all done, recycle what you can and throw away the rest. If you already have a home compost pile established, add your food scraps to this pile. Otherwise, I'll get you set up in chapter 5.

Set a Waste-Reduction Goal

Having a concrete trash-reduction goal in mind is critical to your success. It will take you between one to three months to fully implement this lifestyle. Trying to do too much at once, or trying to quit trash "cold turkey," just isn't a good idea. Give yourself time to research recycling facilities, bulk food stores, and other resources in your area; the chapters that follow will point you in the right direction for all of these tasks.

Now that you know how much trash you produce each day, it is time for you to set your own waste-reduction goal. Throughout the book, I tailor sug-gestions toward three distinct levels of waste reduction: beginning, moder-ate, and advanced. You will find sample goals for each waste-reduction level. I recommend you set a goal that will be challenging but not frustrating—you want to achieve success so you stay motivated to continue shrinking your trash. Remember that whatever goal you set for yourself is excellent—there is no right or wrong way live this lifestyle. You will make a difference each and every time you keep one thing from heading to the dump.

When I first decided to live a zero-waste lifestyle, I spent about a month intensely researching the lifestyle to determine whether it was even possible. Then, when I had a system established that I thought would work, I set a date and decided to stop producing trash. This might work for you, or you might choose a more gradual approach. Zero-waste contributor April Luebbert, a mom from the Seattle area, recommends the latter, saying that, for her fam-ily, "transitioning slowly made the lifestyle more of a habit." Here are some sample goals based on beginning, moderate, and advanced reducing. These are just suggestions; your own goals might be a combination of these levels or look completely different.

Beginning Level

Allow yourself to ease into your trash-free lifestyle. Aim for a 25-percent trash reduction in weight by the end of three months. If you're not keen on constantly weighing your trash, set a "per bags" goal. If you currently fill a 64-gallon garbage can a week, aim to fill it three-quarters of the way instead of to the top each week. Or, if you fill four bags of trash a week, aim for three bags instead.

Moderate Level

Aim to cut your trash output in half, whether you are measuring this in weight, volume, or bags produced. If you don't already have a composting system in place, you can easily achieve this goal by establishing one.

Advanced Level

A 75- to 90-percent reduction goal in less than three months is reasonable. If you choose this level of reduction, you should be producing less trash than would fit in a plastic grocery bag per week—or even per month.

The First Month

I'll be honest with you. The first month of your new trash-free lifestyle will be the most difficult, but that's okay because it's also new and exciting. If you can harness that feeling of purpose you get right after you've resolved to improve your life for just one month, you'll be able to establish habits and routines that help you sustain a zero-waste lifestyle even after the novelty has worn off.

Studies show that it takes only about three weeks to form a new habit, so keep this up for just twenty-one days and your trash-free resolve will become permanently second nature. Remember, too, that although this lifestyle takes a little effort in the beginning, everyone who lives this lifestyle says the same thing, almost word-for-word: After a while, it becomes habitual. After a while, it becomes easy. There are a number of steps you can take and tricks you can employ that will help you set up routines to make your day-to-day life easier.

Set Up Ground Rules

It's important to establish some ground rules or guidelines to follow as you start down your zero-waste path so you know how to handle obstacles when they present themselves. You may start by asking yourself the following questions; remember, there are no right or wrong answers, just answers best suited to your circumstances.

- When you say zero waste, does all trash count? What about pet waste, diapers, vacuum cleaner dust, dryer lint, floor sweepings, hair from haircuts, meat scraps like fat and bone and gristle?

- Will you save and measure your trash to track your results? (A number of the zero-waste contributors—including myself, Rose, and Chris—save our trash to see how close we are to our goal. My trash goes into a shoebox—remember, if you save your trash, it won't be messy or stinky because you've removed food scraps).

- What will you do when someone gives you a gift that includes trash?

- How will you communicate about your project to your friends?

- What will you do when visiting a friend's house? When eating out in a restaurant?

- Do you want to allow yourself a luxury item each week? (After all, contributor Desira Fuqua from Tennessee says, "It's not about punishing yourself. This should be rewarding, fun, interesting.")

- Do you need to allow yourself some leeway at work?

See the sidebar on pages 34–35 for the ground rules Adam and I established during our first zero-waste year.

Make Connections in Your Community

Major benefits of a zero-waste lifestyle are shopping in your community, keeping your local dollars at home, and getting to know the people you live and work with. How so? You'll be frequenting locally owned businesses because these businesses will be the ones most willing to accommodate your purchasing requests. Some of your shopping routines will change, because you are working hard to avoid throwaway packaging. This might mean asking the local butcher to put your steaks in a stainless steel pot you brought with you.

Or it could mean asking the local coffee shop to save coffee grounds for your newly growing vegetables. It could mean having the wait staff in your favorite restaurant put your leftovers into *your* container instead of a throwaway Styrofoam one. It might even mean bringing a reusable drink container to the movie theater to be filled with the snack-bar soda you take in to that epic blockbuster.

Before Adam and I started living garbage free, I spent a lot of time researching this lifestyle. This meant I spent a lot of time on the phone and even more time be-bopping around the local community talking to business owners. I am a naturally shy person, so it's outside my comfort zone to approach community members and strike up a conversation about anything. Approaching

GREEN GARBAGE PROJECT GROUND RULES

1. **Medical products and limited hygiene products:** We will count medical and hygiene waste in our final garbage totals at the end of the year, but we will still be using prescription products, oral contraceptives, over-the-counter medicines, and contact lenses. We will recycle where possible and choose products with environmentally friendly packaging.

2. **What people give us:** We understand that we can't completely control this. So although we ask our friends and family to please try to honor our challenge whenever possible, we will graciously accept gifts as given and try to dispose of packaging as responsibly as possible.

3. **Meat waste, animal waste, hair, vacuum cleaner waste:**

   Leftover meat—We eat very little meat, and we give leftovers to our dog, Kavik, so we don't anticipate having any to throw away. If we end up with leftover meat/bones, they will go into the bin for curbside pickup each week. We will weigh organic waste each week to keep track.

   Cat poop and biodegradable litter—Cat poop is going straight into the trash because, after much research, this seems to be the safest route. From an article on the subject from Grist.com, "Cats can carry the disease toxoplasmosis and pass it on to us via oocysts (a dormant stage of the disease) in their feces. This disease can be fatal to infants and immune-system-deficient adults, and make the rest of us sick. Do not handle cat poop if you are pregnant, and don't let small children do it either. Wash your hands thoroughly after handling cat poop, no matter who you are." It is recommended that cat feces not be flushed, buried, or composted due to the danger of toxoplasmosis. We want to be safe, so kitty litter gets trashed.

people I didn't know and explaining that I wanted to do something weird like live garbage free? Not even within the stratosphere of my comfort zone.

Yet I persevered, because the cause is bigger than I am. And you know what? I'm so glad I had those conversations with employees, managers, and community members. Every single individual I talked to thought my mission was interesting. Sure, to some this was a euphemism for "weird," but so what? No one ever said anything degrading or discouraging to me, and most people were genuinely interested in what I had to say.

So what did I have to say? Basically, whenever I do this, my goal is to establish a relationship with business owners in my community. I introduce myself, shake their hand, and explain my lifestyle. Then I ask that person

Dog poop—No worries here, this will be buried.

Vacuum cleaner dust—Returned to nature, unless our vacuum cleaner dust includes nonbiodegradable items like paper clips or pen caps, in which case we throw it out.

Hair—Returned to nature.

4. **Accidents do occasionally happen,** and although we hope they don't, we may not be able to control disposal of car parts/fluids, appliances, or other hazardous materials. We will dispose of these items as responsibly as possible, if the need arises.

5. **When considering work-related trash, some leeway is necessary.** Although we will make every effort to reduce the amount of trash we create in the workplace, we understand that some may be generated in spite of our best efforts. A teacher can hardly avoid dry erase markers and pens, for example.

6. **All garbage counts as part of the challenge.** It will all be saved (with the sole exceptions of cat litter, meat/bones, and hazardous car/household waste, if this arises), weighed, and cleaned, so that at the end of the year we know how much landfill-bound trash we produced. We will use every means available to us to compost, reduce, reuse, recycle, upcycle, or donate any trash we generate, for one year.

whether I can bring my own containers to the store to buy fresh, bulk, or deli products. The answer has been yes in all cases save one: the manager at a Safeway store told me I could bring my own containers to the meat counter but not the deli counter, as (according to her) a health code regulation stipulated that deli food be sold only in store-sanctioned plastic containers. A typical conversation goes like this:

> *Me:* Hi there! My name is Amy Korst. I wanted to take a minute to introduce myself, tell you that I shop frequently at your store, and make what might seem like an odd request.

> *Manager (shakes my hand):* Okay! Nice to meet you, Amy. How can I help you?

> *Me:* Well, my husband and I are trying to reduce our trash as much as possible right now. I wonder if it would be okay with you if I brought a Tupperware container to the store when I buy things like meat or cheese from the deli, so I can avoid all the plastic and Styrofoam?

> *Manager:* Hmm, I don't see a problem with that. What a neat project you're doing! We try really hard to be green at home, too, maybe not to that extreme, but we know it's important. I'll let the staff know they should accommodate your request.

> *Me:* Thanks! It was nice to meet you.

I make sure I note the manager's name, so if I encounter a skeptical employee when I get back to the meat counter, I can say, "Oh, I checked with Carli, the store manager, and she said it was okay." Sometimes I think clerks don't want to use my container because they're afraid they'll get in trouble for doing something unusual. Others worry it's against health code regulations.

THE FIRST STEP

"The important thing is to begin the journey," says Chris Burger, who has been living this lifestyle for more than two decades. No matter what your waste-reduction goal is, the most important step is the first step. Every piece of trash you don't make is an item saved from the landfill.

When I say it's been cleared by the manager, they have no problem accommodating my request.

Local business owners have much more flexibility in what requests they can accommodate and, I've found, they are more willing to work with me to avoid garbage.

If you frequently shop at chain stores, it's still worth making the same connections, but I'd encourage you to find a locally owned business that provides the same service. Wherever you shop, swing into the store during nonpeak hours. Ask to speak to a manager, and introduce yourself and your zero-waste preferences. Explain simply and politely why you want to avoid throwaway packaging, and ask them if they'd be willing to help. Most people seem fascinated by the goal of personal zero-waste and want to participate however they can.

Once you've made this connection, shop at their store whenever you can. Remember, managers are customer service agents. They want to know what their customers want, and they want to be accommodating. You can help your local economy thrive by shopping at community-owned businesses and building this reciprocal relationship that helps you, your town, and the environment.

Deal with "the Look"

There's no way around the fact that we are social creatures bound by the hidden rules of our culture. Taking a deliberate step away from the norm, like you're about to do, is difficult because it means other people might view you as "weird."

Going garbage free has tons of benefits, but there is one drawback—you must prepare yourself for "the look." All of us who live trash free sometimes get the look, and none of us likes it—you know, that raised eyebrow of skepticism that implies you are weird or stupid. Yet we still persevere because ultimately we believe in the cause—we're making the world a cleaner, greener place to live.

Overwhelmingly the people you talk to about your zero-waste lifestyle will be impressed, amazed, interested, or at least polite. As with any walk of life, however, if you do this long enough you will encounter detractors. There are several strategies that you can use to avoid the look or convince a skeptic about the merits of this lifestyle—for yourself and for anyone else.

Anytime you meet someone new and tell them about your garbage-free life, you have the chance to set the tone of the conversation before they can react. Try a little social experiment: Tell two new people this week about living without trash. To one of them, say it confidently and proudly—stand up straight, speak with conviction, and make the case for why this new way of life is a brilliant one that anyone can embrace. Why doesn't everyone do this?

With the second person, let the shy little kid inside do the talking. Speak meekly, with little conviction. "Oh, I know it's probably crazy, it was really my best friend's idea . . ." Do not attempt to explain why you're doing this or how you're saving the planet one step at a time while others are sitting around on their butts watching TV.

Which person buys into a zero-waste lifestyle? That's right, the first friend.

Be proud! You're making a difference. How many people can say that?

The very small percentage of people who greet this news with "the look" come from basically two viewpoints: surprise or disdain.

You'll get the look at grocery stores when you ask an employee you've not yet met to put your slices of deli cheese in your container instead of a plastic bag. You'll get it from bemused friends and relatives who didn't know you had such radical tendencies. I like getting the look from these people, though, because they usually come back for more. They might think you're odd at first, but later that night, they'll be home brushing their teeth and thinking, "Now, how does that lady use toothpaste without making garbage?" People will say they thought of you while throwing out the trash, and it will become a compliment. Use these opportunities to educate and spread the word—there is a better way.

There is another group of people out there. They think your lifestyle is at best a waste of time and at worst a detriment to society. There's something about living without trash that gets their hackles up. A woman once told me I could "better spend my karmic energy feeding the hungry." Another, angrier person told me I would—singlehandedly—put all the garbage men out of business. A particularly offensive soul said I looked fat, so maybe I was just eating all my garbage, that's where it was going.

Without being a psychologist, I'm going to go out on a limb here and suggest that a number of these detractors feel a little defensive about the garbage they create—like somehow my lack of garbage is criticizing their mound of garbage.

All I can say here is to take the high road and ignore it. Talk to those who are willing to listen. Never take on a "holier-than-thou" attitude. Everyone's lifestyle is a legitimate choice, and in time those who criticize you may learn from your quietly conscientious example.

Embrace the Cumulative Effect of Zero Waste

The old saying "one person can make a difference" is about as tired a cliché as they come. Nevertheless, I do believe that small efforts can and do add up to big change. Let me give you an example of what I mean.

When I was thirteen, I decided to become a vegetarian. On a family cruise celebrating my grandparents' fiftieth wedding anniversary, I met a fellow teenager who was a vegetarian. She clearly inspired me, because as soon as we disembarked at the end of the cruise, I announced to my family that I wasn't eating meat anymore. And I stopped right then, cold turkey. My parents didn't really think I was serious at the time, but to their credit, they were totally supportive of my decision from the get-go.

I informed the rest of my extended family and friends about my new dietary decision, and although some of my more staunch meat-and-potatoes brethren thought I was crazy, everyone went out of their way to accommodate my choices.

Now, fourteen years later, here are some of the chain-reaction effects this choice has had: my mom is now a vegetarian, as is my husband; an aunt is a flexitarian, and all members of my extended family (in-laws included) regularly purchase premade vegetarian meals to keep stocked in their freezer for when I visit. I can't overstress how big a deal this is, especially for some members of my family. My Catholic conservative grandparents, who eat meat every single night and can imagine life no other way, now support an industry they would never have supported otherwise. Because my grandparents love me and want me well fed, they are voting with their dollars to promote the vegetarian lifestyle.

In other words, your choices make a difference, first in your own life, but also in a more cumulative fashion. Those around you see your choices and may choose to emulate them. Even if they don't, they may choose to accommodate your choices, thereby using their consumer purchasing power to buy green products.

Here's one more example of how you can make a difference, directly from my first garbage-free year. Although day to day I didn't feel like I was saving the planet, at the end of the year the cumulative effect was clear. Remember, if the average person creates about three pounds of landfill-bound garbage a day, that's about a thousand pounds of trash in a year, or a ton of trash, literally, between two people. At the end of the year, Adam and I created only 4 pounds of trash between us, saving 2,186 pounds of trash from entering the landfill.

Still not convinced? Check out the sidebar below, which shows how much trash you could avoid just by forgoing disposable products.

Pick Up the Phone

During your first month of a zero-waste life, you're going to have questions—lots of them. Reach out to whoever is available to answer your questions. There are a number of resources at your fingertips.

The first question you will be faced with is the recurring "Is this recyclable in my community?" It's up to you to find out. First, read the next chapter about recycling, and if that doesn't answer your question, locate the phone number or website for your local recycling facility, and find out. Not only are most recycling centers staffed with people who care about the green movement, but many communities also have a waste diversion goal mandated by the state legislature. Recycling facilities have a vested interest in making sure

THE AVERAGE AMERICAN USES . . .

10,000 sheets of copy paper each year

350 to 500 plastic shopping bags each year

8 to 10 diapers per day (average newborn)

584 plastic straws each year

122 yards of floss each year

2,182 tampons each year (American women of reproductive age)

218 bottles of water each year

(Sources: *www.cleanair.org/Waste/wasteFacts.html; www.reusethisbag.com/25-reasons-to-go-reusable.asp; www.femininehygiene.com/tampon-safety/; www.back2tap.com/assets/forms_pdfs/bottled-water-iq-test.pdf; www.bestrawfree.org; www.deltadentalok.org*)

you're recycling properly, and often they have trouble getting the word out about how to do it.

Not sure how to find your friendly local recycling facility? Pull up a search engine and type in the name of your county plus the phrase "public works department." For instance, I would search for "Tillamook County public works department." Typically the public works department houses the solid waste department, which handles your garbage and recycling. These are the people to call with your local recycling needs. Of course, if all else fails, wait until your garbage bill arrives and call the number on your bill.

You may also find yourself holding a product you've purchased for years and wondering "What is this made of?" You see, you can't determine whether something is recyclable until you know what it's made from. I've had this issue with a number of products, including Philadelphia cream cheese and bags of dry dog food. If you encounter this issue, your best bet is to call the company directly. I have yet to run across a product that does not have some variation of "Questions? Comments? Call us today!" printed on the back. Take advantage of this toll-free number and call. Again, as with the recycling facility, it's important to remember that you are not being a burden. Companies like to hear from their consumers—you're the one buying their product, and they want to know whether you are satisfied.

When you're on the phone with a company, it's important to do two things. First, ask your question—what is the packaging made from? Is it recyclable? Second, it's very important to express to the customer service representative how important recyclable packaging is to you. Let them know that if their packaging isn't readily recyclable, you won't be buying it anymore. I usually say something like, "I really love 3 Musketeers bars, but I'm afraid I won't be buying them anymore because the packaging isn't recyclable. The green movement is very important to me as a consumer. I hope you'll pass along my feedback that I'll resume buying your product if your company makes its packaging from recyclable materials."

One more note: Infrequently, when I call a company and ask what their packaging is made from, I'll be given an answer that I think is not entirely accurate. This happened when I called the makers of Philadelphia cream cheese. I wanted to know what the foil-like packaging on a brick of cream cheese was made from. A very nice gentleman answered my call and after checking with another employee, assured me that the wrapper was made from nothing but aluminum foil. Although I wish this were the case, I just don't believe it—I need only to crumple the wrapper to see that it doesn't act the same as foil. I suspect there is some sort of plastic liner involved.

Finally, I urge you to call or write to any companies that make products you will no longer use. It's fair to a manufacturer to explain why you are no longer buying a product you otherwise enjoy. Otherwise, they can't know their customer base would prefer minimal, recyclable packaging.

In the American marketplace, one power that we consumers do have is the power to vote with our wallets. Every dollar we spend sends a clear message to the profiting company: *I like your product and choose to support you with my hard-earned money.* Likewise, a boycott of a product sends the opposite message: *I refuse to spend my money on a product that was not produced with the environment in mind.* The time-honored credo of retailing is "The customer is always right." The way we begin to start a movement is to stop buying products—no matter how delicious, time-saving, or prettily packaged they may be—that do not jibe with our worldviews.

Like a Good Boy Scout, Be Prepared

You never know when a trashy situation might sneak up on you, which is why it's so important to always be prepared. Our daily lives are fraught with occasions filled with disposable plates, cups, and silverware, but you can easily avoid these products with a little forethought.

I keep a kit filled with reusable utensils and the like in both my car and my desk at work. The sidebar below lists the contents of my kits.

ON-THE-GO KITS

Put together two sets of the following items and keep one kit at work and the other in your car.

- Several Tupperware containers plus lids
- One set of silverware: knife, spoon, fork
- Glass straw

- Cloth napkin
- Travel mug for hot beverages
- Water bottle
- Washcloth

The car kit comes in handy all the time. There are many days when I am headed to or from work and I need a little pick-me-up like a cup of coffee. Because I always have my to-go kit in my car, I can just reach back, pull out my travel mug, and stop at the nearest café. Adam and I also tend to order take-out food once a month or so, and we usually decide to do so on the spur of the moment. With those reusables in the car, I can swing into our favorite Thai restaurant, order some drunken noodles, and have my meal placed in my own container, saving the Styrofoam for someone else's use. The other common use I have for my car kit comes after eating in a restaurant. As a person who can never finish a meal, I always have to ask for a take-home container. These are usually made from Styrofoam or plastic, and they're basically garbage when you're done with them. Instead, I bring a Tupperware container into the restaurant with me and use it as my doggy bag.

The desk kit at work is perfect for impromptu office parties. If your office is anything like mine, it's common for coworkers to bring in all sorts of treats on a regular basis. Donuts show up in our staff room once a month, and it's a favorite staff pastime to plan lunch potlucks. I always head down to these events with my plastic plate and utensils in hand. This often becomes a talking point among my coworkers, which is great because it helps raise awareness even more.

When putting your kits together, think cheap. There's no need to buy expensive glass containers unless you want to. You probably have most of the stuff you need lying around the house anyway. If you find you need one or two pieces to complete your set, try checking out outdoor patio dining accessories. Look for materials other than plastic, which is toxic to the environment. You could also head to your local thrift store and comb through the kitchen section—it is easy to find secondhand containers that would work for your car and desk kits.

One final note: Make sure you keep your kits clean and tidy. Wash everything in them regularly, even if they haven't been used. This really goes for all your reusables, from Tupperware to canvas tote bags to stainless steel water bottles. I've heard horror stories from grocery store checkers and restaurant workers about customers bringing in dirty or furry reusables, which doesn't help the cause at all.

Take Away the Trash Cans

A remarkable phenomenon revealed itself to us when we started living garbage free: if you take away the trash receptacle, you take away the trash. Of course, you can't just yank the garbage can from under the sink and expect to suddenly be trash free. But after you've prepared and have a recycling and compost system in place, you're ready to take this huge step.

Remove all the trash cans from your house. Hunt for the insidious ones—in your kitchen, in the bathroom, in the office near the computer, in your kids' bedrooms, inside your car. Clean them out and repurpose the ones you can, perhaps using the old under-the-sink bin to hold your comingled recycling. Put the others in storage or donate them to someone who wants them.

Now, remember the goal you set earlier in the chapter regarding how much trash you'd make over a period of time? Whatever your goal is, locate the container you will designate as your family's single trash can. Put it in a central location and avoid putting anything into it at all costs.

Once the commitment is made and all those secondary trash cans are removed, you'll find yourself automatically reaching for the trash cans, and they won't be there. You better figure out what to do with that piece of waste in your hand, because it is not going to the landfill. Especially in the early days of such a project, you'll be apt to fight tooth and nail to keep a single piece of trash from the landfill. Here, necessity is the mother of invention—work hard to find unique ways to embrace the 3 Rs, and reuse what would usually be trash.

William Rathje, whose archaeology of garbage project I talked about in this book's introduction, found much the same thing. One of Rathje's discoveries earned the title of Parkinson's Law of Garbage, which goes like this: "Garbage expands so as to fill the receptacles available for its containment." (The law is named after C. Northcote Parkinson, who said, "Work expands so as to fill the time available for its completion.") We've found Parkinson's Law to be true—take away the receptacle and, in some very real ways, you take away the trash.

Right now, you're just in the planning stages of your new zero-waste lifestyle. Chapters 3 through 5 will help you establish the systems you need to manage your transition to trash-free living. These systems include tasks such as how to eliminate paper towels from your kitchen, set up a home compost pile, and reexamine your recycling bin so it is utilized to its maximum potential. On your first day of trash-free living, you may find, as we did, that although your life has significantly changed, it doesn't really feel like it has. The only time I consciously thought about our zero-waste lifestyle was when I found myself reaching for something that was no longer there. It's much like trying to break a bad habit—you notice you do it only when you make a conscious effort not to do it. I remember how day one found me reaching for a paper towel to use to cover a dish in the microwave or for the kitchen trash can to scrape food leftovers into.

Rely on the new systems you will establish, and you'll notice right away that this zero-waste stuff isn't so hard after all.

When you find yourself reaching for a trash can that is no longer handy, you'll turn instead to the famous three Rs of the environmental movement: reduce, reuse, and recycle. Together the Rs are strategies you can use to divert your waste. The first R, reduce, helps you pare down the number of products you purchase in the first place. The next R, reuse, asks you to look at would-be trash innovatively. Can you, for example, use clean baby food jars to hold paper clips or rubber bands? The third R, recycle, is the one we're most familiar with—this involves giving an old material new life. The next chapters cover the three Rs in much more detail.

Chapter 3

Reduce and Reuse

We've all heard of the three Rs: reduce, reuse, and recycle. Did you know there's a reason we always say them in that order, with reduce first and recycle last? This arrangement is called the *waste hierarchy*—a way to prioritize how we minimize waste.

The Waste Hierarchy

The waste hierarchy can be considered a sort of environmentalist Hippocratic oath: First, do no harm. The first two strategies, reduction and reuse, do no harm to the environment and therefore should be the first tools an environmentalist turns to. Only when the possibility of those two strategies has been exhausted should recycling be an option. Because recycling does use energy and create pollution—albeit dramatically less than manufacturing new products from virgin materials—a product's usefulness should be fully exhausted before it ever hits the recycling bin.

THE 3 RS . . . AND A FEW MORE

The waste hierarchy gives us ways to decrease the amount of stuff that finds its way into our trash cans and recycling bins. As the Green Movement grows, so does the list of Rs that come before "recycle." Try working these into your green repertoire, too.

Rethink	Repair	Respect
Repurpose	Rot	Reflect
Refuse	Refill	Reinvent

Think of the waste hierarchy as an upside-down pyramid. Reduce is on top, making up the largest third in the pyramid, with reuse in the middle and recycling at the very bottom.

This means that recycling is the least important thing we can do to eliminate trash from our lives. Before we ever think about recycling something, we need to think about how to reduce our waste or reuse what we already have.

This chapter and the next cover the three Rs in detail, giving you practical strategies you can use to eliminate waste from your life. The Rs are covered in the same order as the waste hierarchy, so that by the time we get to recycle, you'll hardly have any waste left to deal with.

Understanding a Product's Life Cycle

How is it that recycling is not the most important thing an environmentalist can practice? The answer lies in the manufacturing of materials as well as in the recycling process.

Any humanmade item in your house, from a bag of Cheetos to the T-shirt you're wearing to the shampoo used to wash your hair, goes through an extensive manufacturing and distribution process before it ever reaches your hands. Sometimes this process is called an object's "life cycle." During an object's life cycle, many things happen: energy is expended, the environment is polluted, and waste is generated, to name a few. Annie Leonard, creator of *The Story of Stuff*, has named the different parts of the life cycle as follows: extraction, production, distribution, consumption, and disposal.

Let's take a quick look at the life cycle of toilet paper—something we all use every day—to better understand the environmental impact of our purchases.

Step 1: Toilet Paper Extraction

We all know toilet paper is made from trees. So, if we want to end up with toilet paper, we have to start by cutting down trees, which takes manpower and energy. Basically anytime we're using machine-generated energy, we're using fossil fuels and negatively impacting the environment. Often pollution is a byproduct of energy use, such as the smoke that comes out of a gas-powered chainsaw.

Step 2: Toilet Paper Production

Once cut down, trees are cut up into chips (more energy expended), then cooked down (more energy) with chemicals. The cooked pulp is washed (more energy), bleached, pressed, and dried. Sometimes chlorine bleach is used to whiten the TP. Chlorine bleach produces dioxins as a byproduct; dioxins are harmful to our health and the environment.

A lot of trash is created in production, too, which has to be hauled away to a landfill or incinerator—more energy, less landfill space, and all-around bad for the planet.

Finally, a bit more energy is used to wind the paper onto cardboard rolls and package rolls together in plastic.

Step 3: Toilet Paper Distribution

Toilet paper is loaded into trucks and driven to grocery stores, where consumers buy the rolls while shopping. More fossil fuels are used by the truck drivers who drive the toilet paper all over the country. More pollution in the form of exhaust is created, too.

Step 4: Toilet Paper Consumption

You know how this works. Enough said.

Step 5: Toilet Paper Disposal

After flushing (more energy), waste-water treatment plants process the soggy paper and use a variety of processes to clean the water. Energy is expended throughout the municipal water delivery system from the moment you turn on a faucet until the water is passing through a treatment plant. Basically any time water is being moved by something other than gravity or the moon, energy is being used.

Assume for a moment that instead of toilet paper, we've been talking about standard white computer paper. After your paper is used (and ideally, if used for a draft, reused on the reverse side), you have two choices for disposal—recycle it or throw it in the trash. Of course the better choice here is to recycle what you can, but do be aware that recycling, although much better than sending something to the dump, does use energy and chemicals and so comes with its own set of environmental impacts (more on this in chapter 4, "Recycle").

When discarded objects fester in a dump, they release methane, a harmful greenhouse gas. Then the whole process repeats itself each time we buy a new sheet of paper.

Keep in mind, too, that this entire life cycle applies to all the products and items used in conjunction with the toilet paper manufacturing process. The cardboard TP roll, the plastic wrapper, the materials used to build the paper factory, the containers that hold the chlorine bleach—and the list goes on—all go through each phase of the life cycle, all using energy and creating pollution.

As you can see, the life cycle of a product doesn't start or end with us. Though it's easy to have an "out of sight, out of mind" mindset, our use of any product doesn't happen in a vacuum. There is a negative environmental impact at every step of a product's life cycle.

This doesn't mean we should stop using all products, stand in one place forever, fester, and die. This is where the waste hierarchy comes in, helping us to prioritize by directing us first to reduce the number of products we rely on, then to reuse what we can, and finally to recycle things when we're done with them.

Reduce, the first third of the waste hierarchy pyramid, is so important because it eliminates all the energy used at any point in a product's life cycle. If you never use another lint brush again, that's one less lint brush a manufacturer has to make, meaning less energy and pollutants expended at each step in the life cycle. Go, you!

The Link between Trash and Consumption

Trash reduction is also called *precycling*. The act of precycling simply means considering a product's worth, usefulness, and recyclability before it is ever purchased. In other words, precycling means standing in a store holding an item you'd like to purchase and asking yourself, "Do I really need this new thing, or do I just want it?"

It took me a while to figure this out: that living garbage free was linked to our habits as consumers. There's no question that we live in a "stuff"-driven society. Daily we are bombarded with advertisements trying to sell us new stuff. I can't open my email, read the newspaper, or turn on the television without an ad trying to sell me yet another new product. Being American is practically synonymous with being a consumer. Our economy is built on consumption. And consumption creates trash.

The two are inextricably linked. If I consumed nothing, I would create no trash. Through consumption—of food, clothes, toys, electronics—I fill up my trash can with packaging, food scraps, and discarded products. Trash and consumption cannot be separated.

At about the same time that we started living garbage free, I read an article in the newspaper that suggested that shopping—consumption—triggers an endorphin rush in our bodies. Endorphins are chemicals released by our bodies during pleasurable moments such as lovemaking or exercise, and they leave us permeated with a sense of well-being.

Wait—we get the same pleasure from buying stuff as we do from sex or a good workout? No wonder advertisers assail us with demands to buy the latest and greatest—they know we're suckers for pleasure.

Since that moment, every time I've stood in a store holding something I "have to have," I've thought about that endorphin rush. I thought about how I didn't like being controlled by a chemical reaction and a bunch of advertising execs. More often than not, I put the item back down and remembered one of my favorite quotes: "Have nothing in your house you don't know to be useful or believe to be beautiful."

Every time, as I left the store without buying my new must-have item, that endorphin rush faded. If nothing else, it would still be there waiting if I went back later. Or, as waste-free contributor Robert Haley says, "You're never going to consume enough to make you happy."

COMBATING INSTANT GRATIFICATION

About a month into her family's garbage-free lifestyle, April Luebbert noticed a change in her son. Prior to living without waste, "We were very much an instant-gratification family," she said. Her children were accustomed to eating when they were hungry—so much so that her son would scream throughout the preparation of instant oatmeal. This became much worse when she stopped buying instant oatmeal and started preparing it on the stove top. The screaming worsened while she cooked and tried to explain that we don't always get what we want when we want it. Eventually April wore him down, and she taught her son the value of delayed gratification. Now he plays with his toys while she prepares meals, and she's proud of the lesson he's learned.

The First "R": Reduce

Prior to the Green Garbage Project, Adam and I considered ourselves conscientious consumers, but we were consumers nonetheless. Our shopping habits never centered around reduction of purchasing, but rather around an attempt to purchase products claiming to be environmentally friendly. For example, we would often buy the Method line of cleaning products, which are touted as eco-conscious. And although it is certainly better to buy cleaning products made with natural ingredients than chemicals that can contaminate the waterway when washed down the drain, there is really no need to purchase separate glass cleaners, shower door cleaners, and drain cleaners when simple white vinegar can perform all three duties—and be used in the kitchen as well.

Reducing the number of products we bring into our homes is important because there is a pile of invisible garbage created during every product's manufacturing process that most people rarely consider. We already know that on average every American produces about three pounds of trash each day that is destined for the dump. But, for every can of trash I hauled to the curb, corporate-industrial manufacturing produced an additional *forty to seventy* cans filled with trash generated during the manufacture of my products. Our personal trash is just a drop in the bucket when compared to the trash generated in the creation of all the products we buy—everything from food to clothing to furniture. For example, manufacturing just one gold wedding ring creates twenty tons of mining waste. The only way we can impact that monumental pile of trash is by resisting the endorphin rush we get when we buy new stuff and focus on reducing the amount we buy in the first place. Buying less means we make less trash, and it means manufacturers make less trash upstream, too. (Read more about corporate industrial waste and what you can do about it in chapter 14, "The Global Zero-Waste Movement.")

There's an editorial cartoon I've saved that really illustrates the purpose of reduction and reuse. The cartoon depicts two men taking out the trash. One man, surrounded by a large pile of garbage and recyclables, says, "We help the environment by consuming lots of environmentally safe products!" His next door neighbor, holding only a single small trash can, says, "We help the environment by consuming less." Prior to our trash-free year, we were the first guy: proud eco-conscious consumers, but avid consumers nonetheless. The better bet is to be the second guy—to completely overhaul our consumption habits to require fewer overall products. This is the simplicity behind the first tier of the waste hierarchy. Reduction means simply buying less. We all want to live more simply; here's the first step.

Strategies for Trash Reduction

Several simple guiding principles can help you embrace reduction. Master this step before moving on to the next tier of the waste hierarchy, and you'll already be a third of the way to trash-free living!

Stop Using Single-Serve Products

Do this immediately. Starting today. It may take a little extra effort, but the packaging you'll save by taking this step will decrease your waste by multiples. For example, if you buy a package of twelve single-serve chip bags, your waste will be twelve empty bags plus a cardboard box plus the plastic wrap surrounding it. If you buy one big bag of chips and divvy it into twelve servings, your only waste will be one bag.

LOSE THOSE SINGLE-SERVE GROCERY ITEMS AND SAVE

When you buy single-serve items at the grocery store, you're paying more money for less food. The extra money you're spending gets you a little extra convenience and a lot more packaging. Save money and resources by boycotting individual packages of

Chips	Granola bars	Pudding or Jell-O cups
Crackers	Yogurt	
Fruit snacks	Apple slices	Rice cakes
Cookies	Baby carrots	String cheese
Juice boxes	Applesauce	Candy
Nuts	Raisins	

Instead, try buying a bigger size, buying in bulk, or making your own. Look for recipes in chapter 6.

Stop Using Disposable Products

Disposable products are things intended to be thrown away after a single use. It takes hardly any extra effort to wash cloth napkins or put real dishes in the dishwasher. Remember that one of the benefits of this lifestyle is a simplified routine—reinvest some of the minutes you'll save into maintaining durable, not disposable, products. April says of disposables, "They're unnecessary. Once you're used to not having them, it just becomes a part of your life."

DISPOSABLE PRODUCTS YOU CAN LIVE WITHOUT

INSTEAD OF THIS...	USE THIS:
Plastic water bottle	Refillable metal or plastic bottle
Tear-away lint brush	Reusable fabric lint brush
Paper towels, paper napkins	Dishcloths, cloth napkins
Sponges	Reusable dishcloths
Take-out chopsticks	Provide your own
Plastic lunch baggies	Reusable plastic or glass containers; washable, reusable baggies
Paper or plastic bags	Bring your own reusable bag
Cotton balls	Squares of a soft fabric like flannel
Plastic silverware	Bring your own
Tissues	Old-fashioned handkerchief
Hand wipes	Hand sanitizer
Paper lunch sacks	Reusable cloth sack
Plastic straws	No straw or bring your own reusable straw
Disposable gloves	Reusable, washable gloves
Pens	Refillable pen, fountain pen, wooden pencil, refillable mechanical pencil
Garbage bags	When you compost (see chapter 5), there's no need for a can liner
Plastic produce bags	Invest in or make a set of reusable mesh produce bags. Use, wash, repeat.
Any household wipes: window, counter, dust, and so on	Rags or washcloths

Buy Big and in Bulk

Buying one bigger bottle of shampoo instead of two smaller bottles means you're recycling only one container and therefore reducing your recycling pile. Buying in bulk using your own reusable container, if possible, is desirable because you drastically reduce the packaging you bring into your home and you can buy as much or little as you need. Read more about buying in bulk in chapter 6, "The Zero-Waste Kitchen," which includes ways to even avoid using those tear-off plastic grocery bags.

Buy Concentrated Liquids

Concentrated liquids come in smaller containers, which, once again, decreases packaging. Use a little less, add some water, and suddenly what's in that small container goes a lot further.

Make Products Multitask

Reduce the number of items on your grocery list by looking for ways to double up. Vinegar, lemon juice, and baking soda can all be used in the kitchen and cleaning bucket, for example. I use bar soap for washing and shaving. This not only reduces garbage but also saves you money.

Remember, There Is Another Way

Most disposable products we rely on today were only invented within the last half-century. Today a garbage-free lifestyle may seem impossible, but only a few decades ago it was the norm. Ask yourself (or the Internet, if you're at a loss), "How did my Depression-era great-grandmother accomplish this task?" Bonus: you may learn a forgotten skill in the process.

REMEMBERING YOUR REUSABLE BAGS, BOTTLES, AND MUGS

"Feedback loops are very big with me," Rose Brown says, describing how she remembers to bring reusable bags to the grocery store and coffee mugs to the espresso stand. "If I forgot a travel mug, I had to buy a new one." Rose connected her reusable bags, water bottles, food containers, and coffee mugs to a financial penalty, and after a while, when she got tired of buying new containers, she remembered to bring them with her.

Make Things at Home

This applies to food, clothes, and hygiene and cleaning products. Depending on how adventurous you are, you can make virtually anything at home. Homemade bread, for example, reduces the amount of plastic packaging you bring through the door.

Use Less

Stretch the products you already buy so they last longer. Instead of using a full-length strip of toothpaste as shown in the commercials, use a pea-sized dab. And do you really need a whole glob of shampoo or a foot-long piece of floss? Make it a game, and see how small an amount you really need.

As you comb through your list of household trash, created during your waste audit, you'll likely find that many of the items you usually buy can be eliminated from the grocery list by implementing these reduction strategies. There's nothing quite like the feeling of seeing your grocery list cut down by a quarter or a third—your shopping trip goes fast, and you spend less money in the checkout line, all because you are buying only what you need and making your products do double duty.

The next step in the waste hierarchy, reuse, will similarly help you cross trashy items off your waste-audit list. The reuse principle is both fun and challenging, because it requires some good old-fashioned ingenuity.

The Second "R": Reuse

The reuse section of the waste hierarchy is all about creativity, because although the general principle stays the same, how you implement reuse in your life is completely up to you.

The basic idea is simple—reuse means taking something you already own and using it for another purpose. There are many reasons you may want to reuse something you already own. More often than not, I reuse something for the following reasons:

- I'm done with an object for its original purpose, but I don't want to throw it away because it's still useful.
- I've broken something, but the raw material it's made from is still useful.
- I need something right away, but I don't want to go to the store—after all, necessity is the mother of invention.

Reuse is fantastic for the environment because it begets waste reduction—it avoids the need to purchase a new product. For example, if I can reuse a glass peanut butter jar as a pencil holder, there's no need for me to go out and buy a new pencil holder. Reuse is as simple as using a plastic grocery bag to pick up dog poop—which eliminates the need to buy brand-new doggie-doo bags—or as complicated as crafting a vase from a burned-out lightbulb.

Strategies for Reuse

Here are some ideas to get you started on your reuse journey.

Stop and think before buying something new: Anytime you find yourself wanting to make a purchase, ask yourself if there's a way you can make it from things lying around the house. Need new food storage containers for leftovers? Instead of buying new ones, wash out margarine tubs and peanut butter jars to use for this purpose. If you need a tarp, how about using an old shower curtain?

Borrow from a friend or service: Rather than buying something new, see if you can borrow it instead. Don't overlook professional borrowing services like Netflix or even your local library.

Search the Internet for ideas: Before you throw something out, check whether there are ways to creatively reuse it. Trying searching online to see whether other people have solutions for you. I type in something along the lines of "How can I reuse a broken [item]," and I'm always surprised at the answers I find.

Keep reuse in the back of your mind when buying something new: Some materials last longer than others. Buying durable products is a good idea anyway, because they last longer. Purchasing items with a second use in mind means they last twice as long.

Upcycling

Upcycling is the term crafters and artisans use when they use recovered, used, or scavenged materials to make an art project. The world of upcycling is a large one, and it's growing all the time. Some crafters work hard to make recycled material into beautiful works of art such as sculptures or murals. Other crafters turn their material into functional items like tote bags and raincoats. Whether the result is functional, beautiful, or both, the only criterion for upcycling is that second-hand materials are predominantly or exclusively used.

It's easy for anyone to join the movement. Depending on your area of interest and ability, you may want to spend some time on the Internet or at your local library to gather ideas for your first project. See the Further Reading section for upcycling books and websites to check out.

The possibilities for upcycling are limited only by your imagination. Type "upcycling" into a search engine and you'll find numerous tutorials or examples of this growing phenomenon. I have created a number of upcycled creations, such as a journal made from recycled printer paper and a plastic-bag cover. Other examples are boxes made from cassette tapes, earrings made from pop-can tabs, and stuffed animals made from old blue jeans.

A number of enterprising upcyclers have turned their love for this new trend into successful and lucrative home or online businesses. The online craft site Etsy.com features a number of upcycled products. Two businesses— Lou's Upcycles and TerraCycle—have been particularly helpful to me on my zero-waste journey.

Lou's Upcycles: Crafter Lou Leelyn from Massachusetts got tired of seeing Americans throw away so much plastic packaging. So she started a crafting business called Lou's Upcycles (lousupcycles.blogspot.com), dubbed herself a *trashionista*, and took the world by storm.

Lou's particular form of upcycling uses what's called fused plastic as a fabric for all sorts of projects normally made from cloth. She has solicited donations of plastic from friends and strangers all over the country. Any foldable plastic packaging will do, including french fry bags, chips bags, hot dog wrappers, shredded cheese bags, pet treat bags, and more. Lou takes this entire waste stream and diverts it from the landfill.

These plastic bags are turned into fused plastic through a very low-tech process. The bags are separated into individual layers. Two layers at a time are sandwiched between layers of freezer paper and ironed at a low setting until they are melted together. Additional layers are added the same way until a thick, tarp-like plastic fabric has been formed.

Lou uses this plastic fabric in all kinds of marvelous creations, including baby bibs, coin purses, messenger bags, checkbook covers, and zippered pouches. She sells these at craft fairs in her area and online through Etsy.com.

Although Lou has turned trash into a booming business, she has a real concern: "I am afraid Lou's Upcycles has become a place where plastic can be delivered so consumers do not have to feel guilty about buying hundred-packs of chips, cases of water bottles wrapped in plastic, tiny candy bars, and other scary overpackaging. . . . I think we may have forgotten that what I make should be unnecessary and unfortunate, in a way. Lou's Upcycles was created by something that is suffocating the planet." She hopes her customers and plastic donaters don't use her business as an excuse to buy and use more plastic packaging.

TerraCycle: Another business that has embraced the upcycling model is TerraCycle. According to the TerraCycle website, "TerraCycle's purpose is to eliminate the idea of waste. We do this by creating national recycling systems for previously nonrecyclable or hard-to-recycle waste. Anyone can sign up for these programs, called the Brigades, and start sending us waste."

After TerraCycle receives your waste, innovative designers turn discarded packaging into clever new products that are sold nationally in chain stores like Walmart and Whole Foods. Ultimately I hope to see stores that sell upcycled products invite people to bring in the original discarded packaging for forwarding to upcycling manufacturers, thereby closing the recycling loop entirely. Whole Foods already does this with its Preserve Gimme 5 program (see page 76); with pressure from customers, hopefully other stores begin to follow suit.

You can get involved by collecting and sending your materials to TerraCycle. You join a brigade based on the type of trash you'll be able to collect. When you send in your trash, you'll earn points that can be redeemed to help a local school or nonprofit organization. Brigades have to be accepting new members for you to join. As of this writing, TerraCycle has openings for people to collect the following materials: Elmer's glue sticks, Capri Sun and other drink pouches, Huggies diaper packaging, and cheese packaging, among others.

These materials and many more are turned into new products like bags, bulletin boards, trash cans, clocks, picture frames, speakers, holiday stockings, and toys.

Learn more about this successful upcycling business at www.terracycle.com.

Donating

Even if you can't reuse a material, that doesn't mean someone else can't. As the saying goes, one man's trash is another man's treasure. If you don't want to be a packrat and stash tons of random material around your house for a rainy day, consider donating it to someone or someplace that can use it. I've donated many a fake houseplant to thrift stores over the years, for example, so I found it pretty funny when I walked into the Goodwill this past October hunting for some fake flowers to make into a Green Girl superhero costume for Homecoming Week at the school where I teach. Some of those fake flowers found a permanent place in my costume box, but most made their way right back to the same thrift store, where they can be resold and used again.

Many charities and organizations are happy to take discarded materials off your hands. Call first to make sure your donations will be put to use. I regularly turn to these venues:

Schools, Girl or Boy Scout troops, or other children's organizations: Teachers or club leaders are often in need of supplies for art projects. See whether they need any items such as empty egg cartons, empty oatmeal containers, magazines, newspaper, clean steel cans, cigar boxes, toilet paper or paper towel rolls, clean glass jars, and fabric scraps. Schools and other children's organizations can also use sheet music and used musical instruments as well as athletic equipment.

Middle and high schools: Check with the front office to see what is needed. Often art rooms, science labs, and home economics facilities will take secondhand materials like old photographic equipment or used cookie sheets.

Animal shelters: Animal organizations can generally use rags for cleaning and old blankets and towels for animal bedding. If you have any unused pet food, treats, or litter that your spoiled pets have rejected, bring these to the shelters, too.

Thrift stores, pawn shops, antique stores: Don't forget these options for giving away your old stuff. Thrift stores like the Goodwill or Salvation Army will take all manner of items off your hands. Most people regularly donate old clothes or household items, but think outside the box, too. (Note: There are some items even thrift stores won't accept for resale; these include mattresses and sofa beds, tires, carpeting, air conditioners, and auto parts.) If you have a more valuable treasure you'd like to part with, consider pawning it or even selling it at an antique store. You never know what odd little item someone might be looking for. I personally frequent antique stores often, and I keep an eye out for strange items that evoke nostalgia from childhood, including Welch's jelly glasses and a bear-in-blue-jeans cookie jar.

Art supply nonprofits: Some communities are lucky enough to have a special kind of thrift store designed specifically to collect and sell supplies used in art projects. Community organizations, clubs, schools, and individuals can shop these donation centers for deeply discounted art supplies. Google "art supplies nonprofits" to see a number of examples and to find out whether there is such an organization in your area.

Check out www.scrap-sf.org and www.mfta.org to see a couple of examples of this type of nonprofit.

Garage Sales and Freecycle

There are two other outlets for moving your unwanted items into the hands of someone who finds them useful.

Garage sales: This time-honored American weekend classic is a great way to clean out your house and earn a little extra spending money besides. I got my first taste of the garage sale experience the summer Adam and I moved from Washington to the Oregon Coast. We had a bunch of items we did not want to haul with us, so we put together our first-ever garage sale. We invited our parents to put their unwanted items up for sale, too, so we had quite a spread of items spilling out onto our front lawn. I was surprised at how many items sold, especially things that were marked as broken or that I couldn't find a use for, including a lawn mower that wouldn't start anymore. At the end of the day, we placed a pile of miscellaneous things on the curb with a sign that said "free" and offered up anything that didn't sell, such as an old NordicTrack exercise machine and four unmatched tires. Within a couple of hours, everything had been claimed.

Freecycle: Freecycle.org is a great website that helps you give away or find a wide variety of goods. Freecycle is basically a network of about eight million people who are all questing to "keep good stuff out of the landfill." There are very few rules site members must adhere to—you must be polite or courteous, and you must be giving something away or seeking something for free. Like any good day of shopping, you never know what you'll find on Freecycle. It's like a giant online flea market. To sign up, you create an account and join a local region so you're interacting with people from your local community.

Look for Creative New Uses for Broken or Obsolete Items

A big part of the reuse tier of the waste hierarchy is personal innovation. This means taking a close look at a broken or obsolete object that you have lying around the house, thinking outside the box, and seeing whether you can devise a new use for it. Let me give you some examples:

- Old fabric drapes make great kids' costumes or can be used for pillowcases.
- A leaky hose can be turned into a soaker hose by adding even more holes.
- Old denim jeans can be torn into strips and sewn into a rug.
- Newspapers can be used for creating papier-mâché masterpieces.
- Plastic yogurt containers can be used to start seeds in the spring.
- Wine bottles can be used as water carafes.
- Pieces from broken plates can be used in a mosaic project.
- Dresser drawers can double as plant pots.
- A bunch of wine corks can make a great bulletin board.
- Junk mail can be shredded and turned into packing material.
- Pizza boxes work wonders as weed killers around the garden.
- An old T-shirt can be turned into a cloth grocery bag.

As you can see, implementing the strategies of reduce and reuse into your daily life will have an immediate, noticeable impact on your garbage can. So, to summarize: There are two simple reduction steps you can take right away. The first is to stop buying disposable products immediately. While it might seem impossible to live without paper towels, try it for a week and see what innovative workarounds you come up with. The second is to stop buying single-serve products. If you can't break the junk food habit, at least buy the big bag of chips instead of twelve individually wrapped single-serve bags. Finally, anytime you go to throw something away, remember the second R, reuse. Before putting anything in the trash can, ask yourself if you can give it a second life.

Meet Your Goal: Reduce and Reuse

Easy

- Stop buying single-serve items.
- Donate unwanted items to thrift stores.
- Wait a day before buying something new that you really want; go back to the store only if you can't live without it.
- Stop buying bottled water; use a refillable bottle instead.
- Bring a reusable travel cup to the coffee shop.
- Borrow rather than buy.
- Buy concentrated liquids.
- Use reusable cloth bags.

Moderate

- Stop using paper towels.
- Join a TerraCycle brigade.
- Hold an annual garage sale to get rid of unwanted items.
- Reuse plastic produce bags—bring them back to the store the next time you shop and fill with produce.
- Pack your lunch with reusable containers, not plastic baggies.
- Buy in bulk.
- Shop at antique and thrift stores.
- Sign up for a Freecycle account.

Advanced

- Eliminate foil, plastic wrap, and plastic baggies from your life.
- Turn your trash into an upcycled craft project.
- Invest in a reusable straw and bring it to restaurants.
- Carry home take-out and restaurant leftovers in your own containers.

Chapter 4

Recycle

Sure, the idea of living garbage free sounds nice, but anyone attempting this lifestyle has to wonder, is it even possible within the confines of modern society? After all, most of us want to save the environment *and* live normal lives—we have no interest in quitting our jobs, raising our own food, crafting our toothbrushes from twigs, and otherwise adopting a commune-worthy hippie lifestyle.

Even with the strategies of reduce and reuse in place, we will all still create *some* waste, and this waste needs to be recyclable. When I first started researching recycling, I realized very quickly that, although Adam and I were avid and educated recyclers, we still had a lot to learn. Some of the items we had been throwing into our comingled recycling bin were actually not recyclable—and some of what we were throwing away could be recycled.

Recycling can be difficult because the system is complicated. There is plenty of information available about waste reduction, but some of that information is contradictory. Different cities, towns, and states all have particular guidelines to follow. What's a person to do?

Recycling is the third tier of the waste hierarchy because, although recycling is inarguably a positive thing, recycling by itself is not enough to save the planet, for several reasons. To better understand the positives and negatives associated with recycling, you need to look at what happens to our recyclables after we haul them to the curb.

What Happens to Recyclables

Most of our recyclables are sent to a Materials Recovery Facility, or MRF (rhymes with Smurf). MRFs are specialized recycling plants that receive and sort materials according to type, which are then sold to manufacturers. At a so-called "clean MRF," which sorts only recyclables (as opposed to a "dirty MRF," which separates solid waste from recyclables), a mixture of household metal, paper, plastic, and sometimes glass is dumped onto a conveyor belt. Workers pick through these materials, pulling out anything that is trash. After this, the materials are swept into a giant sorting machine. Magnets pull out bits of metal, and blasts of air dislodge beverage containers from newspaper. Over time, the comingled materials we put out on the curb are sorted according to type. While it seems a little silly to unsort all our recyclables by placing them in a comingled bin only for them to be resorted at the MRF, research has shown that participation in recycling programs increases when sorting is not required. Commingled recycling is also more efficient because recycling collection trucks can haul more materials if they are not sorted.

Next, recyclables are sold to manufacturers who turn old materials into new. Recyclable materials are like any other commodity. They are a salable product, and the value of these materials increases and decreases according to available supply and consumer demand. The value of a particular material depends in large part on how expensive a recycled material is compared to virgin material. Energy is expended in the recycling process, as bottles and cans are melted down into a raw form, and someone—either taxpayers subsidizing the process or manufacturers paying for materials—pays for that expense. Purity of a material is also a consideration for manufacturers, who put material quality at a premium. When many containers are melted together, contaminants like dyes and chemicals can impact a material's purity. If a manufacturer can buy cheaper, purer virgin materials, they have no economic incentive to purchase recycled materials. Historically metals are lucrative to recycle, whereas materials like Styrofoam are not.

A material's ability to be truly recycled, rather than "downcycled," also helps determine how valuable it is. *Downcycling* means that, over time, some recycled materials lose their integrity. A piece of plastic or paper can be recycled only so many times before it will ultimately have to end up in a landfill (that is, assuming that everyone recycles, and that in its next life the paper isn't thrown away before it can be recycled a second or third time). Paper, for example, consists of long fibers mashed together into sheets. As paper is recycled, the fibers get shorter and shorter. Short fibers can be made into only thin materials like tissue paper, toilet paper, and paper towels. After that, the fibers are too short to be recycled again. Plastic downcycles at an even faster rate than paper; so quickly, in fact, that it can rarely be recycled into the same material. Whereas a sheet of typing paper can be turned into more typing paper before winding up as a paper towel, a plastic yogurt cup cannot be turned back into a yogurt cup. Instead, it's turned into a less valuable material, like plastic lumber. Metal and glass, on the other hand, can be recycled over and over, forever, without losing their integrity.

Once a load of recyclables is sorted and purchased, the old materials must be reformed back into raw material. This happens in one of two ways. Metal, glass, and plastic are melted at high heat; the molten liquid can be molded into new products. Paper is washed and bleached until all traces of ink are gone and the paper is white again.

This final step is why recycling comes last in the waste hierarchy. Recycling plastic, metal, glass, and paper uses energy and chemicals to turn old into new. And although recycling saves energy when compared to manufacturing from virgin materials, it is by no means a clean process. A material should be recycled only as a last resort, after it has outlived its usefulness.

Strategies for Recycling

Recycling is complicated—first, because a simple system for recycling just doesn't exist yet; and second, because every town, county, and state in the country has a different set of rules to follow. As consumers, we often have a hard time keeping our local recycling requirements straight, which is complicated by the fact that we don't know what materials our packaging is made from, we don't know what all the recycling symbols mean, and there is a plethora of misinformation available at every step in the process. Though the logistical problems of recycling are numerous—some things can be recycled curbside, whereas others must be "hand carried"—and recycling is not an end-all solution to the country's trash problem, it is a vastly better option than landfilling.

What you need to navigate this confusing infrastructure and maximize your recycling resources is a system. Use the following steps to set up one that works for you.

Make a List

Your first step is to make a list of products you typically buy. You will essentially be making one giant grocery list as if you were out of absolutely everything in your household—think about pantry and freezer items, cleaning products, and laundry products. Don't include large, durable items like toasters or refrigerators; focus on products you consume or use on a regular basis. I've included a master shopping checklist on the following pages so all you have to do is check off the items you buy on a regular basis. Blank spaces are included for items you buy that aren't listed. You will be using this list later in the book to complete various waste-reduction tasks, so it is important to take the time to fill it out now.

Identify the Trash

Next, go through your list and highlight all the things that wind up in the trash. It is the packaging associated with these items that you are going to be dealing with in this chapter. Chances are, some of the things you've been placing in your trash can are actually recyclable, and it is your mission to find out which ones.

A helpful website for beginning recyclers is Earth911.com, a database that catalogs recycling facilities around the country. Want to know where to recycle Styrofoam in your area? Type in your location, and the site will match you with the closest processing facility. You can also select a recycling depot near you and see a list of materials that site accepts.

Define the Recyclables

Next, you'll need to distinguish between comingled recyclables and what I call "hand-carry" recyclables. Most Americans have access to curbside recycling services offered by their garbage haulers. If this is you, you've received two or three separate bins from your local trash collectors, including your regular trash can, a recycling bin, and perhaps a yard waste bin. What you can place in your curbside recycling bin varies from place to

continued on page 72

MASTER SHOPPING CHECKLIST

Use this form to check off the items you buy on a regular basis, and refer to this list to eliminate waste from your life.

MEAT

- ☐ Bacon
- ☐ Chicken, boneless and skinless
- ☐ Chicken, whole
- ☐ Ground beef
- ☐ Ground turkey
- ☐ Hamburgers
- ☐ Hot dogs
- ☐ Lamb
- ☐ Meat from deli counter
- ☐ Packaged lunch meat
- ☐ Pork chops
- ☐ Sausage
- ☐ Seafood from deli counter
- ☐ Steaks
- ☐ Stew meat
- ☐ Turkey, boneless and skinless
- ☐ Turkey, whole
- ☐ Other: _____
- ☐ Other: _____
- ☐ Other: _____
- ☐ Other: _____

DAIRY AND EGGS

- ☐ American cheese
- ☐ Butter
- ☐ Cheddar cheese
- ☐ Coffee creamer
- ☐ Cream cheese
- ☐ Eggs
- ☐ Feta cheese
- ☐ Half and half
- ☐ Margarine
- ☐ Milk
- ☐ Mozzarella cheese
- ☐ Rice/soy/almond milk
- ☐ Ricotta/cottage cheese
- ☐ Sour cream
- ☐ Swiss cheese
- ☐ Whipping cream
- ☐ Yogurt
- ☐ Other: _____
- ☐ Other: _____
- ☐ Other: _____
- ☐ Other: _____

PRODUCE

- ☐ Apples
- ☐ Avocados
- ☐ Bananas
- ☐ Berries
- ☐ Broccoli
- ☐ Cabbage
- ☐ Carrots
- ☐ Cauliflower
- ☐ Celery
- ☐ Cherries
- ☐ Citrus
- ☐ Cucumbers
- ☐ Garlic
- ☐ Kiwi
- ☐ Lettuce
- ☐ Melons
- ☐ Onions
- ☐ Peaches/nectarines
- ☐ Peppers
- ☐ Plums
- ☐ Potatoes
- ☐ Radishes
- ☐ Spinach
- ☐ Tomatoes
- ☐ Zucchini
- ☐ Other: _____
- ☐ Other: _____
- ☐ Other: _____
- ☐ Other: _____

CONDIMENTS

- ☐ BBQ sauce
- ☐ Cocktail sauce
- ☐ Horseradish
- ☐ Jelly/jam
- ☐ Ketchup
- ☐ Mayonnaise
- ☐ Mustard
- ☐ Olives
- ☐ Peanut butter
- ☐ Pickles

- ☐ Salad dressing
- ☐ Salsa
- ☐ Soy sauce
- ☐ Steak sauce
- ☐ Syrup
- ☐ Tartar sauce
- ☐ Teriyaki sauce
- ☐ Vinegar
- ☐ Worcestershire sauce
- ☐ Other: _____
- ☐ Other: _____
- ☐ Other: _____
- ☐ Other: _____

GRAINS

- ☐ Bagels
- ☐ Breadsticks
- ☐ Cake
- ☐ Cereal
- ☐ Coffee cake
- ☐ Couscous
- ☐ Donuts/pastries
- ☐ English muffins
- ☐ Hamburger/ hot dog buns
- ☐ Muffins
- ☐ Oatmeal
- ☐ Pasta
- ☐ Rice
- ☐ Sandwich bread
- ☐ Tortillas
- ☐ Other: _____
- ☐ Other: _____

- ☐ Other: _____
- ☐ Other: _____

FROZEN FOODS

- ☐ Burritos
- ☐ Chicken nuggets
- ☐ Corn dogs
- ☐ Faux-meat products (veggie burgers, veggie dogs, etc.)
- ☐ Fish sticks
- ☐ Frozen TV dinners
- ☐ Fruit
- ☐ Ice cream
- ☐ Ice cream novelties/popsicles
- ☐ Juice
- ☐ Pie crust
- ☐ Pies
- ☐ Pizza
- ☐ Pot pies
- ☐ Pretzels
- ☐ Seafood
- ☐ Vegetables
- ☐ Waffles
- ☐ Other: _____
- ☐ Other: _____
- ☐ Other: _____
- ☐ Other: _____

DRINKS

- ☐ Beer
- ☐ Bottled water
- ☐ Club soda

- ☐ Coffee
- ☐ Energy drinks
- ☐ Flavored water
- ☐ Juice/juice boxes
- ☐ Soda
- ☐ Tea
- ☐ Wine
- ☐ Other: _____
- ☐ Other: _____
- ☐ Other: _____
- ☐ Other: _____

BABY PRODUCTS

- ☐ Baby food
- ☐ Baby oil
- ☐ Baby powder
- ☐ Baby shampoo
- ☐ Baby wipes
- ☐ Diapers
- ☐ Formula
- ☐ Other: _____
- ☐ Other: _____
- ☐ Other: _____
- ☐ Other: _____

CANNED AND JARRED GOODS

- ☐ Applesauce
- ☐ Beans
- ☐ Bouillon cubes
- ☐ Broth
- ☐ Pasta sauce
- ☐ Soup
- ☐ Tomato paste

- ☐ Tomato sauce
- ☐ Tomatoes
- ☐ Vegetables
- ☐ Other: _____
- ☐ Other: _____
- ☐ Other: _____
- ☐ Other: _____

SNACK FOODS

- ☐ Candy
- ☐ Chips
- ☐ Cookies
- ☐ Crackers
- ☐ Dried fruit
- ☐ Drink mixes
- ☐ Fruit snacks
- ☐ Granola bars
- ☐ Jell-O
- ☐ Nuts/seeds
- ☐ Popcorn
- ☐ Pretzels
- ☐ Pudding
- ☐ Rice cakes
- ☐ Other: _____
- ☐ Other: _____
- ☐ Other: _____
- ☐ Other: _____

BAKING ITEMS

- ☐ Baking powder
- ☐ Baking soda
- ☐ Brown sugar
- ☐ Cake mix
- ☐ Chocolate chips

- ☐ Confectioners' sugar
- ☐ Cornmeal
- ☐ Cornstarch
- ☐ Evaporated milk
- ☐ Flour
- ☐ Food coloring
- ☐ Gelatin
- ☐ Shortening
- ☐ Spices
- ☐ Sugar
- ☐ Sweetened condensed milk
- ☐ Vanilla extract
- ☐ Yeast
- ☐ Other: _____
- ☐ Other: _____
- ☐ Other: _____
- ☐ Other: _____

PET PRODUCTS

- ☐ Bedding for hamster/guinea pig/gerbil
- ☐ Bird seed
- ☐ Canned cat food
- ☐ Canned dog food
- ☐ Cat treats
- ☐ Dog treats
- ☐ Dry cat food
- ☐ Dry dog food
- ☐ Fish food
- ☐ Food for hamster/ guinea pig/gerbil
- ☐ Litter

- ☐ Other: _____
- ☐ Other: _____
- ☐ Other: _____
- ☐ Other: _____

BATHROOM ITEMS

- ☐ Aftershave
- ☐ Birth control pills
- ☐ Body wash
- ☐ Bug repellent
- ☐ Chapstick
- ☐ Cologne/perfume
- ☐ Conditioner
- ☐ Condoms
- ☐ Cotton balls
- ☐ Deodorant
- ☐ Depilatory cream
- ☐ Facial tissue
- ☐ Feminine hygiene
- ☐ Floss
- ☐ Hairspray
- ☐ Lotion
- ☐ Makeup
- ☐ Prescriptions
- ☐ Q-tips
- ☐ Razor blades
- ☐ Shampoo
- ☐ Shaving cream
- ☐ Soap
- ☐ Sunscreen
- ☐ Tanning lotion
- ☐ Toilet paper
- ☐ Toothbrushes
- ☐ Toothpaste

- ☐ Other: _____
- ☐ Other: _____
- ☐ Other: _____
- ☐ Other: _____

OTHER NONFOOD ITEMS

- ☐ Batteries
- ☐ Books
- ☐ Candles
- ☐ CDs/DVDs/video games
- ☐ Coffee filters
- ☐ Disposable cups
- ☐ Disposable cutlery
- ☐ Disposable plates/ bowls
- ☐ Flowers
- ☐ Foil
- ☐ Garbage bags
- ☐ Gift cards
- ☐ Greeting cards
- ☐ Home décor items
- ☐ Lightbulbs
- ☐ Magazines
- ☐ Nails, screws, etc.
- ☐ Office supplies
- ☐ Paper towels

- ☐ Parchment paper
- ☐ Plants/seeds
- ☐ Plastic wrap
- ☐ Sandwich baggies
- ☐ Sponges
- ☐ Stamps
- ☐ Straws
- ☐ Tape
- ☐ Tissue paper
- ☐ Toothpicks
- ☐ Vacuum bags
- ☐ Waxed paper
- ☐ Wrapping paper
- ☐ Other: _____
- ☐ Other: _____
- ☐ Other: _____
- ☐ Other: _____

CLEANING SUPPLIES

- ☐ Air freshener
- ☐ All-purpose cleaner
- ☐ Bleach
- ☐ Cleaning wipes
- ☐ Clothespins
- ☐ Dish soap
- ☐ Dishwasher detergent

- ☐ Dryer sheets
- ☐ Fabric softener
- ☐ Floor cleaner
- ☐ Furniture polish
- ☐ Laundry soap
- ☐ Toilet cleaner
- ☐ Window cleaner
- ☐ Other: _____
- ☐ Other: _____
- ☐ Other: _____
- ☐ Other: _____

CLOTHES

- ☐ Belts
- ☐ Bras
- ☐ Pajamas
- ☐ Pants
- ☐ Shirts
- ☐ Shoes
- ☐ Socks
- ☐ Underwear
- ☐ Wallets
- ☐ Other: _____
- ☐ Other: _____
- ☐ Other: _____
- ☐ Other: _____

place, but typically this includes some plastic bottles, mixed paper, and steel and aluminum cans. The "hand-carry" items require that you transport them to a drop-off point. As you can see from the sidebar below, who can recycle what varies from community to community, so it's important that you do a little research to find out what you can recycle.

Some communities, but not all, have secondary recycling resources at your disposal, but you'll have to hand carry your recyclables to them. These resources, too, will vary depending on where you live, and you'll have to do

WHO CAN RECYCLE WHAT?

Where you live determines what you can recycle because different communities have different recycling facilities. Our team of zero-waste contributors shared what they can recycle in their respective parts of the country.

CHRIS BURGER (Whitney Point, New York):
- Comingled recycling: Paper/cardboard, glass, metal, all plastic (except Styrofoam, PVC, and plastic bags)
- Hand carry plastic bag recycling
- Battery recycling

APRIL LUEBBERT (Bellevue, Washington):
- Comingled recycling: Paper/cardboard, glass, metal, plastics 1 and 2

ROBERT HALEY (San Francisco, California):
- Comingled recycling: Paper/cardboard, metal, aluminum cans, rigid plastics (cannot recycle Styrofoam and PVC)
- Citywide composting: Food scraps, soiled paper, pizza boxes

DESIRA FUQUA (Rutherford, Tennessee):
- Because residents have to pay for single-stream recycling, her family takes recyclables to a Sam's Club where they can sort and recycle for free.
- Can recycle all paper, plastics one through six, tin, glass, aluminum, plastic bags, and Styrofoam. At a different location, can recycle cardboard cartons.
- Saves Malt-O-Meal cereal bags for TerraCycle.

ROSE BROWN (Charlottesville, Virginia):
- Comingled: Glass, cardboard/paper, plastics 1 and 2, metal

some legwork to find them. I suggest you start by calling your local public works department and inquiring whether alternative recycling facilities exist in your community. The Earth911 website is also a great place to find these resources. You could try your nearest metropolitan area, as large metro areas often have better recycling infrastructure established. Although it will take some work, phone calls, and internet research, don't skip this step, because you might be very surprised about what you can recycle in your community. When I did this research, I learned that I could recycle foil, empty aerosol cans, scrap metal, cooking oil, plastics numbers 3 through 7, and Styrofoam.

Set Up Your Recycling System

Once you know what is recyclable in your area, you can start setting up your recycling system. You'll need bins for each separate category of hand-carry recycling resources you intend to take advantage of. The sidebar on page 74 shows what my system looks like. I offer a detailed discussion of what goes in each bin. The different bin types listed are based on a best-case scenario. Not everyone has access to each of the bin types. Each bin type has been labeled to correspond to your waste reduction goal—there are bins for beginning reducers, moderate reducers, and extreme reducers. You should set up whatever bin types work best in your particular community.

Bin 1: Curbside Comingled Recycling

Level: Easy

Like most American households, we have a comingled recycling bin that accepts a variety of materials. When we received our comingled bin from our trash company, it came with a pamphlet that lists the materials we can curbside recycle: cardboard, plastic numbers 1 and 2 (water bottles, laundry detergent bottles, ketchup bottles, and the like), mixed paper, and aluminum cans. We were explicitly told not to recycle these items: plastic packaging, plastic grocery bags, waxed cardboard, Styrofoam, plastic containers larger than five gallons, and hazardous waste.

This is an exceptionally straightforward list, but it does not address the exceptions we all wonder about. For example, what about plastic windows in paper envelopes, waxed paper, plastic bottle lids, paper napkins, plastic without number labels, paper soda cups from fast-food restaurants, staples in paper, straws, plastic spouts in milk cartons, stickers, carbon copies of checks? Are these recyclable?

The list of "what ifs?" is long, and unfortunately the answer varies by region. My solution? Every single time I thought of a "what if?" in the course of a year, I called the local recycling company—before buying a product in question. If the local recycling company was unsure (which happened often), I called the product manufacturer to determine what type of material the questionable item was made from. For example, was the plastic spout in the milk carton made from a number 1 or 2 plastic? This level of minutiae was frustrating at times, but after a couple of months I had a pretty good knack for determining what the answer would be, even if a product wasn't labeled.

Prior to starting the Green Garbage Project, I had often heard that a single unrecyclable item mixed in with recyclables could cause an entire batch

AMY AND ADAM'S RECYCLING SYSTEM

Because we live in Oregon, one of the greenest states in the country, we found we have access to a tremendous number of recycling facilities, and among them we can recycle practically anything that is recyclable. In the end, we set up the following bins:

- BIN 1—Curbside comingled recycling: Contains all materials collected by local hauler, including paper, cardboard, aluminum cans, and numbers 1 and 2 plastic.

- BIN 2—Other hand-carry recyclables: Contains specialty recyclable materials we drive to collecting facilities around the area; includes foil, numbers 3–7 plastic, aerosol cans, and frozen food cardboard.

- BIN 3—Stretchy plastic: Contains number 4 plastic bags, including potato bags, toilet paper wrapping, soil bags, and clean plastic wrap.

- BIN 4—Compost: Contains all food scraps except meat.

- BIN 5—Glass: Contains all colors of container glass.

- BIN 6—Burnable materials: Contains clean, dry, untreated organic matter such as dryer lint and match sticks.

- BIN 7—Bottle bill returns: Contains plastic, glass, and aluminum beverage containers with an Oregon deposit.

- BIN 8—Miscellaneous: Specialty recyclers collect unusual items, usually for craft projects. These include produce stickers, phone books, and crayons.

Most Americans could set up a similar system in their homes, varying our regime according to their regional circumstances.

of perfectly acceptable material to be thrown away, so during one of my numerous phone conversations with my recycling company, I asked whether this was true. The answer is no, in most cases, but it does cause a holdup in the entire sorting process at the MRF. This answer allowed me to draw three simple conclusions:

If in doubt, throw it out (or, in our case, don't buy it in the first place). You can always call your local recycling company and ask whether your material is recyclable.

Composite materials are harder to recycle than objects made from one material. This includes things like chips bags, which are made from layers of plastic coated with aluminum, or milk cartons with plastic spouts. Only if there's a specialized market for it can composite materials be recycled. Composite materials can often be easily identified by looking and touching. An ice cream carton made from cardboard feels different from a cardboard package with a plastic lid. To identify packaging made from a composite material, try to separate it into layers. Can a thin layer of plastic be peeled off, revealing cardboard underneath? Zero-waste contributor Chris recommends subjecting your material to the "tear test"—if it tears easily, it's probably made from cardboard or paper, which are easily recyclable. If it doesn't tear easily, like many chips bags, you may well be looking at a composite material. He says when you're faced with something made from mixed materials, ask yourself, "Do I really want to take responsibility for this? If not, it stays on the shelf." Otherwise, you might be faced with trying to deconstruct your mixed materials to prepare them for recycling. Chris points to his toilet bowl brush head as an example of a product made from mixed materials. He describes the brush as plastic fibers wrapped around two or three strands of metal. The metal inside the brush could be recycled, if only the plastic fibers were removed. For now, the brush head sits in Chris's paper bag of trash, but he hopes to one day feel inspired enough to unravel it.

If you make a mistake and recycle something nonrecyclable, it is not the end of the world. Recycling depots hire employees to sort through the items in our comingled recycling bins, meaning that trash gets picked out from the truly recyclable. These employees also operate under the "if in doubt, throw it out" principle, though the fewer items they have to pick out, the better, because this speeds up the sorting process and more material is ultimately recycled.

Bin 2: Hand-Carry Recyclables

Level: Moderate

In this bin, we place materials not recyclable in our comingled bin and deliver them ourselves to centrally located recycling depots in our area. These depots are often set up in large cities around the country. Some are government-operated, often subsidized by "tipping fees"—the money a county or city collects for disposing of household garbage. Money collected from selling recyclable materials like metals also supports the operation of these depots. Others are independently owned, like the depots we use. These companies collect recyclable materials in such large amounts that it is worth their while to collect and sell traditionally hard-to-recycle items.

One such program is the Preserve Gimme 5 program, through which partner retailers—as of this writing, Whole Foods stores in thirty-six states plus a few cooperatives—accept number 5 plastics for recycling. This type of plastic is common in today's households, yet it is rarely recyclable in comingled recycling systems. If you live near a Whole Foods grocery store, save up your number 5 containers, including prescription medicine bottles and yogurt, sour cream, margarine, and sour cream tubs. The Gimme 5 program will also accept Brita water filters for recycling.

Critics of the Green Garbage Project were often concerned about the extra gas we were using—and carbon emissions we were creating—by hand carrying our recyclables to the nearest centralized depot in Portland, an hour away from our home. We were concerned about this, too—after all, although our primary concern was reducing our trash footprint, our overall aim in embarking on this project was to create a lifestyle that was holistically beneficial to the environment. There was no sense in keeping trash out of the landfill if it meant adding more pollution to the air. We vowed never to make a special trip to Portland for recycling. Instead, we would bring our recycling along with us whenever we made a trip into Portland for different reasons, meaning we never used extra gas to hand carry our recyclables.

Additionally, in a study conducted by Oregon's Department of Environmental Quality (DEQ), researchers found that driving materials to a faraway recycling center is almost always better than landfilling those same materials. The study aimed to answer the question "When are markets too far to justify long haul (of recyclable materials)?" Essentially the study found that all materials are worth recycling even if they are hauled over a long distance. Even glass, being the least-valuable material on today's market, would have to be transported 1,300 miles by truck before reaching its "break-even" point—the point at which enough energy has been expended transporting the material that it is equal to the energy expended manufacturing from virgin resources.

THE "WHAT-IFS"

We all wonder about the recyclability of certain items, such as the ones listed here. Unfortunately there are no universal answers to whether or not these items are recyclable. Nevertheless, here is a list of the what-ifs and my best guess as to whether or not they're recyclable.

- Milk cartons with plastic spouts—Recyclable
- Paper envelopes with plastic window—Recyclable
- Cardboard noodle boxes with plastic window—Recyclable
- Sticky notes—Recyclable
- Plastic straws, cutlery—Not recyclable unless you can recycle plastics 3 through 7
- Paper drink cups from fast-food restaurants—Not recyclable because lined with wax or plastic
- Paper with staples or paper clips—Recyclable
- Paper napkins—Not recyclable but compostable
- Carbon copies of checks—Recyclable
- Swiffer sheets—Not recyclable because infused with cleaning chemicals and dust/dirt
- Spray bottles—The bottom is recyclable but not the sprayer top (so try to reuse instead of throwing out)
- Deodorant containers—Not recyclable unless you can recycle plastics 3 through 7
- Shredded paper—Recyclable, but stuff it into a paper bag, staple shut, and label as "shredded paper"
- Padded envelopes—Recyclable if padded with paper; not recyclable if padded with plastic bubble wrap
- Compostable plastics—Not recyclable
- Plastic bottle caps—This varies so much that you should call and check; some places have you leave caps on, others want them removed.

TRANSPORTING RECYCLABLES OVER LONG DISTANCES STILL SAVES ENERGY

MATERIAL	PRODUCTION SAVINGS	"BREAK EVEN" POINT IN MILES		
	(MMBtu/ton collected)	TRUCK	RAIL	FREIGHTER
Aluminum	177	121,000	475,000	538,000
LDPE	61	41,000	162,000	184,000
PET	59	40,000	157,000	178,000
STEEL	19	13,000	52,000	59,000
Newspaper	16	11,000	43,000	49,000
Corrugated	12	9,000	33,000	38,000
Office Paper	10	7,000	27,000	31,000
Boxboard	6.5	4,400	17,400	19,800
Glass	1.9	1,300	5,100	5,800

Bin 3: Stretchy Plastic

Level: Easy

One of the best discoveries I made during the research phase of the Green Garbage Project was that so-called "stretchy plastic" is recyclable. I say best because this solved what I previously saw as an insurmountable hurdle—toilet paper packaging. Although Adam and I had agreed that using toilet paper was allowed within the confines of our project, I was worried about being unable to find it wrapped in something other than plastic and was afraid I would have to resort to stealing rolls from public restrooms.

A recycling representative told me that any stretchy plastic—like plastic grocery bags, plastic wrap, bread bags, and the plastic wrapped around rolls of toilet paper—is recyclable. Cracker and cereal box liners are usually included in this category, too. The test is to slowly poke a finger into tautly pulled plastic. If the plastic stretches with your finger instead of breaking, then it's probably recyclable.

There are some exceptions to this rule, so it's best to always ask before trying to recycle a plastic of unknown origin. The plastic wrap surrounding blocks of cheese, for example, is not recyclable even though it is stretchy because it is manufactured using several different types of plastic that cannot be separated—something I found out when I called the Tillamook Cheese Factory in Oregon to see whether the company was willing to let me buy unwrapped cheese for our project (they weren't).

The key is finding a facility that takes these materials, because they cannot be recycled curbside. In fact, dealing with plastic shopping bags is a major obstacle for today's recycling facilities. The bags, if placed in a comingled bin, can get tangled inside the sorting machinery and cause a whole facility to shut

ITEMS THAT CANNOT BE RECYCLED CURBSIDE

These items are referred to as "common contaminants" often mistakenly placed in a comingled recycling bin. These cannot be recycled in a traditional manner, though there may be specialized facilities in your area.

GLASS

- Lightbulbs
- Drinking glasses
- Porcelain/ceramic
- Window panes
- Flower vases
- Mirrors

PAPER

- Food-contaminated paper
- Tissue paper
- Waxed paper
- Cardboard packaging from frozen foods; there are some exceptions to this, so check with your local recycling facility (frozen food boxes are treated with plastic or wax spray that renders them insoluble and difficult to recycle).
- Paper towels
- Paper cups
- Paper/boxes with excessive amounts of tape (usually envelope windows and adhesive labels are okay). As long as a package is not completely covered in tape, you should be fine. If in doubt, rip off the tape and throw it away, recycling the box.

METAL

- Any metal with plastic or wood attached
- Metal used to store chemicals or paint

PLASTIC

- Food-contaminated Styrofoam take-out containers
- Plastic bags (take these to your local grocery store; never mix them in a comingled bin)
- Foam meat trays
- Plastic toys
- All PVC
- Bottles that contained hazardous material (motor oil, pesticides, herbicides, and the like)

down while the machinery is untangled. The good news is that many super-markets will accept not only plastic grocery bags but other plastic bags as well. Check with your local store to see whether they accept bread bags and such in their bag recycling bins. If supermarkets don't, local recycling depots probably will. However, plastic bags with zip-locking strips—sandwich bags, deli bags, tortilla bags, and the like—are not recyclable anywhere.

Learn more about plastic bag recycling at www.plasticbagrecycling.org. And I'll have much more to say about this topic in the upcoming section, "Plastics Recycling."

Bin 4: Compost

Level: Moderate

Prior to the Green Garbage Project, I had never bothered to set up a compost bin. The reason for this is ridiculous—having grown up in a composting family, I had often been given the chore of taking out the compost as a child. The whole concept of compost was lost on me as a kid, but it was high time that I got over my compost phobia. There really is no greater waste than scraping perfectly useful food scraps into the trash.

MATERIALS THAT ARE RECYCLABLE IF FACILITIES EXIST IN YOUR AREA

Commonly recyclable curbside:

- Number 1 and 2 plastic bottles OR bottles with necks smaller than their base
- Mixed paper, including cardboard, gray board (cereal boxes, cracker boxes, and so on), magazines, newspaper, junk mail
- "Tin" cans (actually made from steel)
- Aluminum cans

Commonly recyclable if hand carried:

- Any item made from metal (paper clips, jar lids, staples, keys, hangers)
- Depressurized aerosol cans
- Foil
- Aseptic containers like juice boxes
- Cooking oil
- Plastics 4, 5, and 7
- Plant trays and pots
- Glass, which usually must be sorted by color
- Plastic film

My family's composting system always consisted of a big container—made from wood or wire—sitting next to the garden. Food scraps went into this bin on a nightly basis. Whenever we thought about it, usually while pulling weeds in the summer or raking leaves in the fall, some green matter (like grass clippings, corn husks, or carrot greens) and brown matter (like leaves, dirt, and small sticks) went into the container along with the food scraps.

I set up an identical system. Like I said, I'm a casual composter, but this approach works for me. All food scraps except for meat went right into the compost. This included moldy leftovers from the fridge, eggshells, vegetable peelings, even the occasional pizza box. Whenever I thought about it (around once a month), I added a small amount of yard waste to the compost. Sometimes I stuck my shovel stick in the middle and whirled things around. Every once in a while, the sprinkler in the garden got the compost's contents wet. After only six months, the bottom-most material had already decomposed into, well, compost. (Completely processed compost looks much like good garden soil, but is much richer in nutrients that nourish the soil.) Any compost pile, mine included, needs to be completely turned about once a year (usually in the spring, when early garden crops are being planted). To do this, I simply unwired my fencing tube, spilled all the compost on the ground, and raked out all the compost. The food that still needed to decompose went right back into the pile once reassembled.

Composting is clearly most beneficial to those who have backyard gardens, but even if you don't have a garden—or a yard—you can still compost. Composting is tremendously better for the environment than letting food rot away in a landfill. Even if you have no garden of your own, chances are you have a friend who does. In this case, consider giving your compost away. Compost is valuable stuff, after all—at our local feed store, it sells for $35 a yard. Read more about setting up your own compost system in Chapter 5, "Organic Waste."

Bin 5: Glass

Level: Moderate

The glass bin we set up is the most straightforward in our recycling system. We hand carried our glass to a local recycling center only two minutes from our house. This depot accepted green, brown, and clear glass, so long as we sorted the colors ourselves. Some facilities also accept blue glass, though blue glass is so rare these days that we didn't have any at all to recycle for the entire duration of the project.

Glass is rarely recycled in comingled bins for two reasons. First, putting glass in comingled bins is a recipe for breakage when recycling cans are dumped into recycling trucks. Truckloads are again dumped at recycling centers where glass bottles have yet another opportunity to break. Broken glass mixed in with paper, cans, and plastic makes the materials sorting process difficult, and none of these materials can be recycled properly if contaminated with other materials. Second, glass must be recycled according to color, because although all colors of glass are manufactured with the same basic ingredients, the ratios of ingredients can vary, causing different melting points and chemical incompatibility.

Only glass bottles can be recycled. Virtually no recycling centers will accept lightbulbs, window panes, flower vases, mirrors, drinking glasses, ceramics, or other household items made from glass. These materials must be given to a thrift store, reused in some way, or thrown out.

Bin 6: Burnable Materials

Level: Easy

Perhaps one of the most controversial aspects of our project was our decision to burn an extremely limited number of items. Our rule—burn only clean, dry, untreated organic material. Our logic—these materials could be used as fire starter on camping trips when we would be making a campfire anyway. This way, instead of buying wood to be used as kindling, we were respecting the waste hierarchy by reusing a material, rather than throwing it out after its first life. Materials we burned were limited to the following: dryer lint, vegetarian corn dog sticks, matches, toothpicks, wooden chopsticks, caramel apple sticks, and sewing scraps like cotton thread.

In no way do I condone burning garbage rather than landfilling it. But burning a matchstick is a whole lot different from the practice (still followed in many localities) of burning all the chemical-laden materials that are in an average American's trash by facilities called trash incinerators or waste-to-energy recovery plants, which emit pollution.

The debate over whether to incinerate or landfill garbage is a heated one that is not going to be solved any time soon. Although today's trash-burning facilities are far better for the environment than the incinerators of the early twentieth century, it is inarguable that waste-to-energy plants emit toxins into the air. It is also inarguable that our sanitary landfills, though protected by thick liners and surrounded by "leachate collectors" (used to hold liquid runoff from landfills), contaminate our groundwater supply.

This and many other issues face waste management today. They are issues of scale—how to dispose of the vast amount of trash we are creating—and of contaminants—how to safely dispose of chemicals we use in manufacturing our products. That's why learning to decrease our dependency on trash is one of the first steps in reducing our need for toxic landfills/incinerators—and what a zero-waste lifestyle is all about.

Bin 7: Bottle Bill Returns

Level: Easy

I'll discuss the issues surrounding the bottle bill in chapter 14, "The Global Zero-Waste Movement," so here I just want to note that we set up a recycling bin for our can and bottle returns. The *bottle bill* is the collective name given to laws in many states that dictate that people buying certain beverages (ranging from soda to juice, depending on the state) be charged a $0.05 to $0.10 deposit. When the beverage container is recycled at a redemption location, the deposit is returned to the consumer. Bottle bills have been shown to dramatically increase recycling rates of plastic and glass bottles and aluminum cans.

Oregon is a bottle bill state, so we sort our beverage cans and bottles separately from the rest of our recyclables. We return these to the grocery store about once a month for a $0.05 per-item rebate.

Miscellaneous Bins

Level: Advanced

Because many upcyclers ask for donations for their trashy creations, we are happy to oblige. Two artists we donated to are Barry "Wildman" Snyder, or the Stickerman, who creates intricate mosaic art from produce stickers, and Lou of Lou's Upcycles (see page 57).

In addition to upcyclers, nonprofit organizations often collect discarded goods for various charitable efforts. Eyeglasses can be recycled, for example;

they are given to children who can't afford their own. Used cell phones are given to battered women to help them escape desperate situations. Even coloring crayons can be recycled, remelted, and turned into new crayons.

For ideas on how to recycle many unusual materials, turn to An A-to-Z Guide to Recycling (Just About) Anything (see page 248).

Plastics Recycling

In the recycling world, starting a discussion about plastics is like waltzing through a minefield. The issues surrounding this material are laden with emotion, misunderstandings, and sensationalism. At some point in your zero-waste journey, you will encounter some of these issues.

Is Plastic Truly Recyclable?

The truest definition of recycling involves taking a material, melting it down, and turning it back into itself over and over. This can be done with glass and metal, which can both be remelted and remolded into jars or cans forever. This is a closed-loop system, and it's very desirable in the world of recycling. On the other hand, some materials slowly degrade over time, meaning they can be reformed maybe once or twice, but after awhile the chemical composition of the original substance has changed and it can no longer be turned back into what it once was. As discussed at the beginning of this chapter, this is called downcycling.

Plastic is similar to paper in that it downcycles, though it has a much shorter life in the recycling stream—sometimes it's not even recycled once before it is turned into a less-valuable material. Plastic water or soda bottles, for example, are rarely turned back into bottles. Instead, the plastic is used for something secondary like fleece fabric or plastic lumber. This means that virgin plastic (made from fossil fuels) is still needed for the manufacture of new plastic bottles.

The downcycling of plastic is just one of the serious issues surrounding this material. The other is the fact that plastic never, ever biodegrades.

Many materials, newspaper included, will biodegrade at the end of their lives. This means they mineralize, or turn back into their respective chemical components. When paper enters the environment, given exposure to the air, it disintegrates, leaving the world no worse for wear. Plastic, on the other hand, photodegrades, and this is very concerning.

As discussed in chapter 1, in the process of photodegrading, wind, sun, and water break plastic down into smaller and smaller parts that don't lose their chemical composition as plastic. Eventually these particles get so small they are microscopic. Scientists and environmentalists are very concerned about the impact of these microplastics on the environment, especially the role they might play in the ocean ecosystem.

If there wasn't so much plastic in our oceans, this wouldn't be such an issue. The problem is, it is estimated that the volume of plastic in our oceans is six times that of plankton, according to the website TreeHugger.com.

Finally, there is valid concern about heating food in plastic containers—evidence suggests that some chemicals in plastics can leach into our food and cause health problems. While the jury is still out on many of these studies, some precaution seems to be in order. Avoid reheating food in plastic containers in the microwave, and stop covering food with plastic wrap. Avoid products like TV dinners and microwave popcorn. Storing cool food in plastic containers isn't as big a concern, but avoid heating food and plastic together to eliminate the possibility of plastic leaching into your food.

So the downsides to plastic are that it can't really be recycled in the true meaning of the term, it will never disappear from our environment because it can't biodegrade, and it is a vehicle to deliver dangerous chemicals into our food chains.

What about Positives?

Well, there are a few. It's hard to make the blanket statement that all plastics are bad, because the issue is more complicated than that. For one thing, plastic is a tremendous asset to the medical community—think syringes and IV tubing. It is durable, so for things like the plastic grocery carts used in my rainy and windy coastal community, it can be a better choice than a material like metal. It is also lightweight, meaning goods can be shipped farther and less fuel is used during transport.

Plastic may be a beneficial material for long-term applications like playground equipment and benches, but it is not a good choice as a single-use material for things like candy bar wrappers and shopping bags. Ultimately we all need to decrease our reliance on plastic to lessen its impact on the environment. And it's important to be aware that, even if you are recycling your empty shampoo bottles, they may not be as recyclable as you think.

How to Recycle Plastics

Plastics are easily the most confusing category of recyclables today, because (1) "plastic" is a broad category covering a variety of material compositions, (2) all communities have differing recycling systems, and (3) much of the information widely available to the public is inaccurate.

Most of us are familiar with the chasing arrows recycling symbol on the bottom of plastic containers. The chasing arrows contain a number, 1 through 7. Each number stands for a particular type of plastic resin—and each resin has a different chemical makeup. Technically all plastic is recyclable—as long as it is melted down with other plastic with the same chemical makeup.

It is important to note that the presence of a recycling symbol with a number inside it does not mean the plastic container is recyclable in your community. The numbers correspond with the resin identification coding system, which allows recyclers to separate plastics according to resin types. Many communities recycle resin types 1 and 2, others recycle only bottles, and still more recycle only containers with necks that are narrower than container bases. Check with your local recycling center for your community's particular rules.

The following is a guide to the seven types of plastic.

Type of Plastic: # 1 Polyethylene Terephthalate (PET, PETE)
Nickname: None
Common Uses: Water and soda bottles, salad dressing bottles, peanut butter jars, mouthwash bottles, beer bottles.
Recycled Into: Carpet fibers, fleece jackets, new containers.

Type of Plastic: # 2 High Density Polyethylene (HDPE)
Nickname: None
Common Uses: Milk jugs, laundry detergent bottles, shampoo and conditioner bottles, juice bottles. HDPE is also used to create plastic film for grocery bags and cereal box liners.
Recycled Into: Decking, fencing, plastic flower pots.

Type of Plastic: # 3 Polyvinyl Chloride (PVC)
Nickname: Vinyl
Common Uses: Children's toys ("rubber" duckies are often made from PVC); blister packs, disposable battery wrap, vinyl shower curtains, construction materials like pipe and window framing, IV bags.

Recycled Into: Pipe, gutters, packaging. Note: The dangers of PVC are well documented. PVC has an easily identifiable odor often associated with "new car smell," new carpet smell, and new construction in general. This smell is the PVC "off-gassing"—the dangerous chemicals used in PVC production leaching into our environment, the air we breathe, and our bodies.

Type of Plastic: #4 Low Density Polyethylene (LDPE)
Nickname: None
Common Uses: Plastic film for bread bags, dry cleaning bags, garden soil bags, and plastic wrap.
Recycled Into: Shipping envelopes, trash bags, compost bins.

Type of Plastic: # 5 Polypropylene (PP)
Nickname: None
Common Uses: Yogurt and margarine tubs; coat hangers; plastic cutlery, plates, bowls, and cups; medicine bottles; toothbrush handles; rakes; storage bins; shipping pallets. Note: The natural grocery store chain Whole Foods participates in the Preserve Gimme 5 program (see page 76); shoppers can drop off their PP plastic, which is usually not recyclable curbside, at many Whole Foods outlets.
Recycled Into: Ice scrapers, brooms, brushes, rakes, storage bins, shipping pallets, trays.

Type of Plastic: # 6 Polystyrene (PS)
Nickname: Styrofoam
Common Uses: Grocery store meat trays, egg cartons, disposable cups, packing peanuts, protective packaging.
Recycled Into: Light switch and outlet plates, protective packaging, desk trays.

Type of Plastic: # 7 Other
Nickname: None
Common Uses: Cheese packaging, oven baking bags, headlight lenses, safety glasses.
Recycled Into: Sometimes recycled into plastic lumber. Note: This code indicates that a piece of plastic is made with a resin other than 1 through 6 or a combination of resins. Because resins are impossible to separate, recycling of number 7 plastic is extremely difficult.

Up Next: Organic Wastes

Let's say that at this point you've successful adopted the three Rs. I hope you are buying fewer products and thinking of creative uses for things you no longer want or need, and you've discovered the ins and outs of your local recycling system. You've made a good start at eliminating many of the things listed in your waste audit, but there's another whole category of garbage still to address: organic waste. This is the stuff that makes garbage so unappealing. It includes food scraps, the contents of your vacuum cleaner, hair from your hairbrush, kitty litter, and cooking oil. How to deal with these items in a zero-waste way is covered in the next chapter, which is all about composting.

Meet Your Goal: Recycle

Easy

- Participate in curbside comingled recycling.

Moderate

- Hand carry glass.
- Hand carry plastic bags.
- Participate in bottle bill recycling, if applicable.

Advanced

- Save odds and ends for individuals and businesses listed in An A-to-Z Guide to Recycling (Just About) Anything (see page 248).

Chapter 5

Organic Waste

Imagine never needing another trash bag again. Imagine not having to plug your nose when opening the garbage can to avoid the stink. Imagine never having to scrub up the slime at the bottom of the trash when your plastic liner leaks.

If you set up a home compost pile, these three things will immediately become part of your past. You may still be making trash here and there, but if you establish a composting system, you will never need to buy trash bags again.

Why? It's simple. The difference between a wet trash pile and a dry one is food. Everything we put into the garbage can—with a few exceptions such as disposable diapers and cat litter—is dry except for food, which rots, squishes down, and grosses up the rest of the can's contents. Later in the book, I will give you strategies for eliminating these other potential smell sources.

This is a really important idea. Nothing you throw into the trash can is wet or slimy except for food. If you take the food out of the trash can, you take away the mess and the need for those can liners. You'll save money immediately when you stop buying plastic garbage bags that are designed for the dump. Before you forgo the garbage bag completely, however, check with your municipal pickup service to see if it requires you to bag your garbage. In this case, try to avoid the standard plastic garbage bag. Instead, opt for a bag made from biodegradable plastic (though the likelihood of these biodegrading in a landfill is slim) or in paper grocery sacks. Additionally, any smell produced by your garbage will simply be gone—the only thing that smells is decomposing food. Leave the decomposition work for the compost pile, and you'll never have to be afraid of the smell or mess of your garbage can again.

For many, composting is the fourth R, as in rot, but I like to think of composting as another way to *recycle*. In fact, composting is as pure a form of recycling as there is. After all, recycling is really about continuous reuse of a valuable resource such as glass or metal. You start with raw material like metal, melt it down and pour it into a form like a car or a can, and at the end of its useful life as a car or a can, you melt the metal down and return it to its raw material form. Composting is exactly the same thing. You start with a raw material—soil—and grow something from it (food, trees for paper, and so on). When you're finished with the plant matter, you return it back to the earth until it decomposes and again becomes soil.

The simple fact is, you cannot live a zero-waste lifestyle without composting.

But don't despair! No matter where you live—house, apartment, city, suburb, or country—this chapter will help you set up your own compost pile. It won't be stinky or difficult. In fact, I'll focus on what many of us zero-wasters call "lazy composting." It will be as easy as—maybe easier than—recycling.

Composting Fears

Before I get into all that, let me commiserate with you for a moment. Let me tell you I understand your fears about composting. My parents have always been big composters, so I grew up with this concept. And I hated it. I absolutely despised the plastic ice cream bucket under the sink that housed all our family's food waste. I held my nose and made a big production every time I scraped my plate into the bucket or I had to trudge outside and empty the bucket into the backyard pile. Then I had to rinse out the bucket with a hose—splattering myself with food goo in the process—and bring the container inside to wash with soap and water. I found the whole process smelly and disgusting.

I know others share this concern about the home compost pile, plus a few more. Maybe you're worried about bugs or wild animals getting into your compost pile, or maybe you're concerned it will be unsightly. Others worry about the work involved—after all, you may have heard rumors about perfect proportions of brown matter to green matter, and requirements for nitrogen balance and regular turning. Basically our compost worries come in three categories: the smell, the effort, and the unsightliness.

I'm here to tell you that after my early foot-stomping compost initiation, I no longer find my compost pile icky. Instead, I find it fascinating. And I guarantee you, it doesn't have to smell, it doesn't have to be ugly, and it won't require a lot of effort.

Set Up Your Compost Bin

It is absolutely critical that composting become more widespread than it is right now. Composting is the new recycling, and it should be treated by city municipalities as such. Some cities and counties are already making strides in this area by implementing curbside composting pickup. Although curbside pickup of leftover organic matter is becoming more common in communities across the country, it's still not the norm. If you don't live somewhere with a citywide composting program, don't despair. There are still many composting options available to you, including worm bins and backyard compost piles.

Before you select the method of composting best suited to your lifestyle, you'll need to get yourself set up inside. Compost piles usually involve two bins—a small bin inside and a larger one outdoors. Your small bin will probably live under the sink or on your kitchen counter. It should be big enough to hold your family's food scraps for several days; otherwise, you'll be trekking out to the big bin every night.

Stores sell fancy kitchen compost containers. These usually look like miniature metal or porcelain garbage pails. They are designed to be lined with a plastic bag, and they hold next to nothing. Don't buy one. Instead, view your kitchen compost container as a chance to implement some reuse around your house. Any container with a lid will do, such as a plastic quart-sized yogurt container or a plastic milk jug. I've used a one-gallon plastic ice cream container before as well as a giant pickle jar. It doesn't need to be pretty, just functional.

Don't line your kitchen compost container with a plastic bag (you don't need it, and it just creates extra garbage). Empty it into your backyard compost pile a couple of times a week and then wash the container with the rest of your dishes.

Now you're ready to choose the method of composting that's right for you. Here is a list of the most common methods of composting.

City-Operated Curbside Composting

Zero-waster Robert Haley is lucky enough to live in San Francisco, where the city runs a curbside composting program. City residents receive a green bin in addition to their curbside recycling and trash cans. All leftover organic matter can be placed in this cart, which the city picks up on a regular basis and hauls to a centralized composting facility.

Some cities—like San Francisco and Portland, Oregon—have passed legislation requiring citizens to participate in city-run composting programs. In some cities, if residents don't comply, they face citations and even fines from their cities. Although curbside composting is certainly the easiest form of composting, it does come with its own set of problems.

Unlike a backyard compost pile, which should be stirred occasionally and which is usually exposed to the open air, a curbside bin is closed. Even if compost pickup is once a week, a bin of all leftover food waste can still get stinky, especially during the summer months when the inside of the container heats up. Some residents object to the mess and stink involved in a city-wide composting program.

To reduce these concerns, you can try the following tip from San Francisco's Recology website: place compostable items in a paper bag or empty, rinsed milk carton. When the bag or carton is full, fold down the top to seal and place the whole thing, container and all, into the green cart. There will be less splattering and smell this way.

I also find it helps me ignore the unsightliness of a compost pile if I remember just how much good I'm doing by recycling my food waste. Remember how William Rathje's garbology teams uncovered lettuce and other biodegradables way down inside a landfill? Every bit of food waste that is thrown in the garbage goes to waste. In a landfill, food either sits intact for decades, buried away from the sun and never given a chance to biodegrade, or rots in an anaerobic environment, releasing harmful methane gases into the atmosphere. Food scraps are a valuable resource, and I'm happy to tolerate the natural processes of composting unfolding because it means I'm participating in the renewal of life on our planet.

What can be placed in a curbside compost bin: Although this can vary from one program to another, curbside composting bins usually accept food scraps (often, but not always, including meat and dairy discards), eggshells, tea bags, coffee filters, waxed paper and cartons, greasy pizza boxes, yard trimmings, leaves, grass, compostable "plastics," small pieces of untreated wood (like chopsticks), cotton balls, fur, and hair.

What can't be placed in a curbside compost bin: Corks (plastic or natural), linens/rags, foil, feces, dirt and rocks, liquids, cooking oil, Styrofoam, treated wood, aseptic containers.

Lazy Composting

Lazy composting is the method I use. It's also used by Rose Brown and Chris Burger. Basically this method boils down to wanting to compost but not having the time to bother with the finer points of composting, like measuring carbon-to-nitrogen ratios. Right or not, though, this is the method I've used for years, and it works.

Lazy composting involves walking into your backyard (you have to have a small plot of yard to utilize this method) and finding an out-of-the-way place for your compost pile. I usually place mine in a corner of my yard. I try to place it away from any windows so I don't have to look at the rotting pile but close enough so that I can dump food scraps into it two or three times a week. I look for somewhere that will be in the sun come summer (a lazy compost pile in the shade is a disaster), and then I set up my pile.

The easiest method of lazy composting is to just pick a spot in the yard and start dumping food scraps. For myself, I went one step further because I did want to design a simple structure to contain the food waste. I went to a hardware store and bought a length of cheap metal fencing called hardware cloth (something similar to, but sturdier than, chicken wire) about four feet tall by six feet wide. I made a cylinder out of the fencing, secured the sides together with some wire, and stood it in my designated composting spot. To add even more stability to this structure, you can pound a fence post into the ground and thread the fencing enclosure over the post.

Zero-waster Rose Brown used a similar method to set up her lazy composting pile. She nailed four lengths of wooden picket fencing together to set up a square compost pile in her backyard.

At one time, Chris made a compost pile similar to Rose's, but today he has a much more commercial model. "We don't turn it a lot," he says. "We have worms [in the pile], but we didn't introduce them. If you build it, they will come."

Once your pile is ready to go, you start filling it with food scraps. If you're brand new to composting, I'd recommend you start off with vegetable and fruit scraps to see how it goes. Eventually you may decide to do as I do and compost all food scraps except for meat (we even compost dairy and egg shells). Expect to get the occasional nocturnal visitor to your compost pile—it'll attract birds and small animals like raccoons. In twenty-seven years of composting like this, I've never had a single problem with an animal nesting in the pile or strewing the pile's contents across the lawn, nor have I had a larger animal visit.

Once a year, usually in the early spring when I'm planting my garden, I undo the wire on the compost pile and give it a good stir. This part does smell, but it's less than an hour of my life each year, so I live. By this time, the bottom third of the compost pile has decomposed and is turning into a soil-like substance. I pull this part of the compost out and spread it in my garden beds, in my plant pots, and so on. The plants love it. The remaining compost goes back into the fence enclosure and continues to decompose.

Finally, if I think about it, I add some "brown matter," which you'll read about shortly. This includes things like twigs, dirt, and leaves. I stick some of these into the pile every so often to balance the contents.

Keep in mind that I've always lived in rural areas when I've had a lazy compost pile. Some cities or suburbs may classify a pile of food scraps as an eyesore and prohibit you from having one in your backyard. In this case, you can at least set up a lazy compost pile for yard clippings.

What can be composted in a lazy compost pile: All food scraps (except meat), eggshells, tea bags, coffee filters, waxed paper, yard trimmings, leaves, grass, small pieces·of untreated wood (like chopsticks), cotton balls, fur, and hair.

What can't be composted: Meat or seafood, corks (plastic), linens/rags, foil, feces, dirt and rocks, liquids, cooking oil, Styrofoam, treated wood, aseptic containers.

Hot Compost Pile

A hot compost pile is the official "right" way to compost. It requires some basic knowledge of the processes involved in turning food back into soil. Although lazy composting certainly works, a hot compost piles works better, faster, and more efficiently. If you choose this method, you will be a much more "hands-on" composter because you'll be making sure you add compost ingredients in the right ratio of green to brown, and you'll be turning or aerating your pile much more often.

To begin a hot compost pile, you must understand some basic chemistry. For a hot compost pile, you need to maintain a 30-to-1 ratio of carbon- to nitrogen-based materials. All organic materials are composed of lots of carbon and a little bit of nitrogen, so just by establishing a compost pile, you'll already have lots of carbon and some nitrogen. The 30:1 ratio is ideal for the composting microorganisms that break down the compost. They work faster if they have the proper amount of carbon for energy and nitrogen for protein production. Here is where the distinction of brown matter and green matter matters. Brown matter, which contains high amounts of carbon, includes cardboard, dried leaves, twigs, shredded newspaper, sawdust, and straw. Green matter, which is high in nitrogen, includes vegetable waste, food scraps, grass clippings, garden waste such as prunings and weeds without seeds, and coffee grounds. A compost pile that contains more brown matter than green matter produces compost faster and has almost no odor.

It's important to note that you probably won't achieve an absolutely perfect 30:1 ratio in your compost pile. In fact, a typical garden generates far more green matter than brown matter, so you'll have to work hard to add enough brown matter to achieve the recommended ratio. A close approximation works, and as with anything, the more you practice it, the more adept you'll become.

A hot compost pile works best in a turning unit, a wooden structure that looks like a file cabinet turned on its side. A turning unit is a lidded, rectangular wooden box with three side-by-side compartments. You begin composting in the first compartment by adding a 4- to 6-inch layer of moistened brown matter. On top of this pile, add four to six inches of green matter. Mix the two layers together and let stand for five to ten days.

Then the real work starts. You need to monitor your hot compost pile's temperature with a tool called a compost temperature probe. These are available online for $25 to $40. It looks like a meat thermometer with a long metal probe that you stick deep into the core of the compost pile. Take temperature readings from several places in the pile to get an accurate reading. The internal temperature of the pile should peak between 120°F and 160°F during that five- to ten-day period. Once the temperature starts to decrease, move the pile into the second section of the turning bin. In the second bin, the process is repeated. Wait another five to ten days, monitor the temperature until it decreases, and move the pile to the third section of the turning bin. In another week, your compost is ready to use.

After you have moved your compost from the first bin to the second, you can start with new food and garden scraps. Add a mix of green and brown matter, let sit for a few days, and start taking the pile's temperature. Continue rotating your piles through the bins, and soon you'll have a steady influx of fresh garden compost.

What can be composted in a hot pile: All fruit and vegetable scraps; eggshells, dairy products, other meatless leftovers as desired; yard waste (grass clippings, twigs and sticks, leaves, and some weeds); straw; paper.

What can't be composted: Meat or seafood, corks (plastic), linens/rags, foil, feces, dirt and rocks, liquids, cooking oil, Styrofoam, treated wood, aseptic containers, weeds spread by runners or roots (as a hot pile may not kill all weed seeds).

Vermicomposting or Worm Bin Composting

This is the only composting option available to those living in apartments or houses without yards. Worm bins take some effort to set up, and they can't handle as much material as a lazy or hot composting pile, but they yield a high-quality nutrient to add to your plants.

A typical worm bin is basically a box containing a worm habitat that you add food scraps to. Commonly worm bins involve at least two chambers

ACHIEVING THE RIGHT CARBON-TO-NITROGEN RATIO

HIGH-CARBON BROWNS	HIGH-NITROGEN GREENS
Wood ashes 25:1*	Alfalfa 12:1
Shredded cardboard 350:1	Clover 23:1
Corn stalks 75:1	Coffee grounds 20:1
Leaves (dried) 60:1	Garden waste 20:1
Shredded newspaper 175:1	Grass clippings 20:1
Pine needles 80:1	Hay 25:1
Straw 75:1	
Sawdust 325:1	

* If you have alkali soil, ashes should not be used because they are highly alkaline.

Source: http://www.composting101.com/c-n-ratio.html

stacked on top of each other. You can purchase a premade worm bin or you can build your own. See the sidebar on page 98 for instructions for a simple worm bin made from two plastic storage containers.

To construct a worm habitat in your bin, first loosely pack it with a bedding of damp—but not wet—strips of newspaper. Add a couple of handfuls of dirt to the bedding. Now you are ready to add your worms. You can buy these online or get them for free from a friend with an established worm bin (people with worm bins periodically have an excess of worms to share after harvesting a batch of worm compost), but in either case, make sure you're getting a certain species known commonly as red wigglers (*Eisenia foetida*). Red wigglers are ideally suited for life in a worm bin; ordinary earthworms from garden soil won't fare as well. To determine how many worms you need, first estimate how much your daily food scraps weigh. Red worms can consume about half their weight in food each day, so if you average a pound of food scraps a day, you'll need two pounds of worms.

Once you have your worms, add them to your ready-made habitat and cover with a piece of damp cardboard. Give them about a week to settle into the bin. They will start off by eating just bedding. Add food to the bin weekly, burying it under some of the newspaper and placing the food in a different place each time. If you feed the worms more than they can process, you'll be facing a pile of rotting, smelly food scraps.

A productive worm bin will produce a drainage liquid called *worm tea*. This "tea" is brownish and filled with nutrients. Plants love it. If you've purchased a worm bin, it's likely to have a drainage spout. Otherwise, you'll need to make sure your homemade worm bin is elevated over a tray to collect any drainage. Add this to house or garden plants and watch them thrive.

Every couple of months, the compost the worms have made, called *worm castings* or *vermicompost*, needs to be removed from the bin to make room for more newspaper, cardboard, and food scraps. Purchased worm bins are essentially a series of drawers that worms travel through, and make removal of the castings quite easy. The worms start in the bottom drawer, and once it's full, you add your food scraps to the second drawer. The worms move up, and your lowest drawer is filled with compost. If you've made your worm bin (see page 98), your two plastic containers will work much the same way. See the sidebar for compost removal instructions.

HOW TO MAKE A WORM BIN

A worm bin doesn't have to be complicated or store-bought. To make your own, all you need is a couple of ten-gallon plastic storage totes, a drill, and a few other items (see list). Make sure you decide where you want to keep your worm bin before you make it; once you've filled it, it is heavy. Remember, worms in a plastic bin need to live indoors in the winter unless yours is a very mild climate; I keep mine in the garage. You'll probably want to find your worm bin a home in a quiet, dark space not easily visible to your guests.

YOU'LL NEED:

Drill with $1/4$- and $1/16$-inch drill bits

Two 10-gallon plastic storage totes

Lots of newspaper, torn into 1-inch strips

2 cups sand or dirt

1 pound red worms

Small sheet of old cardboard

Four bricks or plastic cups

Using the $1/4$-inch bit, drill 16 to 20 evenly spaced holes in the bottom of each plastic storage tote. Your worms will travel through these holes, so avoid jagged edges. Worm tea will also drain through these holes. (Tip: Drill from the inside of the bin to the outside; the bit will push out a raised ring of plastic around each hole, and if you drill from the outside in, those raised rings will impede full drainage.)

Using the $1/16$-inch bit, drill ventilation holes 1 inch apart on each side of the bin near the top edge.

Using the $1/16$-inch bit, drill 25 evenly spaced holes in the top of just one of the two lids.

Moisten the shredded newspaper and fill each bin with this bedding, loosely packed. Add 1 cup of sand to each bin, mixing it in with the shredded newspaper. Set the second bin aside for now.

Add your worms to the first tote. Moisten the cardboard sheet and place it on top of the worm bedding. Cover the tote with the ventilated lid.

Use the second lid (the one without the holes!) as a drainage tray by placing it upside down on the floor and place a brick or cup in each corner. Stand the filled worm bin on the bricks.

When the worm bin is full, remove the ventilated lid and any remnants of the cardboard. Remoisten the contents of the second worm bin and cover the top with a freshly moistened cardboard sheet. Place the second worm bin directly on top of the bedding in the first bin and cover it with the ventilated lid.

The worms will travel upward into the second bin as you start adding food scraps. After a month or so, the first bin will be filled with compost and empty of worms. The compost is now ready to use.

What can be composted in a worm bin: Breads, grains, cereals, fruit and vegetable scraps, tea bags (staples removed), coffee grounds and filters, crushed-up eggshells, shredded junk mail and paper (avoid glossy and colored paper), cardboard.

What can't be composted in a worm bin: Meat, dairy, oils, feces, smelly foods like onion and broccoli.

Using Your Compost

Now that you have at least one active composting system up and running, you'll need to plan how to use your nutrient-filled compost once it's ready to go. Compost can be used around the yard in a couple of ways: as mulch and to enrich soil. If you really have no use for your compost, offer it around at work or to neighborhood friends—compost is valuable stuff, and if you're giving it away, you won't have it on your hands for long.

Mulch

Mulch is placed around the base of plants to keep weeds at bay, to protect the plant roots, and to conserve moisture in the soil. To use mulch on garden beds, spread compost in rings around each plant in a one-inch layer. For trees and shrubs, clear the area underneath as far as the branches spread, then ring layers of compost around each plant. Compost can also be mixed with sand or sandy soil and sifted over the lawn using a $^1/_2$-inch mesh screen.

NONCOMPOSTABLE ORGANICS

You should never compost the following materials:

- Cat, dog, and bird feces: These contain harmful pathogens that cannot be killed even in a hot compost pile (read on to see how you should properly dispose of pet wastes).

- Meat and seafood leftovers.

- Oils, greases, and fats.

- Treated wood.

- Invasive, fast-growing plants: Weeds such as ivy can drop seeds in a compost pile that can choke out other plants when compost is used in the garden.

- Diseased or insect-infested plants: The diseases and insects may not be destroyed, even in a hot compost pile, and would then be added right back into the environment.

Enrich Soil

When you're doing larger landscaping projects, compost can be mixed with existing soil to improve its quality. Never simply spread compost over existing soil without mixing it in, because the compost will become a barrier to water and nutrients penetrating deeply into the soil. This is how I frequently use my own compost. Each spring, when I'm planting annuals and vegetables, I mix my potting soil or garden soil with my compost to make a nutrient-rich soil for my new plants. The plants love it.

I BET YOU DIDN'T KNOW YOU COULD COMPOST . . .

Anything organic can be composted. Of course this includes food scraps and yard trimmings, but it also includes a number of other common household items. There are a few items on this list that are a bit contentious in the world of composting, so I've added explanatory notes. Just remember that if you'll be using your compost to grow food, you don't want to compost anything questionable.

- Used paper napkins
- Pizza boxes, ripped into smaller pieces
- Paper bags, either ripped or balled up
- The crumbs you sweep off the counters and floors
- Used paper plates (as long as they don't have a waxy coating)
- Cellophane bags (be sure it's really cellophane from cellulose and not just clear plastic—there's a difference)
- Nut shells (except for walnut shells, which some believe can be toxic to plants)
- Old herbs and spices
- Wine corks (made from real cork, not plastic)
- Paper egg cartons
- Toothpicks
- Bamboo skewers
- Paper cupcake or muffin cups
- Used facial tissues
- Toilet paper rolls
- Old loofah sponges
- Nail clippings
- Cotton balls made from 100 percent cotton
- Cotton swabs made from 100 percent cotton with cardboard (not plastic) sticks
- Cardboard tampon applicators
- Latex condoms
- Dryer lint (preferably from nonsynthetic clothing)
- Hair and fur
- Old or stained cotton clothing, ripped or cut into smaller pieces
- Leather
- Rope and string

Other Organic Waste

There are a few other organic items you may be wondering how to dispose of. These include meat scraps (bone, gristle, grease) and cat and dog feces. Although there are people who successfully compost all of these items, it is not recommended for the beginning composter. These organic wastes can carry with them toxic bacteria that must be properly eliminated before they are safe to add to soil. So these are basically the only categories of organic waste that I recommend adding to the trash.

- Sticky notes and masking tape
- Old or stained wool clothing, ripped or cut into smaller pieces
- Shredded paper
- Envelopes (minus the plastic window, which is OK for recycling but not in compost)
- Pencil shavings
- Business cards (as long as they're not glossy)
- Receipts
- Contents of your vacuum cleaner bag or canister
- Newspapers, shredded or torn into smaller pieces
- Subscription cards from magazines
- Leaves trimmed from houseplants (make sure the plants aren't toxic to you or pets)
- Dead houseplants and their soil

- Flowers from floral arrangements
- Natural potpourri
- Used matches
- Butcher paper, waxed paper*
- Soap scraps
- Wood ashes from the fireplace, barbecue grill, or outdoor fire pit**
- Wrapping paper rolls
- Paper tablecloths
- Crepe paper streamers
- Latex balloons
- Raffia
- Jack-o'-lanterns made from real pumpkins
- Feathers
- Rawhide dog chews
- Fish food
- Dry dog or cat food

*There's some debate about waxed paper, as many commercial waxes are petroleum based. If you know for certain your waxed paper is coated in a plant-based wax, add it to your compost pile. Otherwise, throw it out.

** If you have alkali soil, ashes should not be used because they are highly alkaline.

Meat Scraps

Meat scraps can be used to make soup stock before you need to dispose of them. Recipes abound on the Internet, but making stock is quite simple. It involves simmering meat scraps in water for a long time, usually with some vegetables like carrots and onions, then straining off the liquid. Stock can be frozen in plastic containers or glass canning jars so it is ready to use when you need it.

After you (and your dogs) are completely done with bones, you do need to throw these away. There is nothing else safe that can be done with them. The way to eliminate meat waste from your garbage can is to eat little or no meat.

Litter/Poop Patrol

Disposal of dog and cat poop poses some difficulties; the method depends on the animal. In some cases, it might be safer to dispose of these materials in the landfill instead of attempting to flush or bury them, which poses hazards to water tables and soil.

Cat feces pose a problem to the environment because they can contain a dangerous parasite. From the National Resource Defense Council's website:

> Now, here's the scoop on cat poop. EPA brochures and a variety of other publications say you can flush it down the toilet, minus the litter. However, research suggests that the eggs of *Toxoplasma gondii*, a parasite found in cat poop, may survive the wastewater treatment process and contaminate waterways. Although *Toxoplasma* rarely affects healthy people, it can cause defects and brain damage in babies whose mothers were exposed when pregnant. Brain disease can also develop in people with compromised immune systems. In addition, *Toxoplasma* has been shown to harm sea otters and may affect other wildlife as well. As the eggs can last for up to a year in soil, burying cat poop is also problematic. For this reason, researchers working in the field recommend keeping cats indoors and disposing of waste and litter in the trash in sealed plastic bags.

For indoor cats, the best way to dispose of cat litter is according to the NRDC recommendation, though I take issue with their suggestion of a plastic bag. When we clean out our cats' litter, we scoop the waste into brown paper lunch sacks. These are the only things that go into our garbage can. Ultimately, in spite of the fact that not much biodegrades inside a dump, we use paper sacks instead of plastic because there is a possibility of them breaking down eventually.

Cat litter itself should be purchased with care. Most cat litters come packaged in a giant plastic jug. This jug is recyclable, but it's such a waste to buy a new jug each time you need new litter. Instead, consider Petco's scoopable litter program, which saves the environment and money. If you have a Petco nearby, you can go in and purchase a jug of their store-brand litter. When you run out, you bring your container back to the store and refill it from a giant litter "sandbox" display in the center of the store. Each time you refill your container, you get a discount. Your other option is litter packaged in paper bags, such as Swheat Scoop, a natural litter made from wheat.

Dog poop doesn't pose the same environmental or health hazard as cat feces, but you still want to be careful disposing of it around waterways or food gardens. Dog poop can be safely buried in a backyard in small amounts—but check your local ordinances first! Some cities require that all dog poop is bagged and placed in the trash. If you have to pick up after your dog while out on a walk, think about using a paper bag instead of a plastic one.

⚘

Composting is often considered a fourth R, as in rot. Combined with the original three Rs—reduce, reuse, recycle—you've got a solid line of defense in combating waste in your house. As soon as you have implemented each of these Rs, you should notice a reduction in the amount of waste being produced by your household.

Now that you know about waste reduction in general terms, it is time to tackle your remaining trash. Part 2 of this book walks you through trash-generating challenges you will encounter as you adopt this lifestyle—situations such as celebrating holidays (even Christmas!), traveling on an airplane, and meal preparation. If you encounter trash not covered in this book, feel free to email me for advice at the address provided at the end of the Epilogue. I'll help you problem-solve, or we'll pose the question to the garbage-free community at the Green Garbage Project blog.

Meet Your Goal: Compost

Easy

- Participate in curbside compost pickup, if applicable.
- Start your own lazy composting pile.
- Compost your used paper towels.
- Pick up dog and cat poop in paper, not plastic, bags.

Moderate

- Start a worm bin.
- Release small wooden pieces like match sticks, popsicle sticks, and corn dog sticks to the great outdoors instead of throwing them away.
- Compost your nail trimmings, hair, and dryer lint.

Advanced

- Start a hot compost pile.
- Sign up for a Master Composter class, offered in many communities.
- Make your own soup stock from meat scraps.

PART 2

Trash-Free Challenges

This part of the book will help you navigate the various trashy circumstances you are likely to encounter in your daily life. Chapters 6 through 8 are devoted to removing trash from the rooms in your house where it is most likely created—the kitchen, bathroom, and bedroom. These chapters cover problem areas down to the nitty-gritty details. Say, for example, you love yogurt or tortilla chips or mascara, but you don't know how to avoid the garbage they create. Turn to these chapters for specific advice on all of these and many more.

You are also likely to encounter a number of social scenarios that you'd like to approach in a zero-waste way. These include traveling (road trips, hotel stays, eating out in restaurants), going to the movies, and navigating the holiday season. Or perhaps you'd like to know how to encourage your kids to go garbage free, or how to make your workplace garbage free. Part 2 has chapters devoted to each of these likely problem areas. Feel free to skip the chapters that don't apply to you—or read them anyway to see if you can apply any of the tips to your own circumstances.

Chapter 6

The Zero-Waste Kitchen

As a food lover and someone who loves to prepare meals, I was worried that going trash free would cramp my style in the kitchen. The kitchen is a difficult room to make garbage free because so much of our garbage comes from food packaging. With this in mind, I've put together some tips for zero-waste kitchens, covering everything from shopping to storage.

In chapter 2, you performed a home-waste audit and likely found that a lot of your household trash is generated in the kitchen. You're not alone here. Most of us make a lot of trash by preparing three meals plus snacks each day—all the packaging from our ingredients plus food scraps may wind up in the trash can at the end of each meal. Chapter 4, about recycling, and chapter 5, about composting, helped you deal with some of your kitchen garbage in a general sense. Now let's tackle the single biggest source of trash—grocery shopping.

I'm pretty attached to certain items in my pantry—most of us are—and I wanted to see whether I could find viable substitutes for any trash-creating items I didn't want to live without. So I decided to go on a little grocery store reconnaissance mission to find out which food items were in and what were out.

Because the items that a grocery store stocks varies from store to store, I recommend you do your own reconnaissance mission to explore your food choices. Here's how it works:

Step 1: Dig out that master shopping checklist.

You constructed this master shopping checklist on page 68; it lists every food and household item you buy on a regular basis.

Step 2: Go through your list and star all the things you buy that create garbage.

This may be most of the items on your list. If you can't recycle all the packaging after the item is used up, highlight it. For example, I would highlight blocks of cheese, because the wrapper isn't recyclable, but I wouldn't highlight a can of tomato paste because the whole can is recyclable. Pay attention to all parts of the packaging, thinking especially about plastic or foil safety seals under or around lids. It's up to you how nitpicky you'd like to get with your list. Some diehard zero wasters don't accept any garbage in their lives, whether it's big or small. Others let tiny items slide, preferring to focus on the bigger picture. It's up to you whether you want to find a substitute for ketchup based on the small foil seal under the lid, especially if the rest of the bottle is recyclable in your community.

My master shopping checklist is included below. Checkmarks indicate items I bought on a regular basis before I went zero waste. Asterisks indicate items that produce waste. Because your community recycling system may vary from mine, I might be able to recycle some items that you can't (foil and milk cartons, for example) and vice versa.

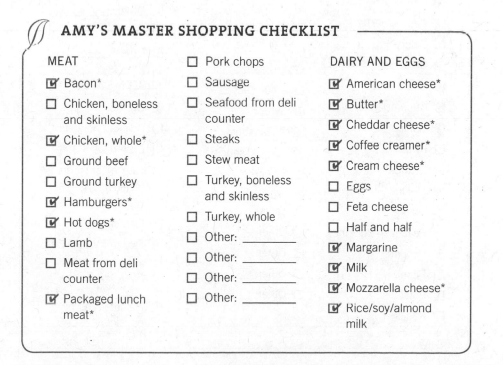

AMY'S MASTER SHOPPING CHECKLIST

MEAT

- ☑ Bacon*
- ☐ Chicken, boneless and skinless
- ☑ Chicken, whole*
- ☐ Ground beef
- ☐ Ground turkey
- ☑ Hamburgers*
- ☑ Hot dogs*
- ☐ Lamb
- ☐ Meat from deli counter
- ☑ Packaged lunch meat*

- ☐ Pork chops
- ☐ Sausage
- ☐ Seafood from deli counter
- ☐ Steaks
- ☐ Stew meat
- ☐ Turkey, boneless and skinless
- ☐ Turkey, whole
- ☐ Other: _____
- ☐ Other: _____
- ☐ Other: _____
- ☐ Other: _____

DAIRY AND EGGS

- ☑ American cheese*
- ☑ Butter*
- ☑ Cheddar cheese*
- ☑ Coffee creamer*
- ☑ Cream cheese*
- ☐ Eggs
- ☐ Feta cheese
- ☐ Half and half
- ☑ Margarine
- ☑ Milk
- ☑ Mozzarella cheese*
- ☑ Rice/soy/almond milk

- ☑ Ricotta/cottage cheese*
- ☑ Sour cream*
- ☑ Swiss cheese*
- ☑ Whipping cream
- ☑ Yogurt*
- ☐ Other: _____
- ☐ Other: _____
- ☐ Other: _____
- ☐ Other: _____

PRODUCE

- ☑ Apples
- ☑ Avocados
- ☑ Bananas
- ☑ Berries
- ☑ Broccoli
- ☑ Cabbage
- ☑ Carrots
- ☑ Cauliflower*
- ☑ Celery*
- ☑ Cherries*
- ☑ Citrus
- ☑ Cucumbers
- ☑ Garlic
- ☐ Kiwi
- ☑ Lettuce*
- ☑ Melons
- ☑ Onions
- ☑ Peaches/nectarines
- ☑ Peppers
- ☑ Plums
- ☑ Potatoes
- ☑ Radishes

- ☑ Spinach
- ☑ Tomatoes
- ☐ Zucchini
- ☐ Other: _____
- ☐ Other: _____
- ☐ Other: _____
- ☐ Other: _____

CONDIMENTS

- ☑ BBQ sauce
- ☑ Cocktail sauce
- ☑ Horseradish
- ☐ Jelly/jam
- ☑ Ketchup*
- ☑ Mayonnaise*
- ☑ Mustard*
- ☑ Olives
- ☑ Peanut butter*
- ☑ Pickles
- ☑ Salad dressing
- ☑ Salsa
- ☑ Soy sauce
- ☑ Steak sauce
- ☑ Syrup
- ☑ Tartar sauce
- ☑ Teriyaki sauce
- ☑ Vinegar
- ☑ Worcestershire sauce
- ☐ Other: _____
- ☐ Other: _____
- ☐ Other: _____
- ☐ Other: _____

GRAINS

- ☑ Bagels
- ☐ Breadsticks
- ☐ Cake
- ☑ Cereal
- ☐ Coffee cake
- ☐ Couscous
- ☑ Donuts/pastries*
- ☑ English muffins
- ☑ Hamburger/ hot dog buns
- ☐ Muffins
- ☑ Oatmeal
- ☑ Pasta
- ☑ Rice
- ☑ Sandwich bread
- ☑ Tortillas*
- ☐ Other: _____
- ☐ Other: _____
- ☐ Other: _____
- ☐ Other: _____

FROZEN FOODS

- ☑ Burritos*
- ☐ Chicken nuggets
- ☐ Corn dogs
- ☑ Faux-meat products (veggie burgers, veggie dogs, etc.)*
- ☐ Fish sticks
- ☑ Frozen TV dinners*
- ☐ Fruit
- ☑ Ice cream
- ☑ Ice cream novelties/ popsicles*

- ☑ Juice*
- ☐ Pie crust
- ☐ Pies
- ☑ Pizza*
- ☑ Pot pies*
- ☑ Pretzels*
- ☑ Seafood*
- ☑ Vegetables*
- ☐ Waffles
- ☐ Other: _____
- ☐ Other: _____
- ☐ Other: _____
- ☐ Other: _____

DRINKS

- ☑ Beer
- ☐ Bottled water
- ☑ Club soda
- ☐ Coffee
- ☐ Energy drinks
- ☐ Flavored water
- ☐ Juice/juice boxes
- ☑ Soda
- ☑ Tea
- ☐ Wine
- ☐ Other: _____
- ☐ Other: _____
- ☐ Other: _____
- ☐ Other: _____

BABY PRODUCTS

- ☐ Baby food
- ☐ Baby oil
- ☐ Baby powder
- ☐ Baby shampoo

- ☐ Baby wipes
- ☐ Diapers
- ☐ Formula
- ☐ Other: _____
- ☐ Other: _____
- ☐ Other: _____
- ☐ Other: _____

CANNED AND JARRED GOODS

- ☑ Applesauce
- ☑ Beans
- ☑ Bouillon cubes*
- ☑ Broth
- ☑ Pasta sauce
- ☑ Soup
- ☑ Tomato paste
- ☑ Tomato sauce
- ☑ Tomatoes
- ☑ Vegetables
- ☐ Other: _____
- ☐ Other: _____
- ☐ Other: _____
- ☐ Other: _____

SNACK FOODS

- ☑ Candy*
- ☑ Chips*
- ☑ Cookies*
- ☑ Crackers*
- ☐ Dried fruit
- ☐ Drink mixes
- ☐ Fruit snacks
- ☑ Granola bars*
- ☐ Jell-O

- ☐ Nuts/seeds
- ☑ Popcorn*
- ☑ Pretzels*
- ☐ Pudding
- ☑ Rice cakes*
- ☐ Other: _____
- ☐ Other: _____
- ☐ Other: _____
- ☐ Other: _____

BAKING ITEMS

- ☑ Baking powder*
- ☑ Baking soda
- ☑ Brown sugar
- ☐ Cake mix
- ☑ Chocolate chips*
- ☑ Confectioners' sugar
- ☑ Cornmeal
- ☑ Cornstarch
- ☑ Evaporated milk
- ☑ Flour
- ☐ Food coloring
- ☐ Gelatin
- ☑ Shortening*
- ☑ Spices
- ☑ Sugar
- ☑ Sweetened condensed milk
- ☑ Vanilla extract
- ☑ Yeast*
- ☐ Other: _____
- ☐ Other: _____
- ☐ Other: _____
- ☐ Other: _____

PET PRODUCTS

- ☐ Bedding for hamster/guinea pig/gerbil
- ☑ Bird seed
- ☑ Canned cat food
- ☑ Canned dog food
- ☑ Cat treats*
- ☑ Dog treats*
- ☑ Dry cat food*
- ☑ Dry dog food*
- ☐ Fish food
- ☐ Food for hamster/ guinea pig/gerbil
- ☑ Litter
- ☐ Other: _____
- ☐ Other: _____
- ☐ Other: _____
- ☐ Other: _____

BATHROOM ITEMS

- ☑ Aftershave
- ☑ Birth control pills*
- ☑ Body wash
- ☑ Bug repellent
- ☑ Chapstick*
- ☐ Cologne/perfume
- ☑ Conditioner
- ☐ Condoms
- ☐ Cotton balls
- ☑ Deodorant*
- ☐ Depilatory cream
- ☐ Facial tissue
- ☑ Feminine hygiene*

- ☑ Floss*
- ☐ Hairspray
- ☑ Lotion
- ☐ Makeup
- ☑ Prescriptions*
- ☑ Q-tips*
- ☑ Razor blades*
- ☑ Shampoo
- ☑ Shaving cream*
- ☑ Soap
- ☑ Sunscreen
- ☐ Tanning lotion
- ☑ Toilet paper
- ☑ Toothbrushes*
- ☑ Toothpaste*
- ☐ Other: _____
- ☐ Other: _____
- ☐ Other: _____
- ☐ Other: _____

OTHER NONFOOD ITEMS

- ☑ Batteries*
- ☑ Books
- ☑ Candles*
- ☑ CDs/DVDs/video games*
- ☑ Coffee filters
- ☑ Disposable cups*
- ☐ Disposable cutlery
- ☐ Disposable plates/ bowls
- ☑ Flowers*
- ☑ Foil*

- ☑ Garbage bags*
- ☑ Gift cards*
- ☑ Greeting cards
- ☑ Home décor items*
- ☑ Lightbulbs*
- ☑ Magazines
- ☑ Nails, screws, etc.
- ☑ Office supplies*
- ☑ Paper towels*
- ☑ Parchment paper
- ☑ Plants/seeds
- ☑ Plastic wrap*
- ☑ Sandwich baggies*
- ☑ Sponges*
- ☑ Stamps
- ☑ Straws*
- ☑ Tape*
- ☑ Tissue paper
- ☑ Toothpicks*
- ☐ Vacuum bags
- ☑ Waxed paper*
- ☑ Wrapping paper
- ☐ Other: _____
- ☐ Other: _____
- ☐ Other: _____
- ☐ Other: _____

CLEANING SUPPLIES

- ☑ Air freshener*
- ☑ All-purpose cleaner
- ☑ Bleach
- ☑ Cleaning wipes*
- ☑ Clothespins

- ☑ Dish soap
- ☑ Dishwasher detergent
- ☑ Dryer sheets*
- ☑ Fabric softener
- ☑ Floor cleaner
- ☑ Furniture polish
- ☑ Laundry soap
- ☑ Toilet cleaner
- ☑ Window cleaner*

- ☐ Other: _____
- ☐ Other: _____
- ☐ Other: _____
- ☐ Other: _____

CLOTHES
- ☑ Belts
- ☑ Bras
- ☑ Pajamas
- ☑ Pants

- ☑ Shirts
- ☑ Shoes
- ☑ Socks
- ☑ Underwear
- ☐ Wallets
- ☐ Other:
- ☐ Other: _____
- ☐ Other: _____
- ☐ Other: _____

Step 3: Transfer your list of starred items to a table.

Now, create a simple chart on a piece of paper. The first column should list your starred items. Next to these, list the trash created by each item. Finally, add a "replacement options" column and fill in as you find solutions. My chart is included to give you an idea of what those options might be (replace, do without, and so on).

TRASHY ITEM	TRASH CREATED	REPLACEMENT OPTIONS
Bacon	Plastic packaging	Do without
Chicken, whole	Plastic packaging	Whole rotisserie chicken; recycle plastic container
Hamburgers	Plastic packaging	Do without
Hot dogs, lunch meat	Plastic wrapper	Do without
American cheese	Plastic wrapper	Do without
Butter	Composite wrappers	Make your own
Cheddar, swiss, mozzarella cheese	Plastic wrapper	Do without
Ricotta/cottage cheese	plastic seal	Make your own
Coffee creamer	Inner safety seal	Half and half, milk, or cream
Cream cheese	Plastic-foil composite wrapper or seal	Do without
Sour cream, yogurt	Plastic seal	Purchase variety with foil, not plastic, seal; recycle foil seal
Cauliflower, celery, cherries, lettuce	Plastic wrap	Recycle plastic wrap
Ketchup, mayonnaise, mustard	Plastic safety seal	Condiments in glass bottles
Peanut butter	Plastic seal around lid	Buy in bulk

TRASHY ITEM	TRASH CREATED	REPLACEMENT OPTIONS
Donuts/pastries	Plastic window in pastry box	Make your own
Tortillas	Plastic bag with zipper	Make your own
Frozen burritos	Plastic bag	Do without
Faux-meat products (veggie burgers, veggie dogs, etc.)	Plastic inner packaging	Do without
Frozen TV dinners	Plastic tray, plastic seal	Do without
Ice cream novelties/popsicles	Plastic wrappers	Make your own
Frozen juice	Composite material—plastic pull-tab, metal top and bottom, cardboard tube	Juice in glass jars
Frozen pizza	Plastic wrap	Recycle plastic wrap
Frozen pot pies, pretzels	Plastic inner liner	Make your own
Frozen seafood, vegetables	Plastic bag	Do without
Bouillon cubes	Plastic or foil wrappers	Canned broth, or make your own stock
Candy	Throwaway wrappers	Do without, or make your own, or buy candy that comes in recyclable packaging (Nerds, Junior Mints)
Chips	Bags	Do without
Cookies	Composite wrappers, plastic trays	Make your own
Crackers	Plastic inner packaging	Make your own
Granola bars	Wrappers	Make your own
Microwave popcorn	Outer plastic bag, oil-soaked popcorn bag	Air-popped popcorn
Hard pretzels	Plastic bag	Do without
Rice cakes	Outer bag, inner wrapper	Do without
Baking powder	Composite materials canister	Buy in bulk
Chocolate chips	Plastic packaging	Buy in bulk
Shortening	Tub made from composite materials	Butter or applesauce in recipes; upcycle shortening container
Yeast packets	Foil-lined pouches	Yeast in a glass jar
Cat, dog treats	Composite bags	Make your own
Dry cat, dog food	Plastic-lined bag	Buy in bulk, or make your own
Birth control pills, prescriptions	Pill packs, plastic outer wrapper, prescription bottles	Buy anyway
Chapstick	Plastic tube	Buy in glass container with metal lid
Deodorant	Composite plastic tube	Tom's of Maine deodorant
Feminine hygiene	Tampon wrappers, tampons, pad wrappers, pads	Menstrual cup or reusable, washable cloth pads
Floss	Used floss is trash	No suitable replacement has been found
Q-tips	Plastic stick	Do without, or buy swabs with a cardboard stick
Razor blades	Replaceable razor blades are made from plastic and metal	Metal safety razor and metal blades

TRASHY ITEM	TRASH CREATED	REPLACEMENT OPTIONS
Shaving cream	Aerosol can	Conditioner, body wash, or soap
Toothbrushes	Toothbrush is trash	Preserve toothbrush, which is mailed back to Preserve company for recycling
Toothpaste	Toothpaste tube	Make your own
Batteries	Dead batteries	Rechargeable batteries
CDs/DVDs/video games	Plastic wrapper	Digital copies, rentals, or buy used (Redbox, iTunes, Netflix)
Candles	Glass containers or plastic wrappers	Do without, or reuse glass containers
Disposable bathroom cups	Used cup	A real drinking glass
Flowers	Plastic sleeve	Potted plants; buy unwrapped flowers or flowers wrapped in paper
Foil	Used foil	Glass food storage containers; recycle with scrap metal if clean
Garbage bags	The bag itself is garbage	Do without, or use compostable/biodegradable bags
Gift cards	The used gift card itself	Recycle the card (see page 250)
Home décor items	Packaging	Buy unpackaged or floor models
Lightbulbs	Garbage when burned out	Compact fluorescent lightbulbs, which last much longer than traditional bulbs
Office supplies	Pens, markers, etc.	Use pencils or refillable pens; recycle staples and paper clips; reuse rubber bands; compost pencil shavings; see chapter 12 for other ideas
Paper towels	Soiled paper towels	Compost used paper towels, or use cloth wipes
Plastic wrap	Used plastic wrap	Clean plastic wrap is recyclable with plastic bags, or use glass food storage containers
Sandwich baggies	Used baggies	Clean baggies are recyclable with plastic bags, or use glass food storage containers
Sponges	Plastic wrapper	Cotton dishcloths
Straws	Plastic straws	Do without, or use glass, metal, or paper straws
Tape	Used tape	Use sparingly, or use string or raffia
Toothpicks	Toothpicks, made from wood, are often thrown away	Compost outdoors
Waxed paper	Wax is usually made from a petroleum product	Compostable parchment paper
Air freshener	Aerosol canisters	Some scrap metal dealers will recycle empty aerosol canisters, or use essential oils or soy candles
Cleaning wipes	Used wipes	Cloth wipes
Dryer sheets	Dryer sheets	Liquid fabric softener
Window cleaner	Spray bottle nozzle	Reuse spray bottle, or use homemade window cleaner

The Zero-Waste Kitchen

Step 4: Take your table to the grocery store.

All you need is a pen or pencil and your list—you aren't buying anything today. Now go through the aisles of the grocery store with your list and stop when you come across an item that's written down. Your goal is to discover whether the grocery store has a trash-free item you can substitute for something on your list. You'd be surprised just how often this is the case. You'll find that many store-brand items are your best bet. They are often packaged with fewer frills, meaning recyclable packaging, and more savings for you.

It's important to be creative at this point. Have fun exploring the grocery store. If you're anything like me, you're probably in a grocery store rut already. You zip through the store, buying the same tried-and-true products every time. Well, variety is the spice of life! Grocery stores contain a plethora of interesting products—so many that I haven't come close to trying them all. Use your new trash-free lifestyle as a way to try new foods that you've always wondered about.

Many trash-creating packaged store products can be made at home, so depending on your time and skill, keep this in mind. Perhaps you could live without store-bought English muffins if you could find an awesome recipe for the fresh, home-baked variety (see page 130).

Finally, remember that you may have sturdy versions of single-use products already at home. Kick those single-use products to the curb once and for all. Save money by forgetting about the paper towels, plates, and bathroom cups.

COMMON ITEMS FOUND IN THE GROCERY STORE BULK SECTION

- Nuts and nut mixes
- Flours
- Sugars
- Cornstarch
- Baking powder
- Baking soda
- Chocolate chips
- Yogurt-covered pretzels
- Candy
- White and brown rice and other grains
- Dried fruit
- Spices
- Animal crackers
- Granola
- Trail mixes
- Dried beans
- Unpopped popcorn

Step 5: Spend some time in the bulk section of your grocery store.

Most stores have at least a small selection of bulk bins containing "granola-y" foods, as my friends like to say. Natural foods stores and co-ops, the pioneers of the bulk food movement, contain an even greater selection of bulk bins. The bulk bins contain an array of wonderful raw ingredients that can be turned into many meals, and many stores stock bulk snack mixes, candies, and nuts. Especially if you've never bought items from a bulk bin before, jot down a quick list of products you think you might be interested in trying. This way, when you get home, you can start planning meals based off bulk foods, which create absolutely no trash at all.

Step 6: After your reconnaissance mission,
head home and look at your data.

You're likely to have found substitutions for many things you commonly buy, but you also probably have some unsolved items still on your list. You now have some decisions to make. Look at the remaining items that you didn't find substitutions for. Are you willing to give up any of these items? Chances are you can live without some of the remaining products. Maybe remembering that many of these food items are processed and filled with chemicals, preservatives, and artificial flavors and colors might help you kick them to the curb.

Remember to be gentle with yourself. You don't have to do everything overnight. Lifestyle changes require sacrifice and adaptation, but if you change too much too fast, you'll start to resent your new lifestyle and long for your old one. Do what I do and allow yourself a weekly luxury item. I let myself buy one garbage-creating product each week as a splurge—it feels like a treat, and even then, I'm only creating one piece of trash a week. Not bad, huh?

Ultimately you're working to simplify your life by buying less. Buying fewer products means spending less time at the grocery store, consuming more whole foods, and having a smaller grocery bill at the end of the month. Keep this goal in mind, and suddenly your sacrifices don't seem quite so onerous anymore.

Get Your Containers in a Row

Reusable containers are a fact of your trash-free life. You'll come to love and rely on these garbage-reducers, but first you need to figure out what you'll be using to haul and house your products. My containers fall into several categories.

Reusable Green Bags

Reusable tote bags should be the first tool in your green arsenal. They are cheap, sturdy, and can be used anywhere. These bags, which are usually made from canvas or synthetics like nylon, come in many different sizes. You can even find some that scrunch down smaller than a tennis ball to attach to your key ring with a carabiner. Stash them in your trunk, on the floor of your car, in your glove box, or in your purse—in other words, carry them with you everywhere. Any time you go into a store, train yourself to remember your green bags. You can use these bags at places other than the grocery store, too—bonus points if you remember them when shopping for clothes, at the department store, for take-out dinners, at thrift stores, and at the library.

Produce Bags

Mesh produce bags are a new product hitting the market, and I highly recommend them. You can find these little bags all over, or, if you're handy with a sewing machine, you can make your own for a couple of dollars. These are simply see-through drawstring bags made from a mesh fabric with a tiny weave. You bring them to the store, and instead of using those tear-away plastic bags in the produce department, you put your produce in the mesh drawstring bag. I even bring my mesh bags to the bulk section of the store for larger bulk foods like peanuts or noodles, simply winding the twisty-tie label around the drawstring. The cashier can still see what product you're buying through the mesh. When you get your produce home, you can wash it while it's still in the bag, or store produce in the fridge in the mesh bag. They are machine washable and very reusable. Don't forget to take these to the farmers' market, too!

MESH PRODUCE BAGS

There are many options if you want to invest in your own set of reusable mesh bags. Here are some of my favorites:

- Flip and Tumble five-pack Reusable Produce Bags—five color-coded bags for $11; www.flipandtumble.com
- Blue Avocado Mesh Pod—one bag for $5.99; www.blueavocado.com
- Earthwise Bags—three three-packs for $9.99; www.earthwisebags.com
- ChicoBags Recycled PET Produce Bags—three bags for $11.99; www.chicobag.com

---

Bulk Bin Containers

Bulk shopping is great, but you have to have something to put all that bulk bin goodness into when you get it home. My favorite way to store bulk foods is in repurposed glass jars. These are sturdy and see-through, so you always know what you're grabbing from the pantry shelf. If you need to invest in some glass jars, remember the waste hierarchy: either reuse jars you already have, such as scrubbed and sanitized pickle or salsa jars (I peel off labels and run mine through the dishwasher), or head to your local thrift store, where you can almost always find old mason jars in near-perfect condition.

Reusable Plastic or Glass Containers

Packing lunches or storing leftovers becomes a new experience when done without waste. It's easy to do as long as you have a stack of reusable containers lying around. Tupperware used to be the go-to choice for food storage, but in the past few years stores have seen an influx of inexpensive plastic or glass to-go containers. Find the type that works best for you, and invest in enough to get you through a week of food storage. Thrift stores are great places to start, but most grocery stores carry these, too. In the case of plastic containers, watch out for the flimsy variety that is intended for just a few uses before it becomes trash. When it comes to this type of plastic, made-to-last is the best.

Make the Most of Bulk Shopping

During your grocery store reconnaissance, you checked out the bulk foods section of your local stores. Now it's time to put those bulk bins to good use. Because bulk shopping can be intimidating for someone who has never done it before, I'm going to walk you through the process step-by-step. The benefits of bulk food shopping are numerous. First, bulk bins greatly reduce packaging and trash. You are scooping dry goods into a plastic bag and tying with a twisty; both of these items can be reused numerous times before being recycled. Or, to avoid the plastic bags and ties entirely, you can make or purchase cloth drawstring bags (usually made from white muslin or cotton fabric). Fill these with grains, beans, or flours from the bulk bin, and then write the bulk item's number directly onto the sack with a washable marker or crayon. You can use your mesh produce bags for larger bulk items like noodles or trail mix, but these won't hold fine products like flour or sugar.

Bulk bin shopping is also often cheaper. You'll need to do some price-checking at your local store, but the price of bulk goods is frequently cheaper than that of prepackaged foods. And bulk food is usually fresher. Because it doesn't sit on the shelf as long and gets replenished often, I've found the quality of bulk products to be fresher than the packaged counterparts. This is especially true with spices.

Here are the three easy steps I use to complete my bulk shopping. Once this becomes a routine, you'll never want to go back to the junk-food-lined shelves of the grocery store's interior aisles.

Step 1: Locate a bulk foods store.

Finding a store with a good bulk foods supply is often the most difficult part of bulk shopping. In my experience, most grocery stores have a small section of bulk bins located somewhere along the store perimeter, often in the produce section. These bulk bins usually stock basic pantry staples like noodles and dry baking supplies. Sometimes they have a limited selection of snacks such as trail mixes, nuts, or candy. I rarely shop from this sort of bulk bin, simply because most of the items sold here already come in minimal, recyclable packaging. Flour is a good example. A 10-pound bag of flour is cheap, and the bag is made from recyclable paper. Buying flour from the bulk bin would move me up the waste hierarchy only if I brought my own cotton bags for bulk foods or reused the plastic bags provided. In my experience, chain grocery stores are not as tolerant of my efforts to reduce packaging as your next option, the local grocery store.

If chain store shopping isn't your style, spend some time exploring your options. In every town I've lived in, from the big city to a small logging community, I've been able to locate a local store with a much better selection of bulk foods than the resident chain outlet. Two options are at your disposal. First, look into locally owned grocery stores. In Washington, Oregon, California, Nevada, Utah, and Idaho, the employee-owned chain Winco is known for its massive bulk foods selection. I've found, too, that these locally owned grocery stores tend to stock an entirely different array of bulk foods than natural foods stores carry. At Winco, I can load up on bulk junk food if I want—everything from dried cheese powder to gummy bears to sweet breakfast cereals.

If, on the other hand, you want to stick with simple, unprocessed health foods, particularly organic choices, look for your local natural foods store or co-op. Natural or health food stores abound near cities and college campuses; I've found them off the beaten path, too. Most communities have a population interested in the simple, wholesome, natural foods stocked at such stores. Pop into your local health foods store and see what they have in stock—some of the foods might be unfamiliar, but often the bulk section is larger than you would find in a chain grocery store.

You'll know you've hit the bulk foods jackpot when you locate a store that sells liquids in bulk. Only the most dedicated natural foods stores carry bulk liquids, but these stores are worth their weight in gold to a trash-free lifestyle. Most of the liquids you rely on each day are carried in this section; products like hand soap, body wash, shampoo, conditioner, and all-purpose cleaner. Additionally you'll likely find liquid food staples like olive oil and honey in the liquid bulk section. With the combination of the liquid and dry goods bulk section, shopping for packaging-free products is much easier, and the range of meals you can make from the ingredients found therein is almost endless.

Step 2: Bring your containers.

Step 2 is where most people chicken out. Shopping in the bulk section isn't weird or unusual at all if you do it the "normal" way, or the way the store intends it to work. The problem is, the so-called normal way results in a lot of unnecessary plastic bag use. Sure, you can reuse your plastic bags for a number of grocery trips, but eventually those plastic bags have to be recycled. And each of your plastic bags has to be tied off with a little paper-coated metal twisty-tie, and really, how many of those things can a person reuse? The solution to all these unnecessary materials is to bring your own containers to the store.

Remembering to bring reusable containers to the store is something many people struggle with. You may wish to use Rose's tip for remembering: each time you forget a container, buy a new one. The negative financial impact will soon have you remembering those containers. Or do what I do and write a reminder on your grocery list. You could also underline all the bulk items on your grocery list. Or stash a bag of reusable containers in your car. Find a system that works for you and use it. A simple, unyielding commitment to the cause may be the best motivator and memory aid.

You'll need a variety of containers for your bulk shopping. First, consider cotton or muslin bags for your dry goods. You can buy these online (try the internet crafting site www.etsy.com) or make your own. Cotton is preferable to plastic because it is easily washable and is biodegradable when your bags reach the end of their lives. You'll need to devise a way to mark the bin number on each of these bags. You could:

- Sew/attach a fabric tag to the bag and write on this tag with a washable fabric marker.
- Carry a notebook to the store and write down the bin number in the notebook. Number your bags so the cashier can quickly ring you up.

If bags aren't your style, some people use glass jars for their bulk purchases. Affix a sticker to the jar and write the bin number on the sticker, and checkout is easy. If you're buying bulk liquids, you'll also need containers for your liquids. Most stores that sell bulk liquids also stock a variety of basic containers in various sizes, so a one-time container investment may be in order. Be sure to keep your food and cosmetic containers separate to avoid cross-contamination.

Step 3: Get the tare weight.

If you are bringing your own containers to the store, you'll want to get their tare weight (empty weight). Knowing the tare weight of your containers is important because bulk food is priced by weight. If you know how much your glass jar weighs before filling it with pasta, for example, the jar's tare weight can be subtracted from the total weight of the jar filled with pasta, meaning you pay for only the pasta. Glass is quite heavy, so you don't want to be charged for it along with your bulk purchases. You can have a cashier weigh it, or do it yourself if there's a scale in the bulk section. You'll need to keep track of this number. I like to affix a sticker to the top of the jar or container lids and write the tare weight on this sticker.

If you bring your own containers to a mainstream grocery store, don't be surprised if a cashier becomes confused or frustrated by your request to take the tare weight of your container. Many chain supermarket employees aren't yet accustomed to the green shopping movement. Use a friendly approach when you ask a cashier at such a store to accommodate your request. Measuring the tare weight of a container does take a little time, so be sure to explain why you're bringing your own containers to the store, and say thank you to a helpful cashier. As long as I've written down the weight of my container, I only have to do it once and then I'm set for the life of that container. If you try and are rebuffed, try again on a different day. It is important to make it clear (cheerfully) that you'll be making those purchases elsewhere. Lost revenue for a supermarket is always meaningful.

One final note: I never worry about finding the tare weight of my mesh produce bags or my muslin bulk food bags. The weight is negligible and quite equivalent to that of a throwaway plastic bag. It's just not worth the hassle.

Pet Food and Treats

When I grocery shop, I spend a good deal of time in the pet aisle, making purchases to feed my cats and dog as well as myself. Dinnertime in my house means I'm preparing food for myself and Adam and our pets. Pet food and treats pose their own set of garbage-related dilemmas. And, as with any other area of your life, making your pets' lives zero-waste is a matter of degrees and commitment. Some aspects of pet ownership are easy to make garbage free, whereas others areas are nearly impossible. Our cats are fed both dry and canned cat food, whereas our dog eats dry food mixed with healthy leftovers. All of our pets get regular treats. The pet garbage we make on a regular basis consists of dry pet food bags and treat bags.

Dry pet food bags look like they are made from paper, but if you submit them to the tear test, you'll find that all are lined with a plastic coating that presumably keeps the food fresh. This plastic coating renders the pet food bags unrecyclable. If you desire to feed your pets dry food, this category of garbage is close to insurmountable. You may be lucky enough to find a bulk foods department that sells dry pet food from bulk bins; however, because I prefer to feed my pets a high-quality food, these bins of unmarked, unbranded dry food aren't ideal for me, as I have no way to know their nutritional contents. This leaves me with two options—either buy bags of dry food in the largest size possible, thereby creating very little packaging waste in relation to the amount of food purchased, or make my own pet food.

Homemade pet food is by no means impossible, though most people have never even considered it as an option. The world of home-cooked pet diets is too large to be addressed in detail in this book, so I'll just give a brief overview. After the well-publicized pet food recall of 2007, consumers began to realize that commercial pet food may not be as healthy as TV commercials suggest. The problem is, pets have different nutritional needs from humans; cats, for example, require more protein in their diets. In designing and cooking a homemade diet of pet food, the mindful pet owner needs to take these dietary needs into consideration. Start by researching your pet's nutritional needs. It is always advisable to consult with your veterinarian. Only after you've gained the necessary knowledge should you begin to explore recipes for cooking homemade food. Most recipes for home-cooked pet food involve a mixture of a grain (pasta or rice), meat (which is difficult to acquire without waste), and fruits and vegetables. The amount of food to be fed is based on your pet's weight. Luckily most recipes I've used can be made in large quantities on a weekend, then frozen until you need them.

Pet treats can also pose problems to a zero-waste household, because most varieties come packaged in composite-material, resealable pouches that are nothing but trash when empty. Your options here are to either donate or reuse these empty bags in an upcycled, fused plastic project, or make homemade pet treats. Some treats, like dog bones, come packaged in cardboard boxes, which are always recyclable.

The Final Challenge: Shopping for Meat and Dairy

Your last hurdle on the path to making your kitchen waste free is the meat and dairy dilemma. Shopping for these two food categories is difficult when living a zero-waste lifestyle, because meat and dairy products generally come in packaging that cannot be recycled. Most of our zero-waste contributors eat little to no meat. Some eat meat only in restaurants; others request for it to be wrapped in paper at the deli counter. Either way, a commonality among most zero-wasters is the understanding that consumption of commercial meat and dairy products is contrary to our environmental values.

It's important to recognize that most meat sold in grocery stores is produced in a factory farm, also called a Concentrated Animal Feeding Operation (CAFO). CAFOs are nasty places by most anyone's reckoning. The goal of a factory farm is the same as that of any factory—to produce as much product (in this case, meat) as quickly as possible. The horrific treatment of animals inside CAFOs is well-documented, but most people turn a blind eye because cheap, readily available meat is so desirable. Inside CAFOs, animals are brutalized, and their living conditions are severely compromised because so many animals are crammed into the space. Additionally, the health conditions inside factory farms are atrocious. When animals are unhealthy, the meat they yield is also not of high quality. Finally, raising animals in feed-lot conditions is harmful to the environment. For example, open-air manure lagoons, which can be as big as several football fields, are prone to leaks and spills. In 1995, a manure spill from a hog farm in North Carolina spilled 25 million gallons of manure into the New River and killed about 10 million fish and closed 364,000 acres of coastal wetlands to shellfishing. There is no real way around the fact that buying grocery store meat (the kind packaged in shrink wrap and Styrofoam) is not good for the environment. So what's an earth-loving carnivore to do?

Rose, who is a vegetarian, appreciates the problem. The dilemma, in her eyes, is that people must choose either quality or quantity. "People are not willing to spend more (on organic meat) and get less," she says. For the most part, I agree with Rose, though luckily there is a growing segment of the population that is willing to pay for free-range meat. The more we, as consumers, vote with our dollars, buying high-quality meat that is healthier and kinder to the animals, the sooner we will see the end of the atrocious CAFO model.

Your best bet for zero-waste meat consumption is to find a butcher who sells locally grown, free-range meat and request that your meat purchase be wrapped in compostable butcher paper. Other zero-waste contributors have taken different approaches.

Chris describes himself and his wife as "quasi-vegetarians." Sometimes meat packaging can be a hurdle. "What we're obviously avoiding is the packaging. The biggest thing we need to avoid is the Styrofoam. Film plastic, if rinsed properly, is not a problem." To avoid the packaging, "don't be afraid of going to the butcher counter and asking for it to be packaged without the tray."

Robert, on the other hand, describes himself as an aquatarian, meaning he is primarily a vegetarian but eats seafood. "I tend to eat vegetarian at home; when I do eat seafood, it's in a restaurant. I make sure it's sustainably harvested." When he eats fish at home, he eats tuna fish from a can or buys fish wrapped in compostable paper from a local fish market.

Desira and her husband are "flexitarians," meaning they don't eat much meat. "I'm not morally against it, but I'd like to get better-sourced meat. It's hard to find." When she buys meat from Whole Foods, she says they're happy to put it in her own container. She eats meat once or twice a week. Although she throws away cheese packaging, she does buy large blocks of cheese and shreds them herself.

I myself am a vegetarian, so I don't face the problem of buying meat. I do eat dairy and eggs, however. Eggs are easy—the carton is recyclable or I can return it to my local farmer for reuse. I make a lot of dairy products at home (see my recipes below), but cheese is still a zero-waste challenge, so I am often left with some cheese wrappers as trash.

Recipes

As you can see, reducing garbage in the kitchen is a wonderful challenge to undertake because it allows you to try new foods and new recipes. In addition, you are spending most of your time shopping the perimeter of the grocery store, meaning you are buying healthful foods like produce and grains as opposed to the highly artificial junk that fills most aisles.

My favorite part about going garbage free has been the challenge of finding ways to make the items I no longer buy due to excessive packaging. Here are my favorite recipes for alternatives to store-bought foods, including English muffins, ricotta cheese, and sandwich bread. If you'd like to do a little experimenting of your own, try an internet search for a recipe for a store-bought item you'd like to try to replicate.

Basic Sandwich Bread

This is the best all-purpose bread recipe I've found. I make it the old-fashioned way, without using a bread machine, because the texture turns out so much nicer. Many homemade breads are great right out of the oven, but they tend to crumble when you try to cut them into even slices. This bread is perfect for sandwiches and French toast. *Yield: 1 loaf*

> 1 cup milk
> $^1/_2$ cup water
> 4 tablespoons ($^1/_2$ stick) butter, melted and cooled, divided
> 3 tablespoons honey
> 3$^3/_4$ cups all-purpose flour, plus extra for dusting
> 2$^1/_4$ teaspoons or 1 envelope instant yeast
> 2 teaspoons salt

Gently warm the milk and water in a microwave or on the stove top—110°F is just right for bread making, just shy of too hot to stick your finger in. Too hot and the liquid will kill the yeast; too cold and the bread won't rise. Whisk in 3 tablespoons of the butter and the honey.

In a separate bowl, mix together the flour, yeast, and salt. Slowly add the liquid ingredients to the flour mixture. Mix with a wooden spoon until a soft dough forms.

Dust a countertop with a light layer of flour. Turn the dough onto the countertop and knead until smooth and elastic, about ten minutes. To knead, push and pull the dough around on countertop, folding it into itself randomly and pushing down.

Form the dough into a round ball. Place it in a bowl lightly oiled with olive oil. Cover with a clean dishcloth and let rise in a warm place until doubled in size, about 1½ hours.

Dust the countertop with a light layer of flour. Turn out the dough, punch it down on the countertop, and press it into a 9-inch square. Tightly roll the dough and place seam-side down in an oiled 9-inch loaf pan. Cover with dishcloth and let rise another 1½ hours.

Preheat the oven to 350°F. Brush the top of the loaf with the remaining 1 tablespoon of butter and place it in the middle rack of the oven. Place another loaf pan filled with hot water next to the bread to increase the humidity. Bake until the bread reaches 200°F inside (I use a meat thermometer to check), 40 to 50 minutes. Turn the bread loaf out of the pan onto a wire rack and let it cool for two hours before slicing.

Sour Cream

Homemade sour cream is the easiest thing to make and it tastes as good as— or better—than the store-bought version. *Yield: 1 cup*

    1 cup heavy whipping cream
    ¼ cup cultured buttermilk

Sterilize a pint-size glass jar by washing it in hot, soapy water. After the jar is rinsed but while it's still warm, pour in the cream, then add the buttermilk and use a metal spoon to gently combine them.

Cover the jar with cheesecloth or a piece of loosely woven fabric. Do not use a jar lid; the liquid must be able to breathe or it won't thicken.

Leave the jar on the counter for at least 12 hours or overnight. (The cream will thicken best if left in a warm environment, so I keep mine next to my stove.)

After the cream has thickened, remove the cheesecloth, cover with the jar lid, and store in the fridge. The cream will continue thickening for another day or so, but it's good to use right away. This stays fresh in the fridge for about 10 days.

Ricotta Cheese

I love lasagna, but I stopped making it for a while because the ricotta cheese came in a garbage-producing container. Now I make my own fresh ricotta whenever I want lasagna. It takes only about half an hour to make, and it's foolproof and delicious. *Yield: 2 cups*

1/2 gallon whole milk
2 cups buttermilk

Combine the milk and buttermilk in a big pot over medium high heat. Stirring the mixture regularly, bring it to 100°F, using a candy thermometer to monitor the temperature. Once it reaches 100°F, stop stirring and let cook for another 10 to 15 minutes until the liquid reaches 175°F. Remove the pot from the heat and let it sit for five minutes.

Meanwhile, stretch two layers of cheesecloth over a colander in the sink. Moisten the cheesecloth with water until damp but not sopping wet.

At this point, the hot mixture will have separated into curds and whey. Using a slotted spoon, gently spoon the curds into the cheesecloth. Let the curds drain for 5 minutes. Discard the remaining liquid.

Gather the edges of the cheesecloth together to form a pouch holding the ricotta cheese. Use a rubber band to securely close the pouch. Hang it by looping the rubber band around the kitchen faucet handle and let drain for another half hour.

Store the cheese in a container in the fridge and use within five days.

Butter

Like the preceding dairy recipes, butter is easy to make and tastes great. There are two methods for churning cream into butter: with a jar or a stand mixer. Both will take some time, but it's worth it! *Yield: 1 cup*

2 cups heavy whipping cream

To make butter in a jar, pour the cream into a lidded glass jar with a clean marble. Tightly close the lid and shake the cream back and forth, agitating it.

The cream will pass through several stages, turning first into whipped cream and then into a liquid and solids as the butter finally appears. This will take a long time (15 to 20 minutes), so you may want to have a friend help you share the shaking duties.

To make butter using a stand mixer, fit it with the whisk attachment and pour the cream into the mixing bowl. Use the splash guard or drape a cloth over the mixer so the cream doesn't splatter. Whisk on medium-high speed for about 10 minutes.

You'll know when the butter has formed because it will look like the store-bought variety. If you use the stand mixer method, the butter will form into a ball inside the whisk. If you are using the jar method, the butter will clump together at the bottom of the jar. Using either method, when butter has formed, pour out the excess liquid and thoroughly rinse the butter under cold water until the water runs clear.

Put the butter in a jar, cover with cold water, and store in the fridge.

Herb Crackers

Homemade crackers are delicious. They taste as good as, or better than, the store-bought variety that come in a bag in a box. Using this recipe means no bag or box to recycle, so it's totally zero-waste. There are endless combinations for flavoring these crackers. Here are just a few: dill and caraway seeds, grated parmesan and basil, rosemary and sage, cumin and cayenne, garlic and onion powder.

For cheese crackers, use garlic powder for the seasoning and stir in $1/2$ cup grated Cheddar cheese with the dry ingredients. *Yield: 5 dozen crackers*

2 $1/2$ cups flour
3 teaspoons dried herbs or other seasoning
1 teaspoon salt
4 tablespoons olive oil
$3/4$ cup cold water
Kosher salt for sprinkling on top

Preheat the oven to 400°F.

Combine the flour, herbs, and salt in a bowl. Add the oil and water; mix with a fork until the dough comes together into a ball. Add more water as necessary to form a rough dry dough.

On a lightly floured surface, turn out the dough and knead just until it comes together into a cohesive ball. Divide into four even portions.

On a silicone mat or piece of compostable parchment paper, roll out the dough as thin as possible until it's nearly the size of a baking sheet.

Cut the dough into squares and prick each square two or three times with a fork. (You can cut them into any size and shape you desire; I cut mine to the dimensions of a club cracker.) Sprinkle with coarse salt.

Place the silicone mat or parchment paper on a cookie sheet and bake until golden brown, about 15 minutes. Repeat this process with the remaining dough.

Let the crackers cool. Store in a tightly covered container.

Vanilla Yogurt

Making your own yogurt is a little tricky and may take a little experimentation. You start your first batch with store-bought plain, unsweetened yogurt—it must contain live, active cultures, or your yogurt won't thicken. Some brands of yogurt work better than others, and I've found that the fresher the purchased starter is, the thicker the yogurt gets. Once you have made your own yogurt, you can use a spoonful as a starter for the next batch. Flavor your yogurt by using extracts, such as lemon or almond.

Note: I use a slow cooker to incubate the yogurt; you can also use a commercial yogurt maker and follow the instructions. I use two pint-size canning jars; you could use a single quart jar or four 1-cup jars instead. *Yield: 1 quart*

1 quart whole milk

¼ cup sweetener of your choice—sugar, honey, maple syrup, molasses, or an equivalent amount of artificial sweetener

1 cup instant nonfat dry milk powder

1 tablespoon vanilla extract

1 tablespoon plain, store-bought yogurt with live, active cultures, for starter

Warm the milk on the stove over medium heat, stirring frequently. When it is hot, stir in the sweetener until dissolved and continue to heat. Just before the mixture boils, remove from the heat.

Stir in the vanilla extract and the instant nonfat dry milk and let cool. While the mixture cools, warm a slow cooker. (I use the "warm" setting for the entire yogurt-making process; once the yogurt goes into the slow cooker to culture, I unplug it.)

When the cooling mixture is 110°F, stir in the store-bought yogurt. Pour the yogurt into clean, warm glass jars. Unplug the slow cooker, add the yogurt jars, and cover the pot to keep in the heat. Incubate the yogurt for 12 hours or overnight. When done, the yogurt will be thick. Screw on the jar lids and refrigerate.

Variation: For fruit yogurt, before filling the jars put 1 tablespoon jam or preserves into the bottom of each, then fill with the yogurt. If you prefer to use fresh fruit, add it to the yogurt right before serving.

Bagels

Homemade bagels far outshine the kind you can purchase in a grocery store. These are easy and delicious. Unlike most bread recipes, they require very little time to rise. Make a couple of batches at a time and freeze some so you have them on hand. *Yield: 8 bagels*

> $3^1/_4$ teaspoons active dry yeast
> $1^1/_8$ cup hot water
> 3 cups all-purpose flour
> 4 tablespoons granulated sugar, divided
> 1 tablespoon molasses
> 1 teaspoon salt
> Cornmeal
> 1 egg
> 2 tablespoons poppy or sesame seeds

Combine the yeast and water in a medium bowl. Let stand for five minutes.

In a separate bowl, combine the flour, 2 tablespoons of the sugar, and the molasses and salt. Add the yeast mixture to the flour mixture and stir until a dough is formed.

On a lightly floured surface, turn out the dough and knead for about 10 minutes, until smooth and elastic.

To form the bagels, divide the dough into 8 parts. Roll each into a ball, then gently press your thumb through the center of the ball and stretch it into a bagel shape. Set the bagels on a baking sheet, cover with a cloth, and let rise for about 15 minutes.

While the bagels are rising, put 3 quarts of water in a large pot over high heat, add the remaining sugar, and bring to a rapid boil. Preheat the oven to 400°F. Sprinkle a baking sheet with cornmeal.

Drop 3 bagels at a time into the boiling water and boil for 90 seconds. Flip them over and boil for another 90 seconds. Transfer to a rack and let cool for a minute. Continue with the remaining bagels.

Beat the egg well with a tablespoon of water. Brush the tops of the bagels with this egg wash and sprinkle with poppy or sesame seeds.

Place the bagels on the prepared baking sheet and bake until golden brown, about 15 minutes. Transfer to a wire rack and let cool.

Store in a sealed container, where they will keep for about five days.

English Muffins

These English muffins are delicious hot off the griddle, or you can freeze them for later use. Your friends will be impressed, as these muffins are as open-crumbed and chewy as the kind you buy in a bag. *Yield: 9 muffins*

   4 cups all-purpose flour
   1 teaspoon salt
   $1\,^2/_3$ cups lukewarm milk
   $^1/_2$ teaspoon sugar
   $^1/_2$ ounce active dry yeast
   1 tablespoon butter, melted

Sift the flour and salt together in a large bowl and make a well in the center.

Stir together half of the milk, the sugar, and the yeast. Add the remaining milk and the butter and stir. Pour the milk mixture into the flour mixture and stir until a soft, smooth, elastic dough forms. Cover and let rise for an hour, until the dough has doubled in size.

Grease and flour a cookie sheet. Punch down the dough and turn it onto a floured surface. Roll out to $^1/_2$ inch thick. Using a plain round 3- or 4-inch cookie cutter, cut out nine rounds and place on the cookie sheet. Cover and let rise for another 30 minutes.

Warm a griddle over medium heat and lightly grease. Cook the muffins on the griddle until golden brown, about 7 minutes per side.

Cool and store at room temperature in a sealed container, where they will keep for about a week.

As you can see, there are solutions to nearly every garbage dilemma posed by kitchen activities. Most of your kitchen waste comes in the form of food packaging, and if you can eliminate this, you've taken a huge bite out of your trash volume. Over and over, people ask me how a zero-waste life is possible. What I tell them sounds so simple, but it's the truth: don't buy trash. Nowhere is this more important than in the kitchen. When you're at the grocery store, do not put anything in your cart that will end up in the trash can. That's it. If you can follow this simple guideline, as well as others outlined in this chapter, your meal prep has gotten simpler, healthier, and trash free.

Meet Your Goal: The Zero-Waste Kitchen

Easy

- Rinse and recycle plastic film from meat trays.
- Eliminate trash, but allow yourself one luxury item a week.
- Replace sponges with washable cloths.
- Replace liquid hand soap with bar soap.

Moderate

- Buy free-range, locally sourced meat.
- Invest in muslin bags for the bulk section; label with a washable marker.
- Use mesh produce bags instead of plastic bags.
- Introduce yourself to local store managers.
- Buy eggs from a local farmer.

Advanced

- Stop eating meat (or drastically reduce your consumption).
- Buy liquids in bulk.
- Make your own pet food.
- Donate used egg cartons to a local farmer.

Chapter 7

The Zero-Waste Bathroom

Although the kitchen may be the room where most trash is produced, the hardest room to make garbage free is the bathroom. From flu season to dental care, feminine hygiene to birth control, the bathroom offers a number of pitfalls for those seeking a garbage-free life.

The problem is that most items we use in the bathroom today are designed to be disposable—some after a number of uses and some after only a single use. Whereas single-serve food items offer mere convenience, sparing us from common preparation tasks that we can easily take on, I believe we use disposables in the bathroom for another reason entirely. Sure, disposable razors are convenient, but we also equate single-use disposables with words like *clean* and *safe*. I think many of us are grossed out by the idea of reusing a bathroom product (washable menstrual pads, for instance).

The first step toward reducing bathroom trash, then, is a mindset shift. To rid the bathroom of single-use disposables, you must embrace the idea of experimenting with alternative products until you find the right ones that fit into your lifestyle. Know that less than a hundred years ago, the disposable bathroom products we rely on today didn't even exist.

One of my personal goals is to live as natural a life as possible, and it helps me to keep this in mind when selecting my personal care products. To me, this means using products made from sustainable resources, not chemicals or synthetics. I want to access ingredients and raw materials that have been on the planet for ages instead of relying on manmade materials. This is all part of simplifying my life—just as I want to be able to pronounce all the ingredients in my ice cream, I want to know what minerals my deodorant is made from.

There are numerous ways to avoid disposables while maintaining modern levels of cleanliness and hygiene, and in this chapter I'll show you how to make the switch.

You should already have a list of the items that create trash in your bathroom, including all the products you buy and use here, from doing your home waste audit in chapter 2 and your master shopping list from chapter 4. These two lists together will give you a good idea of the products in your bathroom that create waste. Because I'm a low-maintenance gal, my list is pretty short: shampoo, conditioner, soap/body wash, contact lens solution, toothbrush, toothpaste, floss, deodorant, razors, and occasionally lotion. You might add makeup, face creams, or hair products to that list and, if you're a guy, shaving cream and aftershave. Contraception such as condoms and other birth control, as well as feminine hygiene products also fall under the bathroom trash heading. And then there are medical products, which we'll discuss in a later section.

Once you have your list, go through it and determine what makes garbage. Take your list to a grocery store, cosmetic counter, or pharmacy, and peruse the many, many personal care products on the market today. While doing reconnaissance for the bathroom, note any products that come in recyclable packaging. Can you replace your makeup remover cloths (garbage) with a liquid remover in a recyclable bottle, for example? You won't need to switch out all or even most of your products. I didn't need to switch out my bar soap, for example, because it comes wrapped in recyclable paper and when the soap is used up, there's nothing left. I can also refill my shampoo and conditioner bottles from the bulk section or recycle the bottles, along with my contact solution bottles, so these didn't need to be replaced. That left me looking for alternatives for deodorant, toothbrush, toothpaste, and floss. Your list may be longer or shorter than mine, of course, so in the sections that follow, I address the most common trash-generating areas of the bathroom and help you find solutions for replacing them with zero-waste options.

Dental Products

Dental products pose a tough problem to those of us living zero-waste lifestyles. Many parts of the dental hygiene routine create trash—the toothpaste tube and floss being the main problem areas. Recipes abound for homemade toothpastes and mouthwashes, and you can buy a toothpaste alternative, tooth powder, from Etsy vendors. The problem is, there is a large debate about which ingredients in (store-bought and homemade) toothpaste are good or bad for your teeth. Because I am not a professional in this area, I recommend you do what I did and speak with your dentist about your desire for an effective, safe, and zero-waste teeth-cleaning routine.

Toothbrushes

Virtually all toothbrushes are designed to be disposable after two or three months of use. And although no one is going to argue for a toothbrush designed to be used forever, this is a lot of waste headed into the landfill each year. The problem is that most toothbrushes are made from plastics, and they are not recyclable. Your better bet is to opt for something recyclable or biodegradable; both options do exist.

Preserve toothbrushes (www.preserveproducts.com): Perhaps the simplest option, Preserve toothbrushes are widely sold in natural food stores. These are regular toothbrushes made from plastic (the handles are made from recycled yogurt containers), but the difference is that the Preserve company not only manufactures the brushes but also takes them back for recycling. So you buy your toothbrush, use it, then mail it back to the Preserve company in a postage-paid envelope. Your toothbrush is melted down and gets another life as a plastic bench.

The only real drawback with Preserve toothbrushes is they're made from plastic (see page 84). Any way you slice it, plastic is not good for the environment. It can't be recycled, only downcycled, and really, humanity can use only so many plastic benches.

Compostable toothbrushes (environmentaltoothbrush.com.au): Toothbrushes made with a bamboo handle and biodegradable bristles are another option to consider. These are sold by an Australian company, so you'll also want to think about your carbon footprint if you choose to order them. They come in sets of twelve packaged in cardboard and paper. After use, these toothbrushes can be placed in your home compost pile, where they naturally biodegrade.

Toothpaste

Until recently, the Tom's of Maine toothpaste company manufactured their toothpaste in recyclable aluminum tubes. The company's switch to plastic toothpaste tubes left a number of zero-wasters in the lurch, for we had long relied on Tom's of Maine products. Today, if you're looking for a zero-waste toothpaste, your options are limited. You can try making your own at home (see sidebar) or look online at Esty, where some crafters sell homemade tooth powders. Otherwise, use your toothpaste sparingly to make each tube last as long as possible. Again, you need only a pea-size dab, not the full-length ribbon that toothpaste sellers recommend.

Floss

Flossing makes garbage, there's no way around it. I have yet to find a biodegradable floss, nor have any of the zero-waste contributors. But flossing is important for good dental health, so if you're going to do it, at least you can use a more eco-friendly floss that comes in more responsible packaging. Eco-Dent GentleFloss and Eco-Dent VeganFloss are unique because they come

---

𝄞 HOMEMADE TOOTHPASTE

I've experimented with a number of homemade toothpaste recipes, and this is my favorite. The flavor is much milder than name-brand toothpastes, but it seems to clean well and keeps bad breath at bay. This recipe is easily doubled or tripled. YIELD: 1/8 CUP

1 tablespoon fresh or 1/2 tablespoon dried, crumbled spearmint leaves
1/4 cup cold water
1/2 teaspoon cornstarch

1/2 teaspoon olive or sunflower oil
2 to 4 drops pure spearmint essential oil, to taste

Place the mint leaves and water in a small saucepan and bring just to a boil over high heat. Remove the saucepan from the heat and let cool for 15 minutes.

In a small bowl, mix together the cornstarch and oil and stir until smooth. Pour the minted water through a strainer into the cornstarch mixture. Discard the leaves.

Pour the water and cornstarch mixture back into the saucepan and add the essential oil. Bring to a boil over high heat, stirring occasionally. Once it reaches a boil, the cornstarch thickens the mixture.

Spoon into a clean container and use like regular toothpaste.

packaged in cardboard, not plastic, making the floss box recyclable. The floss itself is made from nylon and is coated in a vegan wax made from rice bran. Nylon is a material derived from petroleum, so the floss itself is not biodegradable, but at least the packaging can be recycled.

Your other option is a water jet device (two brands are Water Pik and Sonicare), which shoots water jets in between the teeth, allowing you to "floss" with water. I have found a Water Pik to be effective, though not as effective as flossing.

TRASH-FREE MEDICAL AND DENTAL APPOINTMENTS

Trips to the doctor or dentist can generate a lot of trash on site. It is important to let your doctor and dentist know ahead of time that you prefer to be seen by a medical facility that respects and understands your environmental preferences; even if your medical professionals don't currently use green practices, expressing your desire that they do so can help influence the direction of their practice.

At any given doctor's visit, the doctor or nurse will likely generate the following trash while caring for you: plastic thermometer cover, plastic otoscope cover, tongue depressor, one pair of gloves, a paper gown, and a paper table sheet. If you need a shot, lab test, or any other special procedure, even more trash is created.

A visit to the dentist will generate a paper bib, a pair of gloves, floss, and pieces of plastic to cover the light handles. If charting and X-rays aren't done digitally, this creates more waste.

I'm not saying all this trash is bad or unnecessary. I'm very glad my doctor wears a new set of gloves per patient and doesn't reuse needles. However, it is important that both patients and medical staff are aware of the massive amount of trash generated by doctors, dentists, and hospitals. There are steps that medical professionals can take to reduce the amount of waste produced in their profession, but they need to know this is a priority to their patients.

The website www.ecodentistry.org is a great place to start if you're looking for a green dentist in your area or if you're looking to encourage your dentist to go green. Included on the "Green My Dentist" page is a letter you can print off and give to your dentist that expresses your desire to see the practice adopt greener policies and produce less waste. Once you've given your dentist the letter, you let Eco Dentistry know and they follow up by sending an information kit to your dentist. In particular, the organization helps your dentist adopt the use of cloth bibs and eliminate reliance on paper cups and paper or plastic chair covers.

Medical Products

Trash-free over-the-counter medicine is practically impossible to find. Prescription bottles can be hard to recycle. This means your cold season zero-waste toolbox should include preventive care and homeopathic remedies. It's important to think about headaches, stuffy noses, sore throats, and coughing before the winter months hit, because I speak from experience when I say the very last thing you will care about while sick is your zero-waste lifestyle. The whole effort will feel silly and stupid, and you'll just want whatever over-the-counter remedies you've always relied on to make you feel better.

Preventive Care and Home Remedies

So, first comes preventive care. We all know what we need to do to stay healthy, but sometimes these things get put on the back burner because we get so busy. I'm talking about simple steps like eating well, drinking lots of water, exercising regularly, getting enough sleep, managing your stress, and washing your hands. The good news is your new zero-waste lifestyle has already helped you adopt the first step, because eating well and living without trash go hand-in-hand.

Next, make sure to put together a trash-free cold- and flu-season kit before you start feeling sick. Colds pretty much have to run their course, so the focus of my kit is more on comfort than on cure. We keep soup on hand, and I regularly make popsicles in reusable plastic molds to soothe sore throats. Water, tea with honey, lots of naps, a good supply of washable cloth hankies, and some books or movies pretty much get me through my minor sniffles.

That said, sometimes I have to work when I'm sick, and I need something a little stronger than chamomile tea to help me function. In particular, I need something for headaches and for my voice when it's threatening to leave me. Sometimes I have to bite the bullet and buy an over-the-counter drug that creates as little garbage as possible.

Recycling Medicine Containers

In general, when buying over-the-counter medicine, I shop in the same way I do for other grocery products. I check out the packaging before I buy it. With almost all medicines, you'll be throwing away a foil or plastic safety seal (or sometimes both). Ideally, however, the rest of the packaging is recyclable. My aspirin comes in a plastic bottle inside a recyclable box. Under the screw top, I peel off and throw away the foil seal. If there is a wad of cotton inside, this is compostable. I try to buy the biggest bottle available, so I get the most product for the packaging I have to purchase. I avoid medicines that come individually wrapped in little blister packs as well as packets of medicine (such as powders designed to be poured in a liquid). The blister packs and packets are always trash.

Sometimes you'll find a little packet containing a preservative powder inside your medicine bottle. Here's a little-known tip thanks to my photographer husband—you can place these little packets inside camera bags to keep the internal environment drier. You can also place these freshener packs in with stored garden seed packets to reduce their exposure to humidity.

Recycling plastic medicine bottles, especially prescription bottles, can be a tricky process. Most bottles are number 5 plastic, and many communities cannot recycle this plastic. Remember the Gimme 5 program (see page 76); even if you don't live near a Whole Foods or other participating outlet, you can mail your number 5 plastics to them for recycling. Better yet, give those prescription bottles a second life by reusing them (see sidebar for ideas).

Properly Disposing of Expired or Unwanted Medicine

There is no way to recycle expired or unwanted medicine, whether prescription or over-the-counter. Instead, the best bet for a dedicated zero-waster like yourself is to follow federal guidelines for disposal.

REPURPOSING EMPTY PRESCRIPTION BOTTLES

- Call local free clinics and veterinarian offices to see whether they can reuse your empty bottles.
- Store small items like jewelry, buttons, and hardware like screws and nails.
- Store spare change in your car.
- Store a portable mini sewing kit or Band-Aids for travel.
- Just the right size for stashing earplugs in your purse or pack to protect your hearing in a high-volume movie theater or allow you to sleep in a noisy hotel room.

One precaution—do not store candy or other medicines in an old prescription bottle. Candy's a no-no because we want small children to clearly distinguish between medicine and food. Other meds are a bad idea because it can be easy to mistake the contents of the bottle for what the label indicates.

First, check whether the police or fire department in your community hosts an annual drug collection program. You bring your unwanted pills to these collection events, and the officials ensure that the drugs are properly disposed of.

Check also with your local recycling facility for guidelines on hazardous waste disposal in your community. Often hazardous waste departments accept expired medications or hold take-back events.

If you don't have these options, follow these steps to safely dispose of pills.

1. Remove the pills from their original containers. (Recycle or reuse these, if possible.)

2. Mix the pills into a substance like sand, kitty litter, or coffee grounds.

3. Place the mixture in an unmarked, impermeable container and seal it. (This prevents drug seekers, children, or animals from accessing the drugs.)

4. Dispose of the container in your regular curbside trash bin.

Whatever you do, *never* flush pills down the drain or toilet, which allows the medicine to enter our waterways.

Feminine Hygiene

Ladies looking to lessen the waste produced during their menstrual cycle are in luck—there are several effective and comfortable products on the market today. Although the vast majority of women use disposable options each month, there are other ways to take care of your menstrual needs; namely, menstrual cups and reusable cloth pads. Try them, and I'm willing to bet you won't miss your tampons or pads.

The garbage caused by disposable pads and tampons each year is absolutely a problem on a massive scale. The Luna Pad company, which manufactures cloth pads, estimates that approximately twenty billion pads, tampons, applicators, and wrappers are being sent to North American landfills each year. This is an incredible amount of garbage, and continuing the cycle of using menstrual disposables is as senseless as using plastic water bottles instead of stainless steel ones, or plastic shopping bags instead of cloth versions.

If the garbage isn't enough to convince you to give reusables a try, perhaps a cost-savings analysis will be. I've used the same Diva Cup, a reusable menstrual cup, for three years. The Diva Cup costs about $40. Previously I used tampons, and I easily went through a $5 box a month. Over the course of the year, I spent at least $60 on tampons, meaning my initial investment in the Diva Cup saved me $20 the first year I used it. Since then, it's saved me another $120, as I've not bought tampons for two years.

Environmental and cost benefits aside, it's a delightful feeling to not have to wander down the feminine hygiene aisle at the grocery store anymore. Menstrual reusables make life easier because you never have to worry about running out of them. My Diva Cup stays tucked in my purse where I used to keep tampons. It's small and discreet. Buying tampons used to feel like a necessary evil; now the thought feels downright wasteful and unsanitary.

The Diva Cup (www.divacup.com) or the Keeper (www.keeper.com)

Menstrual cups are small, cup-shaped pieces of latex or silicone that are inserted like tampons to collect blood. Unlike tampons, which are absorbent, menstrual cups catch blood and need to be emptied every so often.

Trust me, I understand what a huge leap of faith it is to try a menstrual cup the first time. I have a very clear memory of shopping with my husband after we agreed to try trash-free living. I plucked a Diva Cup off the shelves and put it in the cart. Adam looked at it and said, "Well, if you're willing to try that, I guess I don't have much to complain about when it comes to going trash free."

Of all the things I gave up and of all the new products I tried, the menstrual cup is the one that worried me the most. I'm pretty active, and until that point had never used anything but tampons. I was worried it would be gross, messy, and uncomfortable to wear. Luckily my worry was unwarranted, and the menstrual cup became one of my new favorite things. Forgive me for the overshare here, but I get so many questions about menstrual cups that I'm going to describe my experience with them in some detail. Feel free to skip this part if you're of a delicate sensibility.

Your initial investment in a menstrual cup will run you about $40, and manufacturers recommend buying a new cup every year. I've been using mine for nearly three years and only recently felt like I'm going to need a replacement soon. You'll choose one of two cup sizes depending on whether or not you've given birth. The cup comes in an unrecyclable plastic box, which is a bummer, and it also comes with extensive instructions for first-time users.

Basically you squeeze the cup into a U-shape, insert it, and make sure it pops open. The cup can be worn for up to twelve hours, depending on your flow.

It took me some practice to get the thing in and out the first few times. I also felt some discomfort from the short stem attached to the cup that helps you pull it out, but then I read online that some ladies cut the stem shorter. I tried this and it stopped bugging me. I've also learned that I prefer to remove and insert the cup in the shower. When you remove a full menstrual cup, you do need to dump it somewhere—sink, toilet, or shower—and then wash the cup out before reinserting. This can be a slightly messy procedure, so I just take care of the whole chore while bathing.

I've found that I truly can wear a menstrual cup for twelve full hours, even on my heaviest days. I've not yet had the thing overflow, and I do start to feel a difference as it fills up, so I don't worry this will happen. I've worn my cup camping in the woods while backpacking two days away from civilization. I've gone hiking, running, and swimming with it. I wear the thing just like I used to wear tampons (but with far fewer changes), and I will never go back.

Lunapads (www.lunapads.com) and Glad Rags (www.gladrags.com)

Reusable menstrual pads are your other zero-waste option. Unlike disposable menstrual pads, which are made from a composite of plastic and paper, Lunapads and Glad Rags are made from soft cloth. Like disposable pads, they come in a wide variety of shapes, sizes, colors, and thicknesses, including pantyliners. Instead of a peel-off adhesive side that sticks to your panties, reusable pads have wings that wrap around and snap beneath the gusset of your underwear. Most reusable pads that I've seen are designed like an envelope with reusable liners—pull the pad open and you can replace, stack, or add liners inside the pad to adjust for your flow.

In addition to my Diva Cup, I've also purchased a set of Glad Rags and been quite happy with the results. Occasionally I opt to wear the pad at night instead of the Diva Cup, and I've found these to be much more comfy and reliable than disposable pads. Because they use an actual metal snap instead of a sticker, they do not shift. The fleece fabric feels nicer than the material in a disposable pad, too.

Birth Control

Birth control can get tricky because there are hardly any garbage-free options in this area. Family planning is an extremely personal choice that I think pre-empts any need to be zero waste. Most people I interviewed use some form of birth control that creates garbage because, let's face it, the environmental impact of a few condoms or pill compacts is a lot less than the environmental impact caused by having a child. If and when to have children is up to each individual couple, and I can't possibly advocate zero-waste birth control methods that might be less effective than hormonal or barrier methods. If my husband and I ever decide to have children, we'll talk seriously about how to do so in a way that treads lightly on the earth. Until then, I'll be sticking with my birth control pills.

If you do want to lessen your impact in this area, recycle what you can. Condoms come in boxes that are recyclable. The foil condom packet is not recyclable, nor is the condom (though remember that latex condoms are technically compostable, if you're adventurous and not allergic). I recycle the instruction packet from my birth control pills each month. If your pill compact is made from rigid plastic, this may be recyclable in your community. While it is not as popular today as it once was, the diaphragm and cervical cap are effective methods of birth control that can be reused. Planned Parenthood suggests that a diaphragm can be used for up to two years, making it a markedly low-waste birth control option. Products such as the birth control patch and the Nuva Ring create trash on a monthly basis, but it amounts to about the same as a pack of pills. Some hormonal birth control options create trash at the doctor's office—this includes IUDs and Depo Provera shots. If you are considering these options for birth control, you will have to live with the trash they create.

Earlier in the book, I advocated calling companies and expressing your preferences as a consumer. You should also feel free to express your opinion about the excessive packaging that characterizes most birth control products.

Fertility Awareness and the Rhythm Method

A number of my blog readers have commented that they use natural family planning methods with lots of success. Although I don't trust myself or fate enough to employ this method, certainly other women do. When using the rhythm method, women keep track of the days during their cycle when they are fertile, and they don't have sex on those days. This works best for women who have highly regular cycles, and as I don't, this is another reason I won't use this method. Consult with a doctor about the specifics of using this natural method of birth control.

Permanent Sterilization

For men or women who are finished having children, permanent sterilization—a vasectomy or tubal ligation—is certainly a zero-waste option. For me, at this point in my life, the decision to remain fertile trumps the decision to live without waste.

Makeup

With seemingly bajillions of makeup products on the market, how do you sort through the myriad tubs, pots, and potions to find cosmetics that look great and are great for the environment? Luckily we live in a world where the green movement is growing, so there are more eco-friendly makeup options than ever on the shelves. I can't possibly cover them all, but here are a few companies that I'm excited about right now.

Lush.com

Zero-waste contributor April loves her Lush products. "Everything comes unpackaged," she says, noting that you can place products in tins, then bring the tins back for refilling or recycling. "The shampoo is so natural and good for you that I don't always need conditioner." The company has retail stores around the country or a website where you can order their many products. Lush "loves it naked," meaning a number of their products are sold naked, or completely free from packaging. This includes products like shampoo bars, bath bombs, and massage bars. "If you go solid all the time, you can save over thirty plastic bottles a year from entering our landfills!," Lush's website proclaims. The company takes waste seriously, aiming for "the simplest forms of packaging to do the job and use postconsumer or postindustrial recycled materials that are 100 percent recyclable, compostable, and biodegradable whenever possible."

Alimapure.com

Alima Pure is a company with admirable environmental values. The company makes mineral makeup that is cruelty free. They are participants in the Environmental Working Group's Skin Deep Cosmetic Safety Database (www.ewg.org), a database that catalogues and rates the safety of ingredients in cosmetics. I particularly like Alima Pure for the company's jar return program. Collect your empty makeup jars, and once you have five, send them to the company in biodegradable packaging and you'll earn a free eye shadow. The company recycles the empty jars.

Origins.com

A popular department-store makeup brand, Origins also has a strong environmental ethic. Origins is unique due to its Return to Origins Recycling Program, which encourages consumers to drop off empty makeup containers—regardless of brand—at a local Origins store or Origins cosmetics counter. The empty containers are either recycled or used in "energy recovery" (read: incinerated). Since the program's launch, according to the Origins website, the company has recycled more than seventeen thousand pounds of cosmetics packaging.

If you are a huge fan of your current brand of makeup, trying calling the company and asking what plastic the packaging is made from. Most makeup tubes, pots, and containers are made from plastic number 5. If the container isn't labeled, check with the manufacturer first; these can be recycled in a Gimme 5 receptacle at Whole Foods.

Skin Care

Skin care is another huge arm of the cosmetics industry. Americans spent $33.3 billion on cosmetics in 2010, and a good chunk of this was in lotions and potions designed to give us smoother, younger-looking skin. Among the skin care products available to us: antiaging serums, wrinkle removers, UV protection creams, cleansers, moisturizers, scrubs, and toners. Whether these products really work to make our skin appear younger and healthier is debatable, but they sell like wildfire because they make us *feel* younger and healthier. What to do if you want to pamper your skin and the planet, too?

Avoid facial cloths: As much as possible, avoid any single-use cloths designed to scrub your face or remove makeup. They are treated with chemicals, which means that after you use them, they are garbage. Instead, try to find a similar product in a glass jar or a recyclable bottle. Use your own washable cloth to apply the product to your face.

Avoid scrubbing microbeads unless your product specifically says they are derived from natural ingredients: Most exfoliators, which are touted as the perfect way to slough off dead skin cells, are actually made from plastic. That's right, those little microbeads, used to gently scrub your face, are tiny particles of polyethylene that are washed right down the drain and into our waterways. Some companies do use natural exfoliating ingredients such as walnut shells; these are A-OK.

Check the packaging: As with anything else you bring into your zero-waste home, make sure the packaging is recyclable before you buy it. We know that plastic isn't great, but if you have to buy skin care products, buy them in recyclable bottles. Look for number 1 and 2 plastic containers, glass jars, and cardboard boxes. Steer clear of foil-plastic composite pouches (like those that single-use face masks come in) or anything else made from mixed materials.

Use as few products as possible: Ask yourself whether your skin care regimen really needs to involve more than four or five steps. Perhaps there are one or two products you can part with. Remember the principle of reduce—can one product do the job instead of two?

Take it from me, skin care does not have to involve as many steps as today's skin care lines would have us believe. I had notoriously bad skin as a teenager, but today my skin care routine consists of bar soap in the shower, a dab of blemish cream at night as needed, and a moisturizer/sunscreen combo cream each morning.

Deodorant

Deodorant, like toothpaste, lasts for so long that it doesn't create a ton of waste. On the other hand, a bottle of roll-on or stick of solid deodorant every three months, or four a year, adds up over a lifetime. Most plastic deodorant containers are made from several different types of plastic. Because recycling facilities cannot take the time to separate plastic A from plastic B, deodorant containers are not generally recyclable. (Even if the two types of plastic were separated, the type of plastic isn't always identified, so recycling plants couldn't know how to sort the materials anyway.)

The Speed Stick deodorant website addresses the issue of recyclability: "All of our antiperspirants and deodorants are packaged in polypropylene, polystyrene, or PET packaging. Since they are made of mixed materials, they are not recyclable. Currently it is necessary to use these mixed plastics since the container is exposed to extreme temperatures during the manufacturing process." The Tom's of Maine company does manufacture a deodorant with a case made entirely from number 5 plastic, though you need to either live in a community that accepts this plastic for recycling (most don't) or mail the container back to the Tom's company for recycling.

Aerosol containers, if completely empty, are often recyclable wherever you take scrap metal (but call to check, and remove plastic parts first).

As with every other bathroom product, there are a number of alternatives you might try to reduce your deodorant waste. One benefit of trying an alternative method is eliminating your exposure to a number of questionable ingredients contained in conventional deodorants. Many deodorant/antiperspirant sticks contain aluminum-based compounds as their active ingredient. They also contain parabens. Both of these ingredients have been linked to serious diseases such as breast cancer and Alzheimer's disease. Although the National Cancer Institute states that "there is no conclusive research linking the use of underarm antiperspirants or deodorants and the subsequent development of breast cancer," it also notes that "research studies of underarm antiperspirants or deodorants and breast cancer have been completed and provide *conflicting* [emphasis mine] results." If there is any possibility that conventional deodorant contains ingredients that are unhealthy, I'd steer clear.

Crystal Deodorants (www.thecrystal.com)

Salt crystal deodorants are another product I was wary to try. The idea of a naturally occurring mineral being able to control body odor seemed so far-fetched. Well, because the crystal deodorant is touted to last for a year and its case is made from a plastic I can recycle, I decided to give it a test-drive. I was quite pleased with the results. The crystal deodorant, which is made from the mineral alum, is applied like deodorant to the underarms after showering. It is not an antiperspirant, so it won't stop you from sweating, but it will stop you from smelling. April has also used this deodorant. It took some getting used to, she says, describing the resulting smell as not stinky but "earthy."

Baking Soda

Pure baking soda (the kind that comes in a box in the baking aisle, and sometimes unpackaged in the bulk section) is about the most natural deodorant there is. Find an old powder puff or powder shaker, fill with baking soda, and brush on after showering. Like the alum crystal, baking soda is unscented and does not prevent sweating, but it will prevent odor. Some people find that pure baking soda can be harsh on underarm skin; if you find this is the case, you can cut it with cornstarch. I've also tried adding a few drops of essential oil to my baking soda to give it a little scent.

Homemade Deodorant

Making homemade deodorant is simpler than you might think. For the essential oil, I prefer to use lavender or tea tree oil. And you can find coconut oil with other oils in natural foods stores. When you apply this deodorant, I've found you don't need quite as much as you're used to because it rolls on a little thicker. It also crumbles more than store-bought varieties, so put it on in the shower or over the sink. *Yield: Makes 1 (2.5-ounce) roll-on deodorant*

    10 drops essential oil (optional)
    $1/4$ cup cornstarch
    $1/4$ cup baking soda
    2 tablespoons coconut oil
    Empty plastic stick deodorant container

In a small bowl, mix together the essential oil, cornstarch, and baking soda. (If you have particularly sensitive armpit skin, decrease the baking soda by half and increase the cornstarch to $1/2$ cup.) Add the coconut oil and stir until the mixture has the consistency of cream cheese.

Wind back the central stick in the empty deodorant container. Spoon the deodorant into the empty deodorant container. Press the mixture down with the back of your spoon. Let it firm up for a day or so, or, if you're rushed, put it in the fridge for a couple of hours.

Hair Removal

I think most people expected me to stop shaving when we started our garbage-free life. This, however, is something I have no desire to do. I'm much too attached to my smooth legs and armpits to contemplate letting the hair grow. That said, I've spent some time researching various zero-waste hair removal options to find the one that works best for me.

Razors

The EPA estimates that more than two billion disposable razors wind up in landfills each year. Unlike trying a menstrual cup or a crystal deodorant, which might entail some worry and adjustment, giving up disposable razors in favor of more environmentally friendly options is easy. You have several options.

Switch to a reusable handle: If you haven't already switched from disposable razors to a reusable handle with replaceable blades, do it immediately. I have a razor handle I've been using since I was fourteen. To shave with this, all I need to do is buy replacement blades. I can use each blade a number of times before it's too dull. There are many reusable handle options for both men and women.

Hunt down a safety razor at an antique store: I was surprised at how easy these were to find. The first antique store I walked into had a wide selection of metal-handled safety razors. The one I found cost $32. Continuing the theme, I was also surprised at how easy it was to find blades for my new safety razor handle—my local drug store and my local grocery store both carry 10-packs of metal blades packaged in a little cardboard box for about $6. The handle will last me a lifetime, and I can recycle the used blades with my scrap metal.

Try homemade sugar wax with reusable cloth waxing strips: Although I enjoy waxing my legs, I don't use this method too frequently because it's time-consuming and messy. For a special occasion, it is an effective method of hair removal—it even works on the bikini line. For waxing strips, you can use an old sheet or buy some cheap muslin from a fabric store—cut either one into strips.

To make homemade sugar wax (enough to wax both legs), you'll need: 2 cups sugar, $^1/_4$ cup water, and $^1/_4$ cup lemon juice. Combine the sugar, water, and lemon juice in a saucepan over medium-high heat, stirring constantly, until the mixture reaches 260°F on a candy thermometer or the soft ball stage. It will turn brown and look similar to honey. Pour the wax into a clean glass jar and let cool for about 2 hours.

To use, heat the wax in a microwave for about 30 seconds or heat in a saucepan on the stove over medium-low heat for about 5 minutes. Check the temperature before applying to your skin to make sure it's not too hot. I use a popsicle stick to apply the wax because the stick is washable and reusable, and later it's biodegradable.

Apply the wax to your skin in the direction of the hair growth and lay the cloth strip on top. In a smooth but quick motion, pull the cloth strip back and away, going against the hair. You will probably have to wax the same area a couple of times to remove all the hair. I've used this for my legs and bikini line; others use it for their armpits and facial waxing, too.

To clean the strips, rinse them under hot water to remove the wax and hair, then wash in the washing machine with your regular laundry.

Depilatories

Depilatory creams contain the active ingredient calcium thioglycolate, which, according to its Material Safety Data Sheet, "is toxic to the reproductive system, upper respiratory tract, [and] central nervous system. Repeated or prolonged exposure to the substance can produce target organs damage." Since one of the aims of a trash-free life is to eliminate harmful chemicals from our lives, depilatory creams are not the best choice for natural, zero-waste hair removal.

Aftershave

Aftershave is not normally a huge issue, wastewise, unless you are trying hard to avoid plastic (aftershave usually comes in a recyclable plastic bottle). To avoid the plastic altogether, look for aftershave in a glass bottle or try your hand at making your own. Recipes abound online and use simple ingredients such as witch hazel, glycerin, aloe vera gel, rum, and essential oils.

Toilet Paper and Facial Tissue

Although there are some people who advocate using cloth wipes instead of toilet paper, I haven't made it that far yet. Instead, I recommend you buy toilet paper made from recycled paper. I buy Seventh Generation's toilet paper, which is made from 100-percent recycled paper and at least 50-percent post-consumer recycled paper. According to this company, if every household in the country replaced one twelve-pack of toilet paper with recycled TP, we would save 1.9 million trees, 690 million gallons of water, and 4.8 million cubic feet of landfill space.

Did you know that the outer plastic wrapper that surrounds your toilet paper is recyclable? Add it to your plastic bag recycling pile (see page 78), make sure you recycle the cardboard tube in the middle of the roll, and your toilet paper purchase is zero waste.

As for facial tissue, just stop buying it all together. Channel your grandparents and adopt the habit of carrying a handkerchief. These are washable and reusable over and over again. Carry one in your purse or pocket, or keep one in your glove box for when you're on the road. If you must use a throwaway product for blowing your nose, make your recycled toilet paper do double duty. Don't buy two products when one will suffice.

GROW YOUR OWN SPONGES

Did you know you can grow your own sponges at home? Loofah sponges are actually a plant in the gourd family. Once they reach maturity, they can be dried and turned into fully biodegradable sponges. Neat, huh? Here's how to grow your own sponges:

Buy your loofah seeds (check out www.luffa.info to order online) and start them indoors. Loofahs take a long time to grow, so they need a head start.

Transplant the loofah seedlings outside after the danger of frost has passed. Grow in full sunlight and give them a trellis to climb up.

When the loofah fruits mature (see the website for pictures), harvest, peel, and rinse with spray from a hose. Let the loofahs dry in the sun.

When completely dry, cut off sections to use as sponges.

Hair Products

A discussion of bathroom products wouldn't be complete without touching on hair care. Similar to the world of skin care, there's a plethora of hair products—some useful, others frivolous. If you know what to look for, you'll find many that work for a zero-waste lifestyle.

Shampoos and Conditioners

The vast majority of shampoos and conditioners come in plastic bottles that are recyclable—so buying these and recycling them meets that third-tier requirement. To make each bottle last longer, try using a little less shampoo and conditioner each time you wash your hair—I was surprised at how far a little dollop would go when I started using less.

Even better options include making your own shampoo and conditioner or using a shampoo bar. Shampoo bars look just like a bar of soap, but they are designed specifically for washing hair. If you choose to try a shampoo bar, try it for a good couple of weeks. When switching products, your hair needs a little time to adjust to the new ingredient mixture before it looks its best.

Styling Products

Styling products come in one of three types of containers: tubes (such as the kind hair gel comes in), aerosol cans (mousse), or spray bottles (hairspray). The first category, tubes, is generally recyclable curbside. These tubes are usually made from number 2 plastic (you can often find the resin number at the top of the tube where it was crimped shut). The screw-on lid will probably be made from a different type of plastic, so let your recycling center be your guide here—if you usually leave the lids on your bottles, leave the lid on. If not, leave it off.

Aerosol cans are generally recyclable as long as they are completely empty. Their plastic lids need to be handled separately; they are not usually accepted curbside but can be recycled at a facility that processes plastic 1 through 7. Some municipalities will accept these in curbside comingled bins; others require that you hand-carry aerosols to a centralized recycling depot. A quick phone call to your recycling company will answer this question for you.

Spray bottles made from plastic generally come in two parts: the bottle and the screw-on spray top. Once they are empty, spray bottles are perfect for reuse around the house, especially in the cleaning bucket. If you have no use for another spray bottle, recycle the bottom and throw away the spray top.

Brushes, Combs, and Other Styling Tools

Although you can find eco-friendly hairbrushes (made from sustainable wood or postconsumer waste plastic), the hairbrush most of us have lying around the house is made from plastic (both bristles and handle). When your hairbrush gives up, you cannot recycle it. You can, however, find a new use for it, such as using it as a bristle brush to scrap down muddy shoes or tools, or you can donate it to a little girl in your life whose dolls have hair that needs brushing.

As for combs, these are generally made entirely from plastic or entirely from steel. Metal combs can be used indefinitely and then recycled. It will be harder to recycle your plastic combs simply because the plastic type is not identified on the comb. If you live in a place where you can recycle all rigid plastic, throw the comb in the recycling bin. Otherwise, try to reuse it before it becomes garbage.

Hair Dryers, Curling Irons, and Straightening Irons

When these hair accessories break, they are trash. Your best bet here is to buy high-quality versions so they last longer; otherwise, go au naturel to make your hair care garbage free.

Hair Elastics and Other Accessories

Most hair accessories, once broken or worn out, become trash, simply because they are made from several different materials. Elastic hair bands are trash when they break. Do try to separate materials and recycle where possible (metal parts are always recyclable); plastic parts are recyclable depending on your community's guidelines.

Your Own Hair

And finally, we get to human hair. That's right, even your tresses can have a second life rather than being carted to the local landfill. I first became interested in the idea of hair as garbage when a student in one of my classes asked of my year-long trash-free challenge, "What about haircuts? Does your hair count as trash?"

An interesting question, and one that took some research. I have found two viable options for keeping your hair out of the trash.

Locks of Love (www.locksoflove.org): Locks of Love makes human hair into wigs for children struggling with long-term hair loss caused by cancer or another disease. To qualify for a hair donation, you must meet some requirements. The hair to be donated must be at least ten inches long and gathered into a ponytail before cutting. The hair can be dyed or permed but not bleached. Layered hair is accepted as long as the shortest layer is at least ten inches long.

Composting: If you maintain a hot compost pile, you can put your hair right into it with all your fruits and veggies. (Hair should be added to only a hot, active compost pile (see page 94) because it takes a long time to compost; in a hot pile, decomposition begins right away.) Untreated hair contains lots of nitrogen, a main ingredient in plant fertilizer, which means that hair makes a good natural fertilizer. Don't put hair that's been treated with lots of chemicals or bleached into your compost pile, because then you'd be introducing those harsh chemicals into the environment. Cut it into small pieces and sprinkle them throughout the pile.

To sum up, turning the bathroom into a waste-free zone can be a challenge, because there are so many products to sort through. Look at this challenge as an opportunity to simplify your daily bathroom routine. Your pocketbook will be happier if you can make do with fewer products, and you will have shaved time off your morning rush to tend to your hair, skin, and makeup.

Meet Your Goal:
The Zero-Waste Bathroom

Easy

- Buy exfoliating creams made from natural ingredients, not plastic.
- Switch to a razor with a reusable body and disposable blades.
- Switch to a Preserve toothbrush.
- Switch to eco-friendly tampons with cardboard (not plastic) applicators and paper (not plastic) wrappers—or no applicator at all.
- Use an eco-friendly floss.
- Recycle all containers.
- Recycle the inner cardboard core of each toilet paper roll.

Moderate

- Invest in a safety razor.
- Reuse empty prescription bottles for storage.
- Talk to your doctor and dentist about your desire for them to create less trash.
- Use less makeup.
- Streamline the number of products in your skin care routine.

Advanced

- Switch to shampoo bars.
- Make your own sugar wax.
- Compost your own hair.
- Switch to a menstrual cup or cloth pads.
- Make your own deodorant.
- Grow your own loofah sponges.

Chapter 8

The Zero-Waste Bedroom

Although not much trash is created in the bedroom on a daily basis, it does contain a number of items that will eventually become trash. This includes everything in the closet, from clothes to shoes as well as specialized gear like athletic equipment. When they need cleaning, clothes go into a laundry hamper in the bedroom, where they, too, can be dealt with in a trash-free fashion. Each of these bedroom activities can be addressed to create as little waste as possible.

Clothes

Clothes are not what you usually think about when considering trash produced in your household, because clothes are not usually a weekly addition to the garbage can. There will come a time, however, when some article of clothing needs to be demoted from the closet. Before tossing that holey sock or stained sweatshirt, consider reusing the fabric for another household chore—perhaps cutting old clothing into rags for cleaning.

You might be wondering if clothing trash is really an important thing to worry about. The answer depends on the type of fabric the clothing is made from, whether it is synthetic or natural. Natural fabrics like cotton and linen are biodegradable, but lots of today's fabric is made from petroleum-based polymers—this includes fabric like nylon and polyester. These fabrics pose the same problem as plastic, which is that they never truly go away. Luckily, used clothing is much easier to deal with than other plastics, such as an empty water bottle or an old guitar pick. After you are finished wearing an article of clothing, it's not usually trash. Someone else could wear that old sweatshirt, or you can reuse it in any number of ways.

Purchasing Clothes

When you do need to purchase new clothes, purchasing environmentally friendly products is always your first line of defense against future trash. It's best to buy clothes made from organic, not synthetic, fabrics, because after you're done with them, they will biodegrade—unlike their synthetic counterparts. Fabric made from organic materials includes wool, leather, silk, cotton, hemp, and linen. The treatment of animals should also play a part in your decision whether to wear animal products like leather and silk. Most other fabrics on the market today, from fleece to nylon, are made from petroleum-derived materials. If you buy clothing made from natural fabrics, it is compostable at the end of its life.

When shopping for zero-waste clothing, there are a few other considerations to keep in mind. As with any other purchase, you want your clothing to look good and last a long time. The longer life you get out of your clothing, the fewer purchases you need to make, and because less consumption is better for the environment, this is your best bet. Buy high-quality goods that will last a while rather than cheaply constructed clothing that will not. Because you are hoping to wear your clothing until it wears out, look for styles and colors that are timeless, not trendy. Also, pay attention to the price tags that come with your clothing. You are going to be hard-pressed to find tags that aren't attached with that ubiquitous plastic tab. Nevertheless, some companies do attach their tags with string and a mini safety pin. If you can find clothing with this kind of tag attachment, support this company. A phone call to tell the manufacturers that you appreciate their zero-waste packaging approach is always helpful. The plastic stickers that are sometimes attached to clothing to indicate size are always garbage, but don't forget to recycle paper tags—every little bit helps.

You might also consider buying new-to-you clothing from a secondhand store. It's easy to give secondhand clothes a new life by combing through the racks of thrift stores, vintage stores, antique stores, or yard sales. I head to a local thrift store a couple of times a year to hunt down costume accessories for high school dress-up days, and I always come out with more than I'd planned. Secondhand clothing is very inexpensive, which means you can make your dollars stretch further. Especially for children's play clothes, which are made to get dirty, why not buy used?

Once Clothing Wears Out

The question becomes, what to do with clothing that is old, unfashionable, too big or small for changes in your size, stained, or torn? Cloth is a great resource, because it can always be turned into something new. Your goal is to keep it out of the garbage can by reusing it in some way.

There are many options available for reusing old clothes. The simplest option is probably giving used clothes to a thrift store or a friend. Thrift stores will take pretty much any clothing item in reasonable condition off your hands, and this way you have saved the clothes from the trash. A little-known fact is that some Goodwill locations will even accept clothes that are too stained, torn, or otherwise worn to be resold. Donate these items to the Goodwill in a bag marked as rags, where they will be recycled by a rag dealer. You can also save clothes to sell in a yard sale. This works especially well for unusual clothing items like Halloween costumes, prom dresses, or children's clothes.

You can also organize or participate in a clothing exchange with your closest friends. This simply involves rummaging through your closet for gently used clothing you are tired of. Pull out a handful of items and bring them to a get-together with your family and friends who also bring a number of clothing items to share. Trade your articles of clothing for new to you items brought by others. By the end of the exchange, you'll go home with some free new outfits, and you can feel good about giving old clothing a new life.

Old clothes have a number of reuse applications around the house, too. If you have a set of old, stained clothes you're embarrassed even to donate to the Goodwill, you could certainly turn these into cleaning rags. I keep rags such as these all over the house. A bunch reside in my cleaning bucket, and more live in my garage for messy spills. Old T shirts and sweatshirts make especially good cleaning rags because they are soft and absorbent.

If you are handy with a sewing machine or know a friend who is, you can turn old pieces of clothing into new fabric. To a sewing whiz, there's nothing quite like some new fabric to play with. I have used my old clothing for a number of sewing projects. My favorite to date is a T-shirt quilt. All my old souvenir T-shirts—from the one featuring cats as astronauts from a NASA gift shop to a blindingly lime green atrocity I wore when I worked as a lifeguard—are cut into quilt squares with the T-shirt graphic in the center. The blocks are sewn together in rows, then cotton fabric runs around the border. This is a great use for old T-shirts, because if you're anything like me, some of these are hard to part with because of the memories they hold. Old rags can be used as stuffing, too, especially for something utilitarian like a pet bed.

Shoes

Shoes are hard to recycle because—you guessed it—they are made from lots of different materials, including leather, rubber, and fabric. When picking out new shoes, follow the same guidelines you would when selecting new clothes. Buy whatever shoes you believe will last the longest, and wear your shoes until they can't be worn anymore. Really get your money's worth out of every pair.

You might even consider resoling your shoes. Cobblers and shoe repair shops still exist, and often repairing a pair of shoes is cheaper than buying a new pair. I have an old pair of Birkenstocks that I love, for example, but the cork foot bed is worn to practically nothing, A quick search shows me that I can resole my favorite sandals for about $65, which is cheaper than the $100 I'd pay for a new pair of shoes. When your shoes are ready to move on, you have two options: recycle or donate.

Depending on their condition (they must still be wearable), old shoes can be donated to a thrift store. Some nonprofit organizations also take shoe donations, but again, the shoes must be in decent condition. They shouldn't have holes or be trash-worthy. If you're interested in donating shoes to the less fortunate, check out www.donateyouroldshoes.org or www.soles4souls .org. If you have athletic shoes that are too old or worn for donation, check out Nike's Reuse-A-Shoe program, which grinds old athletic shoes into a material called Nike Grind, used for athletic surfaces. Nike will take all athletic shoes, regardless of brand. Check out the website www.nikereuseashoe .com for more information.

Athletic Equipment

Athletic equipment is usually extremely durable—think racquetballs, baseball bats, inline skates, and basketballs. When you buy new equipment for sports or hobbies, take a look at the packaging it comes in and choose the best trash-free option. It is common for the exact same item to come packaged in very different materials. Tennis shoes are a great example. Some shoes come in a cardboard box with tissue paper wrapping, whereas others have a plastic form inserted into the shoe to hold its shape. The better option here is the shoe that comes without plastic. Additionally, always try to recycle as much packaging as possible—that cardboard box can be reused, and the tissue paper composted.

Because athletic equipment is so durable, you can often elect to purchase it secondhand. I find that athletic supplies are extremely common at both thrift stores and garage sales. If you purchase supplies secondhand, you are saving money, applying the "reuse" principle, and making a purchase without packaging. If you do buy brand-new equipment, look for it without packaging. Tennis rackets, for example, can be purchased loose or in packaging; the loose variety is best for the environment and produces no waste.

Once you are finished with your athletic equipment, try to find a new home for it. People rotate in and out of sports all the time. Just as you are ready to give up inline skating, perhaps you have a friend who has been yearning to try it. Reselling or giving away your equipment is a great way to save it from the trash. The same is true if you donate your used equipment to a thrift store or a charitable organization that could make good use of it (such as a school or youth camp). If you have broken athletic equipment on your hands, try an internet search to see if there's anyone who can recycle it (I use "how to recycle broken [insert item here]" as my search term).

Laundry

Laundry tends to pile up in the bedroom. When it's time to do a load, here are a few considerations for creating a zero-waste laundry room.

Laundry detergent comes in two forms: a plastic bottle or a cardboard box. Because plastic is so harmful to the environment, the best choice is the cardboard box. Once it's empty, it's completely recyclable. Sometimes laundry detergent comes inside a plastic bag in the box. Although this plastic bag can be recycled along with plastic grocery bags, it is possible to find laundry detergent that doesn't contain the bag. Fabric softener comes in two forms, too: liquid or dryer sheets. You should always opt for the liquid form. Those dryer sheets, which seem to be made from innocuous cloth or paper, are in fact made from a chemical-soaked polyester material (read: plastic). They are nothing but garbage, whereas the plastic softener bottle can be recycled. Better yet, skip the fabric softener entirely. While fabric softener manufacturers lead us to believe that their product softens our laundry, what it really does is coat our clothes with a layer of chemicals. These chemicals are linked to health problems like allergies and asthma. To get soft, clean-smelling clothes without the chemicals, rely on that old standby—the clothesline. The only other garbage you're likely to make during your regular laundry cycle is dryer lint. As mentioned in the composting chapter, lint is okay to place in the compost pile, especially if most of your clothes are made from organic materials.

As you can see, achieving a zero-waste bedroom is simple. Like many other areas of garbage-free life, these principles will help you lead a simpler life. Shopping at vintage clothing stores or organizing a clothes swap with friends will help you save money. Removing the chemicals from your laundry room will help you lead a healthier, more natural life. This idea is continued in the next chapter, which will help you remove the chemicals from your laundry basket.

REMOVING STAINS WITHOUT GARBAGE OR CHEMICALS

I avoid commercial stain removers not only because they are often packaged in garbage-generating containers, but also because they are filled with harsh chemicals. Luckily a number of alternative stain-removal options exist using ingredients you likely have around the house.

Natural sunlight is a fantastic stain remover. Hang damp, washed clothes on a clothesline in direct sunlight and watch old stains lighten or completely disappear. This works on all white clothes, even cloth diapers. For more stubborn stains, try the following:

Coffee—Mix some water and borax into a paste; scrub the stain with an old toothbrush

Blood—Soak in cold salt water or hydrogen peroxide

Berries—Soak in white vinegar

Chocolate—Soak stain in a mixture of borax and water

Tomatoes—Soak in white vinegar

Fat and oils—Sprinkle with cornstarch; let sit for twenty minutes. Repeat if necessary.

Meet Your Goal:
The Zero-Waste Bedroom

Easy

- Donate used clothes and athletic equipment to a secondhand store.
- Recycle price tags.
- Purchase secondhand athletic equipment.
- Use natural stain removers.
- Ditch dryer sheets.

Moderate

- Dry clothes using a clothesline.
- Donate to Nike's Reuse-A-Shoe program.
- Use old clothing as rags.
- Buy high-quality clothing.
- Buy clothes made from natural, not synthetic, fabrics.

Advanced

- Make a quilt, stuffed animal, or pet bed from old clothing.
- Organize a clothing exchange.
- Resole shoes.

Chapter 9

Zero-Waste Cleaning

Before my zero-waste lifestyle, I bought all sorts of cleaning products and accessories designed to make my house sparkle and my rooms fragrant. Who doesn't want to live in a clean home, after all? For me, clean equals happy and healthy, so I give my whole house a good scrubbing each weekend.

I've never purchased name-brand, conventional cleaners because most of these companies test their products on animals. I stopped buying products tested on animals at age thirteen, about the same time I became a vegetarian. Instead of the name-brand cleaners, I purchased expensive cleaners touted as environmentally friendly and nontoxic.

It wasn't until I adopted zero-waste as my mantra that it occurred to me to make my own cleaning products. Now that I've discovered how easy it is, I'm a little embarrassed that I didn't start much earlier.

Here's a rundown of the products I used to buy (I buy none of these now): glass cleaner, wood polisher, all-purpose cleaner, surface wipes, and countertop disinfecting spray. I also bought plug-in scent diffusers and quite a few candles to make the house smell good after the cleaning was done.

What I realize now is how much "scent overload" my body was going through. To think that I layered the smell of cleaner with a diffuser and candles burning now makes my nostrils twitch.

A huge benefit of switching to homemade cleaning products is that you force your body to go through a natural period of scent and chemical detox. I mean this quite literally. A zero-waste lifestyle asks you to eliminate practically everything you used to buy in the cleaning aisle of the grocery store. No more toilet cleaner, no more air freshener, nothing. If I do buy something like dish soap or toilet paper, I get these from the natural foods aisle (or a natural foods store). Never visiting the cleaning aisle of the grocery store ever again is an important byproduct of garbage-free living. I didn't realize how significant this was until one day, in an unfamiliar grocery store, I wandered down the cleaning aisle looking for something else entirely. All of a sudden, my eyes started stinging and watering, and I started sneezing. I now notice that I have this same reaction anytime I'm around someone who uses a particularly strong commercial laundry soap, hair product, or the like.

I credit this new intolerance to my detox period. More specifically, I'm certain that before I switched to homemade products, I had been oversaturated by the heavy fragrances manufacturers put into their cleaning products. I had developed a tolerance to them, thanks to overexposure. Once I took that overexposure away, I could see it for what it really was—an unholy mess of artificialness I should never have subjected my senses to.

Once you switch from conventional cleaning products to natural ones made from ingredients around the home, you'll go through the same detox as I did. This chapter covers everything you need to put together a green cleaning bucket and surround yourself with safe, naturally derived, zero-waste products.

Some people worry that green cleaning products do not clean as well as conventional chemical-filled ones. And I'll admit, there are some messes that are so gross that green cleaners can't begin to tackle them. However, I've found that my cleaning bucket filled with homemade cleaning products does the job around my house 99 percent of the time. I use the same philosophy for cleaning as I do for my health; that is, I focus on preventive measures as opposed to fixing a problem later on. In other words, if you keep your house clean, giving it a regular scrubdown twice a month or so, you shouldn't have any need for harsher cleaning agents. Once your house is clean, your focus is on keeping it clean with naturally derived ingredients.

Cleaning Supplies

Before making your homemade cleaners, I recommend putting together an arsenal of green cleaning tools. Every good cleaning bucket needs lots of rags for wiping household surfaces. Prior to my zero-waste existence, I used paper towels to wipe down mirrors, and we also purchased three types of throwaway wipes: wood, stainless steel, and all-purpose. Now I don't buy any of those. Instead, I spray my all-purpose cleaner or glass cleaner or whatever on a cloth rag and wipe away. A well-stocked cleaning bucket should have at least a dozen wipes. You can use old, ratty T-shirts, washcloths, or microfiber cloths. If you need to purchase new cleaning rags, try the auto parts section of a store, where rags are sold in cheap bundles.

You'll also need a broom and a mop. We've used the same bristle broom for years, but we did switch mops when we went garbage free. We used to have a mop that used disposable sheets to wipe up the floor. Today we use a mop and a bucket of cleaning solution, and we mop the old-fashioned way, with lots of elbow grease. If you're having a hard time parting with those disposable static-cling cloths that attract hair, dirt, and dust like a magnet, try this trick: cut an old pantyhose at the knee and stretch the foot part over your broom. Sweep as usual, and watch as the hose attracts hair and dust in much the same way as a disposable wipe.

Making Homemade Cleaners

Most homemade cleaners can be made with just a handful of cheap, easy-to-find ingredients. Some you'll likely have on hand already. This chapter includes instructions for a variety of common cleaning products. You'll learn to make carpet cleaner and deodorizer, all-purpose cleaner, furniture polish, linen spray, and glass cleaner.

Carpet Deodorizer

I use this deodorizer every time I vacuum, and I make sure to use it right before company comes over—it leaves the house smelling so fresh and clean. My mom uses balsam fir–scented oil during the holiday season to add a festive scent to the house. This recipe makes enough for several vacuuming sessions, so I store it in an old pint-size canning jar. I've punched holes in the top of the metal jar lid with a nail so I can use the jar as a shaker. *Yield: 1 cup*

> 1 cup baking soda
> 20 drops essential oil of your choice

Place the baking soda in a bowl and sprinkle the essential oil on top. Mix the essential oil into the baking soda. The essential oil tends to clump at first, so you'll have to crush the clumps with the back of the spoon. Transfer the powder to a shaker (or just use the spoon) and sprinkle the mixture over your carpet. Wait about a half hour, then vacuum as usual. The baking soda will help pull out stains and smells, and the essential oil leaves your rooms smelling heavenly.

Carpet Cleaner

I'll let you in on a little secret—you don't have to use a brand-name cleaning solution in a steam cleaner. Those bottles of carpet cleaning solution can easily cost $20 a pop, but this recipe works just as well. You can use it in a steam cleaner, or you can use it to spot-treat stains in your carpet—just dab on, scrub with a brush or rag, and rinse with water until the stain comes out. *Yield: 1 gallon*

- ½ gallon very hot water
- ½ gallon white vinegar
- 1¼ cups borax

Mix all the ingredients together in a cleaning bucket. Pour it into the steam cleaner, or use it to spot-treat carpet as just described.

Multipurpose Cleaner

I love this cleaner, and I use it for everything—sinks, countertops, toilets, showers, and wiping down appliances and walls. I even use it and a little elbow grease to scrub down soap scum and rust buildup in the shower. I especially like this recipe because the essential oil masks the smell of the vinegar—I'd rather not have my house smell like Easter eggs after I clean it. *Yield: 2 cups*

- 1 teaspoon baking soda
- 1 teaspoon borax
- 2 tablespoons white vinegar
- 1 tablespoon liquid castile soap
- 2 cups boiling water
- 20 drops essential oil of your choice

Mix together all of the ingredients except the essential oil. Allow the mixture to cool, add the essential oil, and pour into a spray bottle.

Disinfectant Spray

Use this like Lysol spray or bleach—it's an effective and eco-friendly way to kill germs, especially during the winter months. *Yield: 1¹/₂ cups*

> ¹/₂ cup water
> 1 cup 3-percent hydrogen peroxide solution

Mix water and hydrogen peroxide together and store in an opaque spray bottle. The opaqueness is essential, because hydrogen peroxide is light sensitive.

Oven Cleaner

I swear this is all I use to clean my oven. It takes some extra scrubbing, sure, but it works, and I don't have to deal with an oven cleaner-y aftertaste in my food for weeks. *Yield: 1 cup*

> ¹/₂ cup baking soda
> ¹/₂ cup water

Mix baking soda and water together until they form a paste. Apply a layer of paste to oven stains and caked-on food; let sit for two hours, then scrub off.

Clogged Drains

This method should be used only for drains that are starting to clog, not drains that are entirely backed up. *Yield: 1 cup (enough for one drain)*

> ¹/₂ cup baking soda
> ¹/₂ cup white vinegar
> 2 quarts hot (but not boiling) water

Pour the baking soda down the drain, followed by the vinegar. Let this sit for about 15 minutes, then pour the hot water down the drain.

Furniture Polish

I make this fresh each time I need it because I don't know how long the lemon juice will stay fresh. A little goes a long way, and the lemon juice smells way better than the artificial lemon so many cleaners use. *Yield: Enough polish for three to five large pieces of wood furniture.*

> 1 teaspoon water
> 1 teaspoon olive oil
> ¹/₂ teaspoon lemon juice or 5 drops citrus essential oil

Combine the water, olive oil, and lemon juice and pour into a travel-size shampoo container. To use, shake out a few drops onto a polishing rag.

Linen Spray

I absolutely love slipping in between sheets that smell like lavender. I used to pay $15 a bottle for fancy linen spray until I found out how to easily make my own at home. *Yield: 1/2 cup*

- 2 tablespoons vodka
- 1/4 cup water
- 10 drops essential oil of your choice

Mix the vodka and water together in a small spray bottle. Add the essential oil; tilt back and forth to disperse. Spray on sheets, pillows, and upholstery as desired.

Glass Cleaner

After much experimentation with the many recipes for glass cleaner found online, here is my favorite. *Yield: 2 cups*

- 1/4 cup white vinegar
- 1 teaspoon cornstarch
- 2 cups warm water

Combine the ingredients and pour into a spray bottle. Shake well just before using, or the cornstarch will clog up the spray mechanism. Use with wadded-up black-and-white newspaper to wipe windows and mirrors (and be sure to compost the newspaper when you're done).

Other Old-School Cleaning Techniques

There are some other cleaning jobs that can't be attacked with the preceding recipes. Luckily some standard household ingredients have mighty cleaning powers to help you with the dirtiest of jobs around the house. Look no further than lemon juice, white vinegar, baking soda, vodka, and salt to cover most of the cleaning chores left in your house.

Five Ways to Use Lemon Juice

1. Mix with salt to make a scouring paste perfect for washing china.

2. Brighten whites without bleach by adding a $1/2$ cup of lemon juice to your load.

3. Cut a lemon in half and dip it in baking soda; scrub countertops (except for marble and stainless steel) and cutting boards to clean and disinfect.

4. Add a teaspoon of lemon juice to your dishwater to help cut through grease.

5. Clean grout by combining a teaspoon of lemon juice with a teaspoon of cream of tartar (sold in the spice aisle, this is an acidic salt). Apply the resulting paste to a toothbrush and scrub away.

Five Ways to Use Baking Soda

1. Sprinkle inside shoes to neutralize foot odor.

2. Set an open box of baking soda in the fridge and/or freezer to control odors.

3. Sprinkle on top of kitty litter for a fresher-smelling box.

4. To clean drains, pour down sink with a little lemon juice or vinegar.

5. Sprinkle on top of kitchen compost pail to eliminate any odors.

Five Ways to Use White Vinegar

1. Clean out your iron by filling the water chamber with vinegar. Let this sit for 10 minutes, then pour it out.

2. Add $1/2$ cup of vinegar to your rinse water for sparkling clean glasses.

3. Mix equal parts vinegar and baking soda and dump down drains to clean out and deodorize.

4. Boil a bowl of 1 cup water, $1/2$ cup vinegar, and $1/2$ cup lemon juice in the microwave to clean.

5. Use vinegar to loosen chewing gum stuck to carpet or clothes.

Five Ways to Use Vodka

1. Add several drops of vodka and a teaspoon of sugar to cut flowers to keep fresh.

2. Spray on caulk and scrub to keep mold and mildew at bay.

3. Spray weeds with a mixture of one tablespoon dish soap, three tablespoons vodka, and one cup water.

4. Use in place of fabric softener when ironing. Mix equal parts water and vodka in a spray bottle and add 12 drops of lavender essential oil. Spritz on clothes before ironing.

5. Pour a little vodka onto a scouring pad and use to scrub away stickers or adhesives. Rinse with dish soap and water.

Five Ways to Use Salt

1. To remove smells like onion and garlic from your hands, rub your hands with salt and vinegar.

2. If a dish boils over in the oven, sprinkle the baked-on food with a layer of salt. When the oven is cool, the salt layer makes cleanup easy.

3. To remove grape juice or wine stains, sprinkle a liberal amount of salt onto the stain as soon as the liquid is spilled. As soon as you can, soak in cold water and launder as usual.

4. To brighten brass or copper, mix equal parts salt, flour, and vinegar into a paste. Apply, let sit for an hour, then wipe clean.

5. To clean out buildup in your coffee pot, fill it with ice cubes and stir in a tablespoon of salt. Swirl around the pot, scrub, and rinse clean.

EVERY ZERO-WASTE CLEANING BUCKET NEEDS

- All-purpose spray
- Carpet deodorizer
- Window cleaner
- Wood polish

- An old toothbrush for scrubbing
- A stack of old towels for wiping surfaces

- Newspapers for cleaning glass (compost these when finished)

Be sure to label your containers of cleaners. After awhile, you'll have a number of these crowding your cleaning bucket, and it's easy to forget which is which.

Cleaning your home regularly with eco-friendly, homemade products means you will live in a home that always smells fresh and is free from harsh chemicals that are harmful to you, your children, and your pets. You can rest assured that the cleaning solutions you are washing down the drain are not going to pollute the environment. Plus, you no longer have to buy cleaning supplies, meaning you are saving money, and you are no longer making any trash when you spruce up your home. What could be cleaner than that?

Meet Your Goal: Zero-Waste Cleaning

Easy

- Use newspaper instead of paper towels to clean glass.
- Stretch the foot of a nylon stocking over a broom to collect hair and fur.
- Empty vacuum cleaner and broom dust outdoors or in the compost.

Moderate

- Replace a Swiffer-style mop with the sponge variety.
- Make old clothing into cleaning rags.

Advanced

- Clean the oven with baking soda, water, and elbow grease.
- Clean the house every two weeks to prevent messes requiring harsher chemicals.

Chapter 10

Zero-Waste Kids

Diapers. String cheese. Broken toys. So many adhesive bandages you've lost count. Sure, a zero-waste lifestyle might be easy without children, but it might seem practically impossible when you add kids to the mix.

Although children add another element of difficulty to a trash-free life, they by no means make it impossible. Like any other aspect of life without waste, all you really need is a good system in place. Luckily there are parents among the team of zero-waste contributors, and we're here to share all our tips.

Kid trash comes in a number of different categories, and it starts in infancy with a big bang—diapers. As infants turn into toddlers, they start playing with—and breaking—new toys. They grow out of their clothes faster than you can turn around, unless they've ripped or stained them first. Snack wrappers of the instant, disposable variety litter the house, the car, and the playground, and first-aid supplies for scraped knees and elbows abound.

Living trash free with kids is the biggest concern of many would-be zero-wasters. When you're low on spare time and energy, the perception of adding one more hassle to the daily routine might just be too much for you to contemplate.

I don't have children of my own, though as a high school teacher I'm surrounded by the teenaged variety every day. One of the reasons I teach high school is the same reason I believe many people have children: we want to help kids find their own way in life while still influencing their values and ethics. Because you're reading this book, I know we share a belief that the environment is important. Just as it's worthwhile for me to take extra time to prepare a homemade meal instead of ordering takeout, or to rinse out a shampoo bottle for recycling rather than tossing it in the trash, I think it's worth taking the extra time to instill the value of respect for the planet in our children. After all, we all want the same thing—to watch our children grow up and raise their own families on the earth we so love. Before we get into the nitty-gritty, then, a few thoughts on why you may want to consider bringing your children in on your zero-waste project.

Defining Family Values

It's both awe inspiring and frightening to watch a child or teenager interact with an adult they trust and respect. The ability we have to shape and teach a child is huge, and every moment a child spends with a role model is a teachable moment. This is the biggest reason I can think of to lead a zero-waste life with children. Regardless of your political or religious beliefs, the idea that all of us should respect the planet that gives us life is one that all children should learn.

The question becomes, how do I instill these values in my children? The first step, you've already taken: to make sure your lifestyle reflects your values. Simply through your living a zero-waste lifestyle, your children are already learning what you value—nature, family, health—and what you don't value—convenience, consumption, and keeping up with the Joneses.

No matter where you live, you have a profound chance to teach your children to love the outdoors. Children are naturally curious about plants and animals and how things work, and there's no better classroom than nature. Teaching children to respect the planet can be as simple as planting a tree on Arbor Day or observing insects at the park. Consider making nature time a priority. As Bree, a reader of the Green Garbage Project blog, says, "My son has no idea what video games are. We do a lot of outdoor activities with our dog (we live in Hawaii, how could we not?), and we don't take him to toy stores. He doesn't ask for toys; he asks to go to the park or ocean and play."

Sometimes a zero-waste lifestyle can seem frustrating or like one extra thing you don't have time for. The way I remember its importance is to spend some time outside. Each year Adam and I participate in a beach cleanup along the Oregon Coast. We also routinely pick up trash when we're hiking or backpacking in the mountains. It never fails: when I'm in the great outdoors, I see some vista or scenery that stops my breath just for an instant, and I breathe in the fresh air and feel like I'm part of something greater than myself. This moment of awe-inspired breathlessness is what I want to share with our future generations.

Start Them Young

Although it's certainly possible to get toddlers and preteens on board with a change to a waste-free lifestyle, all of our zero-wasters recommend raising your children in a zero-waste home from birth, if possible. This way, your children don't know any different way of life, and zero waste is just normal. Chris says, "We kind of kid that 'glass,' 'paper,' 'metal,' and 'plastic' were the first words [our children] recognized." Because Chris's children grew up living zero waste, they never knew anything different.

Avoid Exposure to Commercials That
Depict Consumption as Paramount

Bree's son has no idea what video games are. Jessica, another blog reader, points out that children are going to want stuff that creates garbage, "unless we completely isolate them from peers, TV, and the world."

In chapter 3, I talked about how we live in a "stuff"-driven society—a society in which we are encouraged to buy, buy, buy! We are inundated with advertisements that connect our self-worth to how much stuff we buy. Any clothing, perfume, or makeup ad makes this instantly apparent—the woman is more beautiful, vibrant, desirable, and happy as soon as she uses the product she just purchased.

Children are bombarded with advertisements just as adults are—if not more so. Children are a goldmine for advertisers because they are frequently a captive audience and they have several adult caregivers emotionally invested in seeing to their happiness. The volume of advertising that children are exposed to is frankly appalling. TV commercials are especially to blame, though even today's schools are displaying some ads for kids' products.

April strives to break this cycle of consumerism with her kids. "I want them to value not objects, but education and their health," she says.

Although it would be nearly impossible to shield children from all forms of advertising—not to mention it would be naïve to expect to be able to—it is fair to say that the more advertising kids take in, the more they desire to participate in our consumer culture, regardless of family values like thrift, conservation, and contentment with what we already have. Instead, try to limit the amount of advertising children are exposed to. When your kids do see something on TV they "have to have," this becomes a teachable moment. I find that one trait high schoolers totally lack is the ability to delay gratification. Our kids are truly a "gotta have it now" generation. Although there's arguably nothing wrong with getting your children the latest, greatest toy on the market, there's also nothing wrong with talking to them about the environmental impact of the toy they want.

Finally, when acquiring new items, help children anticipate the eventual disposal of that product. Teach them to ask, "How do I responsibly dispose of this toy when it breaks?" By including your kids in making a plan about how to recycle a new toy, you can teach them to think beyond instant gratification and develop a life-cycle awareness.

You Don't Have to Be Perfect All the Time

Whatever zero-waste efforts you are making right now are enough. You can always add in more later, but don't berate yourself for not doing enough today. Life is busy and stressful, especially with kids, and we could all use an extra hour or two a day to do just a little bit more. Give yourself permission to do the best you can, because every effort helps the cause.

It helps me to remember, too, that only a hundred years ago parents didn't have access to disposable diapers, plastic army men, or little plastic packets of apple slices. At one point, zero waste wasn't an extreme lifestyle choice, it was the norm. There is a solution to all our no-garbage dilemmas; sometimes it just takes a little elbow grease and ingenuity to get there.

The process of approaching a zero-waste lifestyle with children depends on the age of your children. Trash generated by babies (diapers, formula canisters) is very different from the trash generated by elementary and middle-school-aged children (art projects, snacks), which differs from trash created by teens (cell phones, homework, food, athletic gear). In order to reduce the garbage generated by your children, it is helpful to take the same "waste audit" approach.

Start by taking stock of the garbage your children produce on a regular basis. Again, this is going to vary by their ages as well as where you live and how active you are. Having a list of trash in front of you will help you see trends and patterns. Is most of the trash coming from fast food, for example, because your family is on the go all the time? Noticing garbage trends can help you set goals for waste reduction based on your family's specific circumstances.

If you have older children (not babies), it is important to talk with them about your new zero-waste goals. Kids love projects and challenges, so if "who can create the least garbage?" can become a competition, your children will feel some ownership of this new lifestyle. Early in our Green Garbage Project, we spent some time with two of our nephews who were eager to help us make no trash.

This chapter is divided into those three age groups mentioned earlier—babies, children, and teenagers. Feel free to turn to the specific age group of your children, or read straight through to see how the tips can apply to your life.

Babies

Babies aren't responsible for as much trash as you might think. Of course, the ubiquitous disposable diapers do take up their share of landfill space, but ultimately baby waste comes only from diapers (and accessories like wet wipes) and baby food. There are ways to eliminate even this waste from your household.

Diapers

The average newborn baby uses eight to ten diapers each day, and most children are still using diapers when they are three years old. There are eighteen billion disposable diapers thrown away each year in the United States—that's a lot of unnecessary trash. If you opt for cloth diapers, you will be helping the planet, saving money, and most importantly, positively impacting your baby's health.

Disposable diapers are a composite product made from both plastic and paper-derived products. After they are used, they are trash, because the two materials cannot be separated from each other. Even if you compost, using disposable diapers would necessitate lining your diaper pail and garbage can with an unnecessary plastic bag. More worrisome, however, are the chemicals used in the manufacturing of most disposable diapers. Dioxin, one of the nastiest chemicals we are ever exposed to, is a byproduct of the bleaching that happens in paper mills. Dioxin is a known carcinogen, and the EPA has determined there is no safe exposure level for this toxic chemical. What we're doing strapping it to newborn babies is beyond me. Most diaper manufacturers also use an absorbent gel called sodium polyacrylate, a poisonous substance that has also been linked to a number of dangerous side effects in animal studies.

If the health benefits of switching from disposable to cloth diapers aren't enough to convince you, consider this: cloth diaper companies estimate you'll save $1,200 over the course of potty-training your child. More conservative estimates still estimate you'll save $500 by choosing cloth over disposable.

When most people think of cloth diapers, I think they picture the diapers I was reared in—flat, shapeless pieces of cloth fastened around the hips with diaper pins. Although these did the job, I understand parents' hesitation to use this model of diaper—they look like they'll leak at any moment. As with most modern baby equipment, this is just not the case anymore. Cloth diapers are "in," meaning you have an array of cloth-diapering systems to choose from.

The top-of-the-line cloth diapers mimic disposables almost identically. They are fitted and fasten around the hips with a Velcro or snap closure, and after they are soiled you rinse them off in the toilet and put them right into the washing machine. Other cloth-diapering systems work similarly to a washable menstrual pad, with diaper absorbency controlled with stackable inserts. Still other designs start with an approximation of the original cloth diaper secured with safety pins. Once secured on your baby, a pull-up style cover keeps the diaper in place.

If washing lots of baby diapers isn't your style, you can always consider a diaper service if one is available in your area. Diaper services provide you with clean cloth diapers on a weekly basis, and they even pick up the soiled diapers. Some services don't require that you rinse the diapers first—they just go into a diaper hamper until the service takes them away for washing. Prices vary, but one such company in the Portland, Oregon, area offers 70 diapers a week for $18.50.

Diapers are one item that zero-waster April has struggled to cut from her family's trash can. Her son is potty training and still wears pull-ups at night. April accepts this garbage as something that needs to be a part of her lifestyle right now, adding "it's not very green to wash sheets every day either." She is working to get her infant daughter used to cloth diapers so she and her husband don't have to go the disposable route a second time.

Baby Food

There are many different types of baby food on the shelves today. Some come in disposable packaging; others are more recyclable and eco-friendly. Your best bets are the glass jars of baby food with metal lids. These jars/lids are easily recyclable, and you can also use them for storing many small items like paper clips, coins, bobby pins, and more.

Baby Toiletries

Baby powder, baby shampoo, baby lotion—all of these come in easily recyclable bottles.

Baby Toys

Toys, which are made from a wide variety of materials, are usually garbage as soon as they get broken. Your best bet is to choose durable toys made entirely from one material. Toys made from wood, which are rarely broken, can be passed down from child to child and family to family. Ultimately they are biodegradable. The same thing goes for stuffed or cloth toys. If you choose soft toys for your child that are made from natural fabrics, they can be composted at the end of their life. This is not the case for soft toys made from synthetic fabrics. We all know how quickly babies and toddlers put toys in their mouths; it is worth considering the kind of materials their toys are made from. Natural materials seem like the safer bet when it comes to what is put in a child's mouth.

HOMEMADE REUSABLE WET WIPES

YIELD: 6 TO 8 WIPES (depending on how wet you want the wipes)

3 cups water
2 tablespoons olive oil
5 drops essential oil
2 tablespoons unscented castile soap
6 to 8 standard-size cotton washcloths

Combine the water, oils, and soap in a blender on medium speed until well mixed. Pour the mixture over the wash cloths and store them for up to a week in a covered plastic container.

Toddlers through Preteens

As soon as children start to walk and talk, their routines change. Suddenly they are involved in playtime, hobbies and activities, and preschool or school. All of these activities come with their own zero-waste challenges. The following guidelines can be customized to your own household's circumstances.

Playtime

No childhood is complete without toys, and parents and grandparents love showering children with playthings. But as much fun as toys are, they are sometimes manufactured with toxic chemicals, they come overpackaged in lots of garbage, and many break all too quickly. It's important to consider both your child's health and the environment when selecting toys.

First, ask yourself what makes up quality play time. The answer is rarely the quantity of toys a child has. Instead, an active imagination and a loved one to play with often leads to the most fun.

Buy good-quality, eco-friendly toys: Just like for babies, the best toys for young children are ones made from biodegradable materials like cloth or wood. Plastic toys come in near the middle of the pack because, although plastic is a bane to the environment (see page 84), these toys are often durable and long-lasting—think LEGO sets or My Little Ponies. The worst toys, environmentally speaking, are made from several materials that, once broken, are impossible to separate from one another—think cheap electronics, like handheld games. Most of these toys are flimsy plastic knickknacks that really should never have been made. Birthday party favors fall into this category, as do fad toys like the once-popular Silly Bandz. Teaching children to distinguish between a well-made product and a cheap one with poor workmanship is a good lesson they can learn at this point.

April's children are young enough that she employs the following system: "My son can have three toys. The rest hide away for a couple of months, and then I roll them out and—tada!—he thinks they are new toys." She recommends toys that are versatile and built to last, like blocks.

April's strategy will not work on older children, of course. Instead, get your children involved in finding zero-waste toys. Make this a game. The next time they get to pick out a new toy, help them select several eco-friendly options and allow them to choose among these. If your children are older, make finding a garbage-free toy a game or a challenge. Let them loose in a toy store and have them find as many zero-waste toys as possible, then assist them in choosing one to bring home.

Buy or donate secondhand: Toys can also be purchased from antique stores, garage sales, or thrift stores, or they can be handed down from one family to the next. Often the toys you find secondhand are of high quality; they have already stood the test of time, so you know they're durable. Children have none of the squeamishness over secondhand items that some of us adults seem to have; a new toy is exciting, wherever the toy comes from. When you no longer have use for a toy in your home, pay it forward and donate your old toys, too, so that they may bring happiness to some other child.

Video games: Most households have either a video game system, computer games, or both. Eventually video games wear out and no longer work properly, they are no longer wanted, or the video game system is replaced by a newer version. In any case, video games need to be disposed of properly.

Many video game stores offer buy-back programs to their customers. Once you are finished with a video game, and as long as it isn't broken, the store will buy back your game for a portion of the original price. Sometimes older video games become "classics" and so will sell for a bit of money; check out eBay to see the going rate. If your video games or consoles no longer work, your best bet is to take them to an electronics recycling drop-off center. From there they will go to a facility (in the United States or overseas) where they will be taken apart; metals and plastics will be recycled, and some materials will be treated as hazardous waste.

PET TOYS

When purchasing and disposing of pet toys, follow the same guidelines established for children's toys. It is very important to ensure that your pet toys are made from safe, nontoxic ingredients, because your pets carry them around in their mouths. Therefore, opt for pet toys made from organic, biodegradable ingredients. These include rope toys made from hemp or organic cotton, toys made from recycled and recyclable materials, and plush toys made from organic cotton and natural dyes.

Hobbies and Activities

As children get older, they get involved in many hobbies and activities, from ballet to Little League to karate and everything in between. Each activity a child is involved in requires its own set of specialized equipment, and it is good to keep waste in mind when purchasing this new gear. Children naturally cycle through many hobbies as they explore the world and find their niche. Many places allow you to rent equipment before you buy it, which is a green and frugal way to go.

Basically the "buy and sell secondhand" principle applies here, too. Finding secondhand gear means you are spending less to invest in the new equipment, and you are doing something for the environment, too. Once it's no longer needed, sport and hobby equipment can be redonated to a thrift store.

School

A child's school life can generate waste, though often this is in the form of recyclable paper projects. But paper cannot be recycled if it is covered in materials like glue, glitter, or pasta. Perhaps these types of projects can go into your child's scrapbook or memory box for enjoyment in the future. These days, at the elementary level in particular, teachers tend to laminate many student projects. Laminating takes something that is recyclable (a paper project) and renders it permanently unrecyclable. It is not unreasonable to speak with your child's teacher and ask him or her to avoid laminating your child's projects for this reason.

Clothes

Children can be hard on their clothes. They commonly wear two or three outfits in a single day, and often these outfits hit the laundry basket worse for wear, ripped or stained. And it's common knowledge that kids outgrow their clothes in the blink of an eye. As soon as the teen years set in, fashion consciousness becomes the highest priority. In sum, children's clothing consumption has the potential to cost their parents an arm and a leg—and to generate a lot of discards to be dealt with. Luckily there are many inexpensive, green, and garbage-free solutions for tackling this aspect of raising children; most issues surrounding clothing were covered in the Zero-Waste Bedroom chapter, and some more specific details follow.

You may be interested in organizing a clothing swap with other parents in your neighborhood. Children frequently outgrow clothes before they are worn out, so many parents have piles of clothing on hand they are more than happy to part with. To organize your clothing swap, send invitations to any parents or guardians in your neighborhood. Invite them for a potluck at your house one evening, and request that everyone bring all the children's clothes they would like to part with. Enjoy drinks and dinner; afterward, have everyone lay out their unwanted clothing. Other parents follow behind and pick up clothing in their children's sizes. Whatever doesn't get picked up can be either taken back by the person who brought it or donated to a thrift store.

Teens

Teenager trash falls into slightly different categories from younger kids': there are fewer toys and more gear from activities, electronics, and schoolwork. Teens also create a lot of food-related trash, especially food eaten on the go.

Today's teens are discarding lots of cell phones and MP3 players as the technology that powers these devices is ever-improving, and everyone wants to have the latest and greatest. Cell phones are easily recyclable through a number of different organizations (see page 248). Apple will also recycle iPods at their stores or any mobile device through a mail-in program.

The best way to handle eating out is covered in the next chapter, Zero-Waste Traveling, which will give your family, including your teens, strategies to use when eating on the run.

❧

Although many people think that a zero-waste life with children is nearly impossible, it clearly isn't. As with any other aspect of this lifestyle, you need to find garbage-free solutions that work for you and make them part of your regular routine. Once they become habit, you no longer need to spend time thinking about them. Children tend to like the challenge of looking at things from different perspectives, so you may be pleasantly surprised with their response when you ask them to try out garbage-free living.

Next up is a look at that traditional American summer activity, the family vacation. With or without kids, vacations present a number of trash-related obstacles, from eating out in restaurants to souvenir shopping to sleeping in a hotel room.

Meet Your Goal: Zero-Waste Kids

Easy

- Buy baby food in glass jars; reuse or recycle.
- Purchase clothes, toys, athletic supplies, and so on from secondhand stores.
- Donate used clothes and toys to secondhand stores.
- Recycle empty bottles of baby powder, lotion, shampoo.

Moderate

- Make your own wet wipes.
- Purchase durable toys made to last.
- Buy soft toys made only from natural fabric.
- Limit exposure to TV commercials and other advertisements.
- Avoid cheap plastic knickknacks at all costs.
- Send video games and consoles to an electronics recycling facility.

Advanced

- Use cloth diapers instead of disposables.
- Request that your child's teacher stop laminating assignments.

Chapter 11

Zero-Waste Travel

The family road trip—or plane trip or boat trip—is a time-honored American tradition. Many of us find ourselves hitting the road at least once a year for a weekend getaway or a longer vacation. And these trips present us with a unique set of zero-waste considerations: traveling to your destination, eating out at restaurants, enjoying the sights and local entertainment, sleeping in hotels or campgrounds, shopping for souvenirs, and packing car snacks.

Our first effort to have a zero-waste vacation came one August, when we visited the Oregon Shakespeare Festival in Ashland, Oregon, and spent a long weekend camping at Crater Lake National Park. This particular vacation, a combo road trip and camping trip, taught us a lot about how to travel without creating waste. Of course, there are many other types of vacations out there, but the lessons we learned on our road trip are applicable to any vacation, whether you are traveling by car or plane, camping or staying in a five-star resort.

Vacations come in many different forms, but no matter where you are traveling, there are some considerations that you must address when vacation planning. You will have to travel to your destination, of course, so the first section of this chapter addresses the different forms of transportation you take while on your vacation. You'll also need accommodations—a place to relax and sleep after a fun-filled day. Your days will include eating out, sightseeing, shopping, and other forms of entertainment, all of which create some trash. From the simple-to-recycle (like paper ticket stubs) to bigger conundrums (supplying yourself with drinking water after passing through airport security), this chapter has you covered.

Vacation Planning

Planning for a vacation can be complicated, with arranging for pet sitting, the mail to be stopped, automatic bill pay, and so on. Planning a zero-waste vacation adds an extra layer of preparations to this already hectic process.

Start planning your zero-waste vacation by thinking about your destination in terms of the waste you are likely to create. Consider where you are headed, how you are getting there, what and where you'll be eating, where you'll be sleeping, what you'll be doing for entertainment, and any obstacles you are likely to encounter. Your destination determines a lot about the garbage you'll be concerned with. A short list by trip type might look like this:

- **Plane travel:** Food waste while eating in the airport, beverage containers, snack wrappers while on the plane, throwaway headsets provided for the in-flight movie.

- **Road trip:** Waste-free car snacks, public restrooms or roadside rest areas.

- **Hotel stay:** Individually wrapped plastic cups, toiletries garbage (like the wrapper on the complimentary soap), the plastic garbage can liner.

- **Amusement park:** Ticket stubs or park entry passes, food wrappers, parade giveaways/freebees, cheap souvenirs.

- **Camping:** Food scraps, food packaging (aluminum cans, wrappers, pop cans, oatmeal paper packets, and so on), paper plates, plastic cutlery.

FINDING A BALANCE

"Travel can be tricky," says Rose Brown, "but so far I have been able to continue with my zero-garbage challenge—although I have had to let it go a few times here and there. One example is when I visited some friends in Tucson. When I started living zero garbage [there], I don't think that they could wrap their minds around it. They are very sweet, and they love providing for their guests, so they stocked up the guest room with packaged items like granola bars, nuts, chocolates, soaps, etc. I gently dropped hints about what choices would have made my zero-garbage choices easier, but I also tried not to be an ungrateful, obnoxious houseguest! I did not want to make them feel guilty for trying to make me feel at home. So I did have some of the treats and threw away the wrappers. It felt strange for sure, but I try to put my relationships ahead of my dogma."

Consider what recycling resources might be available to you on your trip. Luckily the world we live in today is filled with companies wanting to capitalize on the growing green movement. Hotel, amusement park, and restaurant owners are all touting their establishment's green practices, especially if the business in question is involved in eco-tourism. A phone call to your vacation destination before you leave isn't a bad idea. Asking about green amenities will help you plan your trip and express to the business owners that you care about their environmental practices.

Getting There

Traveling to your vacation destination is often filled with much excitement and anticipation—and trash. It is often hard to avoid convenience store food packaged in throwaway wrappers whether you are traveling by car or plane. Luckily, with some forethought, you can easily avoid making trash while getting to your vacation spot.

Traveling by Car

Classic Americana—the much-loved road trip. Setting out on the open highway with or without a destination in mind, stopping at bizarre attractions like the world's biggest ball of string, and sleeping every night in a different campground—although these may pose their own garbage-y challenges, they are certainly surmountable when the call of the road beckons.

Public restrooms are the easiest garbage aspect of the road trip to handle. The only garbage typically created in a public restroom is the paper towel used to dry your hands. It is easy enough to forgo the paper towels and let your hands air-dry. You can also use the hand blow-dryer if one is available.

Gas stations pose a problem that is just as easy to remedy. Simply filling up the fuel tank creates no trash (though it certainly causes another set of environmental problems). It's the ancillary gas station activities that need to be addressed. There can be no bell chiming over the swinging convenience store doors, beckoning you into aisle upon aisle of junk food. Instead, you have to anticipate these needs and plan ahead.

Like my mom says, what's a road trip without good car snacks? When you live garbage free, you give up all your favorite convenience store snacks—barbeque chips, candy bars, bite-sized donuts, Corn Nuts. Plan ahead for this inevitability: pack trail mix, bulk candy, carrot sticks, and metal water bottles in a cooler.

This will probably mean a trip to your local bulk foods source. Stock up on everyone's favorites, from trail mix to chocolate-covered raisins to dried apples.

After packing the suitcases and loading the car, stock up the cooler with ice and other snacks assembled at home. Cut-up veggies from the farmer's market or your own garden make excellent car snacks. I always make a big jar of sun tea, which we pour into a small army of stainless steel water bottles.

If you're traveling with children, getting the kids involved in the snack prep process works wonders to stave away the inevitable "Can you buy me this, pretty please?" conversation. We took our two nephews to a drive-in movie theater recently, and, of course, movies aren't complete without snacks. To avoid paying the exorbitant theater prices, we popped up a batch of air-popped popcorn at home. The boys helped, and we put them to work decorating paper lunch sacks with names and illustrations for each of us. After the popcorn was popped, we drizzled it with some butter, salt, and Parmesan cheese, filled the bags, and headed out the door. The boys were eager to dive into their homemade, garbage-free snacks as soon as we got settled at the drive-in, and we didn't hear a peep about needing to visit the snack stand.

ROAD-TRIP SNACKS

- Rice Krispie treats—recycle the plastic marshmallow bag and cereal box liner with your plastic bags
- Apple slices in a plastic or glass container—no need to buy pre-packaged; cut up an apple ahead of time and sprinkle with a little lemon juice to prevent browning
- Grapes or cherries
- Homemade crackers
- Cherry tomatoes, carrot and celery sticks, and dip—package each in a reusable plastic container

- Trail or snack mix from bulk bins
- Candy from bulk bins
- Granola
- Homemade cookies
- Air-popped popcorn sprinkled with Parmesan cheese
- Beef jerky—many local butchers will wrap this in paper or put it in a container for you
- Sunflower seeds or in-shell peanuts—bring a container for the shells
- Dried fruit

Traveling by Plane

Air travel is getting more and more difficult, what with all the security rules now in place. Air travel does not in and of itself create trash, but many of the activities accompanying flying do generate waste. Like with any other aspect of trash-free living, heading into the situation prepared is the best way to create zero waste.

According to the National Resource Defense Council, "The U.S. airline industry discards enough aluminum cans each year to build 58 Boeing 747 airplanes." And aluminum waste is just the tip of the iceberg: the airline industry discarded nine thousand tons of plastic in 2004 and enough newspapers and magazines to fill a football field to a height of more than 230 feet.

Your first obstacle will be the security checkpoint, where no liquids in an amount over three ounces can be carried onto the plane. This sure seems to put a damper on your use of reusable water bottles or coffee cups. The good news is that you can pass through security with *empty* to-go cups and water bottles. Once you get through security, using those reusable containers is as easy as locating a water fountain or coffee shop.

Airports are filled with restaurants, especially fast-food establishments. Food purchased on the go often creates waste that can easily be avoided with a little preplanning. First, pack snacks to ward off the munchies. When mealtimes roll around, try to pick a sit-down restaurant where food will be served on real plates with silverware. If this is not feasible, you can still make smart choices at a fast-food restaurant. Ultimately purchasing a burger wrapped in paper or a cardboard box is better than buying a sandwich wrapped in cellophane (of course, I'm talking strictly about being better for the planet, not your waistline). When you finish a meal, recycle what you can (see more on eating out later in this chapter). Rose says, "When I travel, I make sure to bring my own water bottle and snacks because when I fly, the airport and plane food and drinks are mostly garbagey—and when I drive, most of the gas station and restaurant options are also garbagey. I try to find local grocery stores so I don't have to eat out so much—but when I do eat out, I make sure that I'm ordering a small enough dish so I can eat the whole thing."

Finally, when you board the plane, you'll be trying to avoid amenity garbage. Bring your own headphones rather than buying the disposable ones provided by the airline. Refuse the little plastic cups that drinks come in;

instead, ask the attendant to let you finish a can of soda. Hang onto little glass liquor bottles to recycle after you get off the plane. If you are served a meal, well, there's no way around the fact that this is basically all garbage. It certainly can't hurt, however, to let the airline know you'd like to see it create less waste.

Other Modes of Travel

Although traveling by air or car are the most common forms of vacation transportation, you might find yourself traveling by train, boat, hot air balloon, or rickshaw. Regardless of the travel situation you find yourself in, follow the same guidelines as above. Trains and boats are likely to have dining cars or snack stands. Most of the food from these types of places creates trash and should be avoided. Instead, plan ahead and bring trash-free treats with you for your travels. Forgo freebees if they create trash. Also, remember that you can stash some small items for recycling later on. Cardboard coasters are recyclable and paper napkins are compostable. Being conscientious of potential trash will help you avoid any pitfalls.

Accommodations

Once you arrive at your destination, your overnight accommodations will also be a source of potential trash. No matter where you stay, whether it is a hotel, a campground, or a condo, you can avoid creating waste by again anticipating possible problem areas. The only potential garbage you are likely to encounter comes in the form of amenities, which you don't have to use.

Hotels and Resorts

Hotel garbage comes mostly from the individually wrapped amenities. You can easily avoid using these, leaving everything in pristine condition for housekeeping when you leave. We bring our own shampoo and don't ever have any need for plastic shower caps or lotions. We use our own water bottles when brushing our teeth, in lieu of the plastic-wrapped plastic cups that hotels always provide. That thin paper wrapper on the toilet paper roll? Just recycle it.

Condos and Cabins

If you are on an extended vacation, it may be beneficial to consider getting a room with a kitchenette unit. It's much easier to control the trash you generate in your own kitchen. This is a cost-effective option, too. If your vacation plans include renting a condo or cabin, living trash free on the road will be just about as easy as it is in your own home. From chapter 6, you already know how to shop for and prepare zero-waste meals. Because rental homes come equipped with a kitchen, it is easy enough to apply the same meal-prep principles to your vacation. You can save money by bringing food from home. If this is impractical, try to locate a nearby natural foods store or a grocery store with a bulk section and stock up on ingredients for your favorite garbage-free meals. If there's room in your suitcase, you can even pack a couple of mesh produce bags or canvas totes specifically for this purpose.

And although it might be tempting to save time by using disposable plates, cutlery, and cups—don't. Make doing the dishes a group task so that you can socialize while cleaning up. You'll save a lot of unnecessary waste this way.

Staying with Friends or Family

Maintaining the zero-waste lifestyle on the road can be tricky, especially if you are staying with family or friends who are a little more reliant on trash than you are. It is a balancing act to stay true to your zero-waste aspirations while at the same time being a good house guest. Here are some tips to help you survive:

- Bring your own toiletries.
- Ask about local recycling, and adhere to your host's system.
- Ask about your host's composting system, if applicable, and adhere to it.
- Look into community composting programs and take your food waste to a nearby location.
- If necessary, save room in your suitcase to tote recyclables home.
- Explain your zero-waste choices and give tips if your hosts seem interested.
- Don't let your zero-waste lifestyle get in the way of having a good time with friends.

Camping

A camping trip in the great outdoors lends itself perfectly to a zero-waste lifestyle. Here are some tips to increase your enjoyment.

Bring a compost bin: I know it sounds crazy, but this makes camp life easier than ever. When we camped in bear country, all our food scraps went into the bin, which was then locked inside the bear locker. We brought it home and emptied it in our backyard pile. Rose, too, finds that dealing with compost can be a difficult part of zero-waste traveling: "The hardest thing about travel is finding compost facilities. Some of the friends that I visit have compost bins, so that's easy. But other times, I have to find alternatives. Sometimes I can find public or neighborhood compost bins. Once I actually kept all of my compost in a bag during the trip and brought it home with me in a container in my suitcase. That was pretty gross, but it was the best solution I could think of. I have done the same with recyclables when I'm not sure about local recycling options. So—I do usually try to leave extra room in my suitcase for the trip home!"

Plan your menus ahead of time: Most car-camping prepared foods come in easy-to-recycle containers, such as canned pastas and soups. Fresh foods like fruits and veggies can be easily packed or cut up ahead of time and brought in reusable containers. Produce may create compost, but it is certainly zero waste. After the produce is eaten, those same reusable containers can be used to hold compost. Cereals and crackers are great, too, as long as you recycle the inner liner with your plastic bags.

Bring snacks: To avoid temptation in a gift shop or gas station, pack healthy, garbage-free snacks in an easily accessible cooler.

Bring items from home for fire starters: In chapter 4, "Recycle," I talked about our small container of burnable trash, which included things like match sticks, dryer lint, and toothpicks. Make sure you're burning clean organic material only.

Dining Out

Dining out is a highlight of many vacations. Sitting in a lovely restaurant surrounded by good company and not having to do dishes? Sounds perfect. Eating out does generate a lot of trash, however, and whether you are on vacation or eating at a restaurant in your home town, most of the same considerations apply. The only difference will be that when you are on vacation, you may not be able to bring home leftovers. All zero-waste tourists need some strategies in place to manage eating out in a trash-free way that doesn't put a damper on their fun.

During our hotel stay in Ashland, we approached our first meal with some trepidation, hoping our vacation wouldn't prove to be the project's undoing only weeks after we had begun. We found a small deli in the basement of a wine shop. The atmosphere was more sit-down than fast-food—it was dark and oaky, with wooden tables set between wine barrels. Adam and I both ordered sandwiches, declined the bag of potato chips that came with the meal, and picked out a can of soda. So far, so good.

The waitress delivered sandwiches to our table in red plastic containers lined with recyclable deli paper. The restaurant would reuse the sandwich boat again and again. This left just the plastic-topped toothpick sticking out of our sandwiches. The toothpicks we would burn in a campfire at Crater Lake, but the plastic decorative tops wound up being our first pieces of vacation trash.

At the end of the meal, we gathered up our disposables—empty soda cans, toothpicks, deli paper—and made a pit stop at the car, where we dropped off our load.

We found it surprisingly easy to eat garbage-free in restaurants, by keeping these simple guidelines in mind:

Think about garbage before ordering: We've all been to restaurants before, and we have a pretty good idea what to expect. Look for items on the menu that don't come with disposables. When you order a sandwich, if you opt for a side of chips, those chips usually come in a bag. Ask whether you can get unbagged chips on your sandwich plate (that used to be the standard form) or whether there's an unpackaged alternative, or just pass on the chips. A glass of water generally comes without a straw.

If you're not sure what garbage to expect, ask! It is important for restaurant owners and staff to understand their customers' preferences. If you prefer no trash, voice your concern. Hospitality industry workers are often quite accommodating of special requests.

Specifically request no disposables: This includes straws, napkins, paper wrappers around sandwiches, and the like. Sometimes the wait staff will forget, but it's a bonus if they remember.

Bring your own silverware and reusable straw: Again, this depends on your comfort zone, but the more vocal you are about your activism, the more resources you save and the more people you educate about alternatives to disposables.

Opt for sit-down restaurants over fast food and local over chain establishments: Sit-down eateries are much more likely to serve with metal cutlery,

COMMON RESTAURANT DISPOSABLES AND THEIR RECYCLABILITY

- Plastic cutlery—Wash and reuse; typically number 6 plastic; recyclable in limited communities
- Plastic cutlery plastic wrapper—Garbage
- Napkins—Compostable
- Plastic straws—Wash; make great cat toys; typically # 5 plastic; recyclable in limited communities
- Paper straw wrappers—Recyclable
- Plastic condiment cups—Recyclable in limited communities (check the number on the bottom)
- Paper condiment cups (often containers for whipped butter)—Compostable
- Condiment packets (ketchup, mayo, honey)—Garbage
- Sugar packets—Recyclable
- Paper tray liners—Recyclable
- Paper cups (for coffee or soda)—Recyclable in limited communities; wax/plastic liner considered a contaminant
- Plastic cup lid—Soda lids are generally # 1 plastic and recyclable; coffee cups lids are generally # 6 plastic and not recyclable
- Paper coffee cup sleeve—Recyclable

real dishes, and cloth napkins. Local business owners are more flexible in serving guests with individual needs.

Tell people you're allergic to plastic: Okay, I'm half-joking, but I've found that people are much more accommodating of health restrictions than they are of ethical preferences. Don't want to deal with "the look" when telling people you want no disposables for the environment's sake? Tell them no plastic for your health (as you saw in chapter 4, you're not stretching the truth all that much).

Bring your own container for a doggie bag: Although clearing your plate at a restaurant means no food waste at all, if you do have leftovers, see if restaurant staff would place your food in your container instead of a Styrofoam one. Some will refuse for vague "health code reasons," but many will be happy to comply. This step is so much easier if you plan ahead and keep an extra container with you.

- Individual coffee creamer—Garbage
- Individual syrups or jams—Garbage
- Paper sandwich wrapping (around sub sandwiches, tacos)—Recyclable
- Disposable plastic meal containers—Recyclable in limited communities (check the number on the bottom)
- Paper silverware wrapper—Recyclable
- Foil-wrapped butter pats—Garbage
- Plastic-topped toothpicks—Plastic is garbage; toothpick can be burned or composted
- Paper umbrella—Paper is recyclable; wood can be burned or composted
- Cardboard drink coaster—Recyclable
- Styrofoam food containers—Always garbage, even if your community can recycle # 6 plastic. Styrofoam can be recycled only if it was never used to carry food.
- Pizza box—Recyclable if no grease is present; compostable if grease is present
- Fortune cookie wrapper—Garbage
- Fortune cookie fortune—Recyclable
- Plastic after-dinner mint wrapper—Garbage

WHOLE FOODS

Some businesses are going out of their way to promote the idea of a zero-waste meal. One such establishment is the chain natural foods store Whole Foods. Eating at a Whole Foods restaurant, which caters to the environmentally conscious and trash-free consumer, is a gratifying experience (and one that's fairly unusual now, but other natural foods outlets are beginning to offer a similar experience). Customers have the choice between using an actual dish, which they can pile with food and have weighed at the register (minus the weight of the dish, of course), or selecting a to-go container made from recycled paper. The bioplastic silverware is all compostable. Even the napkins are made from recycled paper.

After finishing a meal, customers sort their leftovers at the trash station—and here is where Whole Foods gets my unadulterated praise. There is not just one single trash can here, oh no. There is an entire sorting system: recycling bins for aluminum, glass, and paper; a compost container; and a trash receptacle.

What's really neat is the display that goes with the various containers. Three columns of Plexiglas, labeled "trash," "compost," and "recycling," respectively, encase examples of what goes where. The consumer doesn't have to understand recycling—the visual aid explains it for them. A display like this, and the accompanying trash station, should be in every single restaurant in the entire country. The simpler we can make recycling, the more people will participate.

When you're through with a meal, take any recyclables with you: All paper products can be recycled or, if contaminated with food, composted. Plastic cutlery can be washed and reused. Even plastic condiment tubs and trays are often recyclable; check with your local facility to see whether you can recycle them in your area.

As we discussed in chapter 4, a material that is recyclable in one community may not be recyclable in another, which makes deciphering the system while eating out or on vacation a murky prospect indeed. Knowing your home system and being willing to tote your recyclables back to your bin is one surefire way to make sure the materials are sorted properly.

For example, we established the following routine on our Ashland trip. At each restaurant we ordered wisely, refused single-serve items that would create trash (bags of chips, ketchup packets, pats of butter wrapped in foil), and carried out whatever the restaurant would have trashed. Occasionally this was inconvenient, necessitating an extra trip to the car to drop off recyclables, but it never cost us more than five minutes' trouble. By following these guidelines, our recyclables were essentially clean and free of food debris. We kept a cloth bag in the car to hold these.

At night, we emptied our purses, pockets, and the car of all collected recyclables, brought them into our hotel room, and washed them with the little bar of soap provided by housekeeping (the paper surrounding the soap was recycled). I still chuckle to think about the maid's reaction when she came into our room each day to clean and discovered a vanity lined with plastic frozen yogurt spoons, empty soda cans, empty sugar packets, and plastic condiment containers.

By and large, this seems like an easy step anyone can adopt on a road trip. It's one we continued even after the project was completed. It makes perfect sense to carry home paper napkins and toss them into the compost bin where they will go to good use.

In Ashland, we found that some restaurants were better than others when it came to conscientiousness about meal-generated waste. We always made sure to request "no disposables" from our server, but after that, the waste we were left with was out of our hands. Although wait staffs were generally accommodating of this request, thanks to Ashland's tolerant culture, we were still frequently served drinks with straws or given a plastic-wrapped mint with the bill, mostly because this was the *hospitality* industry so actions like providing a mint at the end of the meal are considered good manners. Other times, the servers simply forgot our request, and only upon setting our iced teas on the table would they smack their heads and say, "Oh, I'm sorry! You requested no straws, didn't you?" We tipped higher when servers honored our no-disposables request, and we left remarks, both positive and negative, on comment cards about the restaurant's use or avoidance of disposable items.

Shopping

Shopping, like dining out, is obviously something that you do both at home and on the road. Whether you're buying exotic souvenirs or more mundane household items, there are some strategies you can use to ensure you aren't generating waste with what you buy.

During our camping trip, I thought at first that garbage-free souvenir shopping was great! All the stuff lining the shelves of the touristy shops was unpackaged and ready to take home—all I had to do was bring my own bag and walk out with a cool new memento. I have a specific memory of stumbling across a business called the Northwest Nature Shop. Tucked away from the major shopping strips, it looked like a tree house fallen to the ground. Adam and I left this store and others with our hand-picked treasures—bags of books, Tibetan prayer flags, and solar lanterns for our porch—hoping to take some of the peacefulness that infuses the town's atmosphere with us to our new home. I was feeling pretty good, too, because in addition to my supporting local shops rather than corporations, all these souvenirs came without packaging. I could buy whatever I wanted for a change, a feeling I'd not experienced for two months. Because gift shops display their wares instead of boxing them away, the only garbage we had to contend with was a price tag here and there.

Or at least I *thought* this was the case.

Upon returning home, I received the following email from a blog reader who wrote about the time she spent working in retail: "Every single thing that came from China (our entire inventory) arrived individually wrapped in plastic bags that were grouped in larger plastic bags (for inventory counting purposes), surrounded by Styrofoam peanuts or bubble wrap. ... I don't think that many people realize that every free hanging Chef'N spatula and kitchen gadget, or bamboo dish cloth, or big block of soap comes to the business wrapped in plastic."

I checked with Adam, who did a few stints in retail stores back in high school, and he confirmed this ugly truth—merchandise comes to retailers wrapped individually, sometimes in several layers of plastic or foam. Although it certainly depends on the store owner, a lot of this packaging waste ends up as exactly that—waste. It's an extra step to sort recyclables, and many business owners—especially small business owners—simply don't have the time or interest to make this effort.

In a case like this, the question becomes, do I have to assume responsibility for this trash even though I didn't create it? I think I do, because if the items I bought had been placed on the shelf in their original packaging, I wouldn't have purchased them. The packaging is garbage either way, regardless of who disposes of it. That said, although we can assume the ethical guilt for this trash if not the physical guilt, there's not much we can do about it. We can only control what we buy, not how something is packaged in the factory or unpackaged in a store. This is one case where recycling isn't the solution, because the problem—overpackaging on the part of the manufacturer—needs to be dealt with by that manufacturer. Because we can't recycle packaging we never see, we must continually be what another blog reader called "little green thorns" in the sides of these companies, calling manufacturers and speaking with business owners about our desire to buy only green products packaged in recyclable materials (see chapter 2).

Ordering items online isn't any better than shopping in stores, because mail order shipments frequently come overpackaged. How many times have you ordered something small in the mail only to have it show up at your door in a giant box filled with Styrofoam peanuts and plastic film? The plus side of doing some shopping online is that some businesses, especially those run by a single person or family, are willing to accommodate special packaging requests. When you place an online order, look for the text box during checkout that says "notes" or "special instructions." Request only recyclable packaging and no foam peanuts.

Here are some tips for waste-free shopping:

Buy items that were handmade locally: Seek out items made by local artisans. These unique items make great souvenirs because they are one-of-a-kind and they are made by an individual, not a factory. Handmade souvenirs often come with a neat story you can tell people, too. Look for farmers' markets wherever you're visiting; these are a treasure-trove of locally made goods created by people who also care about the environment.

Look at the item's packaging before buying it: If a store owner isn't comfortable with my opening up a box to see the inner packaging, I don't give him or her my business. Before you buy anything packaged in a (recyclable) box, open it up to make sure the inner contents aren't trash. Don't buy anything containing Styrofoam because, as mentioned previously, it's always garbage. Always check plastic bags to make sure they are recyclable, and avoid buying products with disposable batteries included.

Buy nothing wrapped in "suicide" plastic: You know, that stiff plastic you can hardly open without cutting yourself? It's nasty stuff and is not recyclable. Don't buy it unless you absolutely cannot avoid it.

Buy items made of durable materials, preferably metal or wood, over plastic: Buy products that last a long time and that can be recycled when they wear out.

Repurpose packaging: Occasionally an item we purchase is wrapped in bubble wrap or packing peanuts. If this happens to you, don't throw these materials away; save them until you need them to mail a package or transport something breakable. And when you mail or give these materials away, ask the new recipient to reuse them, too, if possible. See page 250 for ways to recycle Styrofoam peanuts and other packing material; many shipping stores will also accept packing materials for reuse.

Refuse the bag or bring your own: You shouldn't have to take bags from merchants, because you are remembering to bring your own, right? If you forget, just carry the unwrapped item to your car.

Presenting gifts: If you are gifting items, wrap them in recycled or recyclable materials like fabric, newspaper, old brown paper bags, and so on. And of course, encourage the recipient of your gift to reuse the wrapping material, too.

Entertainment

Vacations are usually packed full of entertainment—that's the point! The form of entertainment you enjoy on your vacations can vary widely, however. Contrast the ever-popular "lying on the beach drinking alcohol" variety with the "trek through the wilderness for days without seeing any sign of civilization" variety. Or you could be seeing Broadway shows, cruising the Riviera, on safari in Africa, or smiling with Mickey and Minnie at Disneyland. Whatever you do for fun on your vacation, trash will probably be a consideration at the back of your mind.

If you're anything like me, your vacations will generate a lot of paper: brochures about local attractions, ticket stubs, and show programs. All of these can be recycled or used in a scrapbook. Deal with each piece of vacation trash in the same way you approach the rest of your zero-waste lifestyle—look at packaging before you buy, recycle what you can, and before you take possession, ask yourself whether you really need this thing you want. Try to strike a balance between denying yourself anything enjoyable that generates waste and abandoning your lifestyle choices while on vacation.

Remember, too, to take lots of pictures. These are the best souvenirs, after all—photographs and memories.

Packing

Before you head out the door on your vacation, you'll have to pack. I've found that my zero-waste lifestyle lightens the load I choose to pack in my suitcase. My toiletries kit is much smaller, and I'm getting better at reducing the amount I bring, making wardrobe items work in multiple outfits. I always leave a little extra room in my suitcase in case I need to tote home some recyclables. Depending on where you travel, of course, you may or may not be able to haul around recyclables or a compost container, but it's worth thinking about this possibility before you leave.

Like any other aspect of your new zero-waste lifestyle, vacationing without trash is entirely possible with a little bit of planning. Now I believe we all deserve a break, and it would be rather miserable to spend an entire vacation obsessing about trash. Nevertheless, implementing even a few of these easy tips will help you tread lightly on the earth while you're having the time of your life.

In the next chapter, you are home from vacation and back to the daily grind. I cover ways to help you avoid creating trash in the workplace, no matter what your profession.

Meet Your Goal: Zero-Waste Travel

Easy

- Air-dry hands in public restrooms.
- Frequent sit-down instead of fast-food restaurants.
- Recycle brochures and receipts.
- Request "no disposables" from restaurant servers.
- Pack zero-waste snacks for the trip.
- Refuse single-use amenities in hotels, airports, and the like.

Moderate

- Take an empty water bottle through airport security; fill up before boarding plane.
- Hand-carry recyclable items from a restaurant; recycle when you get home.
- Tip higher when restaurant servers accommodate your "no disposables" request.
- Leave comments on comment cards regarding how much or little trash your visit generated.
- Bring your own canvas bag when souvenir shopping.
- Purchase handcrafted souvenirs from local artisans.

Advanced

- Carry a compost container for leftovers.
- Rent a cabin or condo and eat in, not out.
- For camping, bring items for fire starters (toothpicks, chopsticks, and so on).
- Reuse packaging like foam peanuts and bubble wrap.

Chapter 12

The Zero-Waste Workplace

When Adam and I established the ground rules for our Green Garbage Project, we both acknowledged that our work life had to be different from our home life—we knew that a total zero-waste lifestyle wasn't necessarily possible while we were at work. We would limit our garbage as much as possible, but we decided we would use the office and occupational supplies we needed to effectively do our jobs, and if that meant creating garbage, we would live with it.

There are millions of different jobs in our country, which means that targeting this chapter to the specific kinds of trash you generate in your workplace would be nearly impossible. That said, you can use many of the techniques discussed in earlier chapters to customize your approach to workplace trash reduction. Specifically you will start with another waste audit, but this time you'll be looking in your workplace trash can.

Doing a Workplace Waste Audit

I find that work-related trash comes in two categories—general office supply trash (paper, paper clips, used-up pens, and so on) and occupational supplies (items specific to the job at hand). To start your workplace waste audit, sort your results into those two categories. Go through your items systematically and see what you can reduce, reuse, recycle, or compost. Start by replacing garbage-generating items with the solutions you have already instituted at home. Chances are, you'll be left with a small list of workplace garbage conundrums, and that's where this chapter comes in.

Office Supplies

Offices are loaded with the essential tools of the trade: ream upon ream of paper, pens and pencils, highlighters, staplers, paper clips, and many more. Copy machines run through toner cartridges almost as fast as they spit out paper. Just the day-to-day operations of a business or office creates a respectable amount of trash that can be easily reduced.

Paper

The amount of paper we use each year in the United States is astronomical—seventy-one million tons, according to the EPA. Of this, about forty-five million tons was recycled in 2010, meaning that we recycle just over 60 percent of the paper we use. Obviously American workplaces are responsible for a large amount of the paper used. Paper is a valuable resource, and it will save money and the environment if you're able to cut down your consumption. Luckily there are lots of easy ways to reduce your paper consumption at work.

My first suggestion is probably the easiest—use both sides of a piece of paper. I keep a tray by my desk for paper used on one side—paper goes in the tray face-down, and I pull out a piece whenever I need scratch paper. I also cut this paper into quarters and keep a stack by my phone for jotting down phone messages. Single-sided papers can be used to print and send faxes, because no one ever sees the previously used side. We also regularly load our copy machines with paper used on only one side to maximize this resource. Only after you've used both sides should you recycle it.

Next, stop printing emails and other digital files. If at all possible, keep electronic copies of everything you can. Encourage others to do the same by saving a message under your email signature that reads, "Please think about the environment before printing this email." If you must print emails, make sure you do so on paper that's already been used on one side.

Pens, Pencils, and Highlighters

An estimated 1.5 billion ballpoint pens wind up in landfills each year—that's a lot of waste. Ballpoint pens fall into the nonrefillable disposable category we should try so hard to avoid. Yet pens are a necessary tool. What to do?

Your best bet is to invest in a nice pen or two with refillable ink cartridges. I have a fountain pen I use to grade papers. Every so often I have to change a little plastic well inside the pen, but this is a lot less plastic than what a whole pen is made from. Fountain pens can be messy and stain your fingers, but they're fun to use. If you're looking for something a little cleaner, try a regular refillable ink pen. If you must buy nonrefillable ballpoint pens, invest in the ones now being made from recycled plastic.

Many office tasks don't actually require that you use a pen—in fact, the only time a pen is really necessary is when you're signing a document. Other times, consider using a refillable mechanical pencil, an old-fashioned wooden pencil, or colored pencils. I also often use colored pencils to grade papers and write notes—and office supply stores now make mechanical pencils with colored lead. Shavings from sharpened pencils can be composted in your yard.

Staples and Paper Clips

Paper clips and staples are, of course, both made from metal, which is a valuable and recyclable resource. The problem is, both of these items are too small to put into a regular recycling bin. In large quantities, however, they can be recycled at a scrap metal facility. Zero-waster Robert Haley keeps a ball of staples at his desk that he continuously adds to after removing staples from paper destined for the recycling bin. Right now it weighs about ten pounds and is the approximate size of a cantaloupe. Eventually he'll take this to a scrap metal recycling facility. (Note, however, that removing staples and paper clips from paper before recycling is not necessary, because recycling plants are equipped to filter out these items.)

Toner and Ink Cartridges

Toner cartridges from copy machines and ink cartridges from printers are always recyclable. Manufacturers usually make this easy: all you have to do is package the cartridge back up in its original packaging, attach the supplied return label, and plunk it in the mail. Shipping is usually covered, too. Cartridges are returned to the manufacturer, where they are inspected for errors or flaws, then refilled with ink, resealed, and reused.

I will never forget the time I went into my school office to request a new toner cartridge from our secretary. After I replaced the old cartridge with the new, I returned the used one to her. I asked her what the school did with empties. She said she recycles them when she has the time, but usually she just throws them away. I offered to take the old one off her hands and recycle it myself to ensure it wound up in the right place, but that's not the point. The point is that recycling is always worth the small amount of extra effort it takes. If someone else isn't going to do it, step up, or at least work to appoint someone to be in charge of your workplace's green efforts.

Occupational Supplies

Here's where workplace garbage gets tricky. Each occupation comes with its own set of specific disposable supplies that are needed for daily tasks. As a teacher, for example, I routinely use dry erase markers, crayons, glue sticks, glitter, paint, and other art supplies (yes, even in a high school). Doctors' offices fly through supplies like paper sheets, paper bibs, gloves, masks, and paper cups. These items are usually the hardest to eliminate from your workplace or figure out how to recycle. Whatever your particular occupational supplies are, though, there are some principles you can keep in mind that can help you reduce, reuse, and recycle.

Look for Alternatives

You'll do this item by item, and it's a slow process. Identify an item in your work trash that is constantly filling up the bin. For a plumber, this might be spare sections of PVC pipe, or for a restaurateur, broken water glasses. For

---

SOCIAL HOUR

If your workplace is anything like mine, any excuse will do to host a party, potluck, or water-cooler chatting session—in other words, anything to get you out of doing work for a few minutes. All these events, from donuts in the staff room to working lunches to afternoon meetings with to-go coffee carafes, come with plenty of food and disposable paraphernalia. Here are some ways to avoid social hour trash:

- Use your to-go kit: a reusable plate, reusable silverware, a mug, and a cloth napkin.
- Bring your own water bottle to avoid the paper cups at the water cooler.
- Stop buying from vending machines—pure trash and junk food.
- Buy beverages in recyclable containers.
- Stop raiding the candy dish—wrappers are usually garbage.
- Stock your own candy dish with loose bulk candy.

---

me, this was dry erase markers. I use these every day, and they really are necessary to my daily routine. The thing about dry erase markers is that, like pens, once they're dry, they're garbage. Could I find an alternative? A shopping trip to an office supply store led me to a new product—dry erase crayons! I bought a pack to try out.

Sometimes you can find an effective new product on the market to replace your usual disposables; other times you'll find that your replacement doesn't work so well. Unfortunately that was the case with the dry erase crayons. These were not a good replacement for my regular dry erase markers because they wrote in too fine a line, so my writing couldn't be seen across my classroom. This just means I have to keep searching for a new option, using the throwaway one in the interim.

Be Old-Fashioned

Asking myself "What did the pioneers do?" has helped me solve many a garbage dilemma. Good ol' chalkboards would have been used in lieu of dry erase markers, which hadn't been invented yet. I do have a chalkboard in my classroom, albeit one that isn't well-situated. Nevertheless, knowing that chalk is a garbage-free way to avoid the dry erase markers is an incentive for me to use the chalkboard as often as possible. All fields have their specialized equipment, and all used to be handled in a largely zero-waste fashion. Florists used to wrap flowers in paper rather than plastic, as did butchers with meat and bakers with bread. Packages used to be shipped in brown paper and string instead of so much packing tape.

Replace Disposables with Reusables

There's no denying the fact that disposables are convenient, but if you look hard enough, you'll often find there's a reusable product that can take its place. Fountain pens are a great example from my profession. Using the doctor's office example, paper products like bibs and sheets can be replaced with real, washable cloth versions. Dentists could allow patients to drink from real glasses rather than plastic ones. Factory workers can invest in reusable ear plugs and ventilation masks rather than using disposables daily.

If you've been putting all these suggestions into practice, by now you are almost there! Your day-to-day life is largely garbage-free, and you are probably no longer amazed at how slowly the garbage is piling up. Especially once you tackle all your lifestyle-specific challenges—things like leading a busy life filled with children or putting on makeup without trashing the planet—this zero-waste lifestyle becomes a habit. There's only one area left to tackle, and in our consumer-driven American culture, it's a behemoth: the holidays. The next chapter shows you how to handle wrapping paper, fireworks, Halloween candy, and more.

Meet Your Goal:
The Zero-Waste Workplace

Easy

- Use both sides of a piece of paper before recycling.
- Reuse paper clips, binder clips, file folders and more.
- Avoid printing emails.
- Bring your own refillable water bottle.
- Buy loose candy in bulk to stock your candy dish.

Moderate

- Use a colored pencil instead of a pen whenever possible.
- Recycle toner and ink cartridges.
- Add a "please don't print" message to the bottom of your email signature.
- Keep a to-go kit in your desk with a plate and utensils.
- Stop buying snacks from the vending machine.

Advanced

- Use a fountain pen.
- Compost pencil shavings.

Chapter 13

Zero-Waste Holidays and Special Occasions

About three months into our first trash-free year, I discovered that the traditional American holiday experience is synonymous with trash. All through the year, with each holiday I spent time coming to terms with the fact that if I wanted to live without waste, my traditions had to change.

I almost never feel deprived by living trash free. As I've said throughout the book, the benefits of a zero-waste lifestyle far outstrip any drawbacks. Sure, I've given up convenience food, but locally grown, homemade meals taste better and are healthier to boot. But during the holidays, suddenly I felt deprived—of Girl Scout cookies, backyard fireworks, candy canes, Halloween candy, shiny Christmas wrapping paper—the list goes on.

Since that first garbage-free holiday season, I've learned to shift my perspective about what celebrations are really all about. Do I need the plastic grass to celebrate Easter? No. I've also found many alternatives to those trashy celebration centerpieces, including a number of ways to make the things I couldn't buy.

Don't be like me, spending your first zero-waste holiday season feeling sorry for yourself. Use these tips from the trash-free squad to make your family celebrations better than ever.

Planning for a Celebration

With each passing holiday comes a new opportunity to plan a celebration. And although celebrations often create a lot of trash, they certainly don't have to. Celebrations are about gathering with family and friends in a house decorated for the occasion, perhaps for a good meal or to exchange gifts. Party planning is your first line of defense when it comes to throwing a memorable bash without creating much waste. No matter what holiday you are planning for, chances are you'll want to have friends or family visit, and you'll want both good food and good entertainment. Your first step is to send out zero-waste invitations, and then the real planning begins. As with any other aspect of waste-free living, planning a holiday celebration just takes a little creativity. Largely the trash you create at a holiday celebration comes under only a few headings: gifts, food, traditions, and disposable serving ware. It is easy to update your holiday celebrations to avoid trash while still preserving cherished family traditions.

Decorating

Zero-waste decorating during the holidays is quite easy if you let your décor be inspired by nature. Many of our traditional holidays have their origins rooted in nature. We decorate for the winter holidays with evergreen boughs, cranberries, and oranges. Easter is all about tulips, daffodils, and the blossoming spring. Holidays in the summer heat, like the Fourth of July, usually involve outdoorsy traditions like making homemade lemonade, eating watermelon, and gathering around crackling campfires. The fall is filled with

INVITATIONS

Zero-waste invitations are one of the easiest parts of celebrating a waste-free holiday. To get your celebration started off right, you have a couple of options:

- **Send an e-card:** To create absolutely no waste, send an electronic invite to family and friends. I frequently use www.evite.com; there are many other useful—and free—electronic invitation websites online. Invitations are sent instantly, and guests RSVP online. There is no waiting in line at the post office, no money spent on stamps, and nothing left over when the party is done.

- **Send recyclable invitations:** When purchasing or making your invitations, make them from recyclable materials. Include a sticker or a note requesting that your guests recycle the invitation when it's no longer needed.

- **Pick up the phone:** An old-fashioned phone call is a great way to invite guests to a party. It saves time and money and allows you to make a connection with another person, something we all too often forget to do these days.

nature's bounty—orange pumpkins for Halloween and a plethora of local food for Thanksgiving. In many ways, the work is done for you—our holidays are already filled with evergreens and pinecones, crisp fall leaves, beautiful flowers, and delicious summer fruits.

Use What You Have

Most of us have a collection of well-loved and well-used holiday decorations we pull out year after year. If you're tempted to buy new decorations to put up something different for a change, there are other good options. Each year I go to the public library and check out all the newest books on decorating for the holidays to flip through for new ideas. Often all I need is new inspiration, not new stuff. These books have taught me to repurpose what I already have in my home to suit my holiday decorating.

Look through Thrift or Antique Stores

For new-to-you decorations, don't discount the possibilities awaiting you in thrift stores or antique malls. My mom, for example, has several pieces of ruby red Depression glass—candlesticks, vases, bowls—that she's found at antique stores. Not only have these pieces been fairly inexpensive, but she can use them to decorate for Christmas, Valentine's Day, the Fourth of July, and even in a blood-red Halloween display.

Organize a Decoration Swap

If you need new decorations for your holiday celebration but don't want to run out and buy expensive new ones, try organizing a swap with friends or family members. Most of us have holiday decorations lying around our houses that we've grown tired of. Rather than let these decorations go to waste in an attic or garage, why not pull them out and see whether someone you know has a use for them. And who knows? Maybe you'll find something new-to-you from an old friend.

Use Live Plants

No holiday is complete without flowers, fruit, trees, wreaths, or festive garlands. Live plants, not the fake plastic ones, make great holiday decorations. Each passing season brings with it a new abundance of flowers and greenery that could be used to decorate inside and out. For spring celebrations, consider using spring flowers like daffodils, tulips, lilacs, or hyacinths. Often you can purchase these flowers in pots from local nurseries, so after you are done using them for your celebration, you can plant them outside. For the summer months, wildflowers and hanging baskets overflowing with flowers can add fragrance and color to your party decorations. Fall leaves are beautiful on any table, and bundles of dried cornstalks help set the mood for a harvest-themed party. Winter greenery lends itself perfectly to Christmas, Hanukkah, solstice, or Kwanzaa celebrations—consider evergreen boughs, wreaths, and garlands. A few years back I made Christmas candleholders from ice, holly, cranberries, and evergreens. At the end of the night, all I had left was water and some miscellaneous greenery I tossed out into the garden. Real, not artificial, is always your best bet, because after the holiday festivities are over, garlands and greenery can be useful in another capacity, but artificial cannot.

Try Edible Displays

Consider using food to deck out your house for your upcoming celebration. Once you are finished with your edible displays, they can be either eaten or composted, creating absolutely zero waste. The winter holidays already have a number of edible decorations associated with them, such as gingerbread houses or strings of popcorn or cranberries as garlands. In my family, we frequently dust pieces of fruit with a mixture of sugar and meringue powder, which gives the fruit a sparkling sheen that looks beautiful when the fruit is bunched together for a table centerpiece. A fall cornucopia of Indian corn, pumpkins, and gourds looks lovely and will last a long time. In the summertime, fresh fruit is mouthwateringly appetizing as a centerpiece.

Food

There's no doubt about it, holiday food can cause waistlines—and garbage cans—to expand. Many holiday favorites, like candy canes, popsicles, and Peeps, come wrapped in packaging that creates garbage. The good news is that by following the principles outlined in chapter 6, you can have a fun, festive, and zero-waste feast at your celebration. Try your hand at making your own holiday goodies, and consider switching to sustainable, locally grown crops for the food that graces your table.

Stick with Homemade Treats

A lot of holiday cooking centers around old family recipes for tried-and-true baked goods. Nearly all baking ingredients come wrapped in recyclable packaging or are available in the bulk aisle of the grocery store. See the sidebar below to review which holiday baking ingredients are sold in recyclable packaging, the bulk section, or must be homemade.

HOLIDAY STAPLES: HOW TO AVOID GARBAGE

STAPLES	RECYCLABLE PACKAGING	MAKE YOURSELF	BUY IN BULK
Baking chocolate squares	X		
Baking powder			X
Baking soda	X		X
Brown sugar			X
Butter		X	
Confectioners' sugar			X
Cornstarch	X		X
Eggs	X		
Flour	X		X
Milk, evaporated	X		
Milk, sweetened condensed	X		
Pie filling		X	
Spices			X
Sugar	X		X
Whipping cream	X		

I'm constantly surprised to discover that I can make nearly anything from scratch. Last Christmas when I was craving candy canes, I searched online for a recipe and gave it a try. Making candy canes took some specialized equipment, but they turned out wonderfully. My zero-waste lifestyle does not stop me from filling my home with delicious holiday goodies for every holiday, including fudge, way too many cookies, peanut brittle, candy canes, candy corn, marzipan (an Italian candy we always make for Easter), biscotti, and pies of every variety.

Use Humanely Raised Meat

Many holiday tables wouldn't be complete without the crowning glory of a baked turkey or ham. Yet the traditional turkey or ham comes wrapped in layers of trash. Is there a zero-waste way to purchase holiday meat?

The short answer is yes, if you're willing to work for it. Our panel of zero-wasters is concerned with the trash generated by meat consumption but more concerned with the treatment of the farm animals before slaughter. The least-green thing you can do during the holiday season is to buy a commercially prepared turkey or ham from your grocery's freezer case.

HOMEMADE CANDY CANES

This is probably the most difficult recipe you'll find in this book. It's time consuming and requires some special equipment. That said, if you want a rewarding challenge, these candy canes taste just like their store-bought counterparts—and you're guaranteed to impress your holiday guests. YIELD: 1 DOZEN

SPECIAL EQUIPMENT NEEDED:

Metal baking sheet (that you're not afraid to scratch) or a marble slab

Glass baking dish

Rubber gloves

Heavy-duty metal spatula or bench scraper

INGREDIENTS:

3 cups sugar

$1/2$ cup water

$3/4$ cup corn syrup

$1/4$ teaspoon cream of tartar

1 teaspoon peppermint extract

1 teaspoon red or green food coloring

Coat the baking sheet and glass baking dish with cooking oil; set aside. Preheat the oven to 200°F or your stove's warming setting.

In a saucepan over medium-high heat, combine the sugar, water, corn syrup, and cream of tartar. Stir until the sugar is dissolved and the mixture reaches the hard ball stage (269°F on a candy thermometer). Remove from the heat and stir in the peppermint extract.

Divide the mixture evenly between the baking sheet and the glass baking dish. Place the baking sheet in the oven to keep the mixture warm. Add the food coloring to the mixture in the baking dish and stir well until the color is even.

To pursue a zero-waste, environmentally friendly turkey or ham, you'll need to spend some time talking with local meat farmers or butchers before the holiday season starts in earnest. Call up your local butcher or farmer and ask whether they sell farm-raised turkeys or pigs and if they would be willing to wrap their products in paper instead of plastic. I've talked with a few people who think this is an odd request, but rarely do they actually say no. Tell people you're allergic to plastic if you have to. You can also get in touch with your local co-op, which is a good source for sustainable meat.

Know that there are limited numbers of farm-raised and heritage animals available at Thanksgiving and Christmastime. This is because pasture-grown animals are given much more space compared with animals raised in CAFOs, so each farm can raise only a limited number. Plan to speak with your local farmers or butchers several months before the holiday rolls around.

Using the metal spatula, begin swirling the hot candy around and around. Move the hot candy around the tray like you are swirling a wooden spoon through cake batter. You are keeping the candy in a semiliquid state until it cools enough to pick up while wearing rubber gloves. This should take just one to two minutes. Put on the rubber gloves and rub them with cooking oil. As soon as the candy is just cool enough to handle, pick up the whole amount of candy and pull and stretch it until it loses its gloss. This is very similar to kneading bread in the air. You'll see the candy begin to turn opaque pretty quickly, and the whole process will take less than 5 minutes. Form the candy into one long rope, approximately 1 inch in diameter, and then cut into 1-inch chunks and put the pieces back in the baking dish.

Switch the pans—the candy you just worked goes into the oven, and the other mixture comes out. Repeat the above steps with the second mixture, omitting the food coloring. Once you've cut the second batch into pieces, return the baking sheet to the oven.

Remove one piece of each color from the oven to shape each candy cane; leave the remaining pieces in the oven to stay warm as the candy will cool quickly once it's out of the oven. Working quickly, roll out a white chunk of candy and a colored chunk of candy into 4-inch-long ropes (about the thickness of a store-bought candy cane). Twist the ropes together and curve into a cane shape. These cool down almost instantly and can be placed on a plate while you finish working with the other pieces.

Store at room temperature in a covered container (or wrap in parchment paper).

Gifts

Forget about the wrapping paper, ribbons, and gift tags for a moment. Think instead about the things inside the pretty paper. These things come wrapped in their own packaging, and this is a huge contributor to the excess waste of the holiday season. Take a desk fountain that Adam received for Christmas as an example. This fountain came packaged inside a cardboard box, which wasn't so bad because it was recyclable. Inside the box, however, we found a Styrofoam frame wrapped around the fountain's plastic parts, presumably to protect it from breaking. Inside the Styrofoam, the fountain was wrapped in a clear plastic bag that was secured with tape and several twist-ties. That's a lot of garbage!

Most store-bought items are the same way. DVDs and CDs are wrapped in unrecyclable plastic. Computers and other electronics come wrapped in their own nesting-doll-style packaging. Children's toys are often the worst, as many toys are packaged in see-through plastic to be visible in the store. This plastic, affectionately known as "suicide plastic" in the recycling world, is nasty stuff. Made from PVC, it's actually harmful to the environment to recycle it (see chapter 4 for more about the dangers of PVC), and it's nearly impossible to cut through it without cutting yourself on the resulting sharp edges. It should be avoided at all costs.

HOW TO FIND LOCALLY RAISED MEAT

- Local Harvest (www.localharvest.org): This website is the mother lode if you're looking for local farms, farmers' markets, or other sources of sustainably grown food near you. A map pinpoints each location in your state, and every continental state has dozens, if not hundreds, of listings. You can also do a product search to look for local pig or turkey farmers, for example, and the site will turn up anything close to you and provide you with contact information and a website, if applicable.

- Heritage Turkey Foundation (www.heritageturkeyfoundation.org): The organization is dedicated to bringing about a revival of heritage breeds in the holiday turkey market. The vast majority of turkeys sold in supermarkets today are a single breed—the Broad-breasted White. This organization is working to reintroduce other breeds into the American marketplace to support greater biological diversity. Listed on the site are a number of places you can go to purchase your own heritage bird.

Clearly giving new things isn't the best way to help the environment. In addition to all the packaging, buying anything new has its own impact on the planet (see chapter 3, "Reduce and Reuse"). Staying true to the waste hierarchy, it's important to buy new things only when you can't find a used version or you can't repurpose something you already have. When giving gifts, it's rarely necessary to buy a new item—there are so many other options.

Give an Experience

An "experience" gift can come in many styles, can fit into any budget, and works for singles, couples, and families. These are lovely to receive for any occasion, whether it is a bridal shower, a Valentine's Day gift for your sweetie, or a Christmas gift for a coworker you hardly know. To gift an experience, think about what your recipient's hobbies are, then start looking around their city or town to see what unique excursions you can find. For instance, I have an aunt and uncle who are wine lovers. Because they live in Oregon, which has many outstanding wineries, I started looking on various Oregon winery websites to see what sorts of events each locale hosted. I found the perfect event—an evening of wine tasting, salsa dancing lessons, and a bottle of wine—for $50. Not only did this gift suit the recipient to a tee, but it also supported a local business and produced no more packaging than an envelope to enclose the gift certificate.

GIFT EXPERIENCES

Consider giving these sorts of gifts in lieu of gifts wrapped in layers of packaging:

- Movie tickets
- Family fun center tickets
- Wine tastings
- Hotel getaways
- Spa gift certificates
- Fitness center memberships
- Zoo memberships
- Skydiving
- Lessons of any sort (golf, music, cooking)
- Restaurant gift cards
- Hot air balloon rides
- Tickets to a local museum
- Tickets to local sporting events
- Ballet, theater, opera, or orchestra tickets
- Palm readings

Give an Antique

I wouldn't usually give someone a thrift-store find, but antiques, although they are used, are classy enough to give as gifts, and nearly everyone has an interest in some era of history. In my family alone, I have a brother-in-law who collects antique razors, a mother-in-law who loves Depression-era glass, and my own mother who loves old apothecary bottles. My husband, a photographer, loves antique cameras.

Looking for the perfect antique for your recipient is a lot like going on a scavenger hunt. Some antiques are pretty, others are practical. You never know what you're going to find. Spend some time reflecting on your recipient's interests before heading out to an antique store; when you get there, just poke around. Maybe an antique cookie jar for your grandmother, a hand-cranked butter churn for a chef, a set of comic books for a child, a piece of jewelry for your girlfriend, or old vinyl records for the music buff in your life. If all else fails, consult with the shop owner, who is most often extremely knowledgeable about her store's stock. The owner can usually point you toward something that might suit your recipient, and sometimes they can tell you a story that goes along with the item you're interested in, making the gift even more personal.

Give a Homemade Gift

This sort of gift depends on how crafty or handy you are, but most anyone can come up with something they're good at making. Knowing a loved one took the time to make the gift you're holding in your hands makes the handcrafted work a treasure.

Crafters may want to think about making homemade bath products, sewing a quilt, knitting a scarf, or painting a picture. Cooks might whip up some jellies or jams, cookies or candy. If hand-crafted gifts aren't your forte, consider gifting your time in another way. Anyone can give things like an hour of weeding or cleaning. An hour with a handyman would be welcomed by most anyone.

Give Gifts that Support a Nonprofit

Make your money do double duty by purchasing an item that supports a nonprofit organization. You can either donate to a charity in your recipient's name outright or purchase a gift that supports that charity. Virtually every charity holds some sort of fundraiser or stocks a store with proceeds going toward the organization. I've given a number of charitable gifts in the past, and they are always well-received. A favorite is supporting a local "empty bowls" drive, in which our local restaurants team up with local pottery artisans. The event lasts only a day, usually around Thanksgiving. You, the patron, pick out a hand-thrown bowl or bowls that strike your fancy. You buy the bowl, you get free soup, and proceeds benefit local homeless and hungry populations. Recipients love to receive these bowls because they are beautiful *and* they come with a neat story to share.

If you're looking to give a charitable gift, consider your interests as well as the recipient's. Perhaps the recipient is an animal lover. Then a membership to an animal rights organization or an adopt-an-animal program might be good bets. The key is to customize your gift giving to suit your loved one.

Gift Wrapping

A beautifully wrapped gift is a joy to receive, but all the wrapping paper, ribbon, boxes, and tags add up to a big pile of garbage. Some is recyclable, some reusable, but most is garbage. Here's the rundown:

Wrapping Paper

If the wrapping paper is truly made of paper, not foil or plastic, it is generally recyclable as long as all ribbons and bows have been removed. A few pieces of tape are usually acceptable; check with your local recycling facility to be sure. To check for foil or plastic, simply try to tear the wrapping material in half. If it tears easily, like newspaper, it can probably be recycled. When buying wrapping paper, opt for recycled paper and avoid any fancy extras like glitter, velveteen, or raised embossing, which can make otherwise recyclable paper unrecyclable.

Gift Tags

The guidelines for wrapping paper also apply to gift tags. These are recyclable as long as they are made from paper or cardboard with no extra materials thrown in. I've seen gift tags with pompoms posing as snowmen, or glitter standing in for snow, and these sorts of embellishments often render tags unrecyclable. Stick-on tags adhered to wrapping paper are usually fine to recycle if attached to recyclable wrapping paper.

Ribbon

Ribbon is never recyclable, though if you're careful when opening a gift, it is often reusable. I keep a gift bag full of used ribbon, and this comes in handy all the time when I need last-minute wrapping materials. Pretty ribbons can also be used for holiday decorating projects (on wreaths, for instance).

Gift Boxes

Most gifts come packaged in boxes that are both reusable and recyclable. The best way to deal with a traditionally wrapped gift you receive is to separate the wrapping components and either recycle them or reuse them. But what about when you're wrapping your own gifts to give?

After much experimentation, I have found many different ways to wrap gifts without disposable material. When I'm wrapping a present in an eco-friendly fashion, my wrapping must meet several criteria. First, I want something that is equivalent in price to wrapping paper. I have no interest in the wrapping adding to the cost of the gift. Next, I want wrapping to be as easy and straightforward as possible. Finally, I do want my gift wrap to be pretty to look at.

Go the traditional route but buy recycled/recyclable materials: Buy wrapping paper and tags that are easy to recycle. Instead of ribbon, try raffia, a plant-based fiber that is compostable. I usually make my own gift tags, and on the back of the tags I ask the recipient to "Please recycle!"

Use found materials: A number of materials that you already have sitting around the house can be useful for wrapping. Be creative. Small gifts can be wrapped in newspaper—especially the funny pages—or try cutting open a paper grocery bag. My brother, a helicopter pilot, uses old aviation maps as wrapping paper. You could also use pages torn from a book or dictionary, or try cutting up an old scarf or T-shirt. Got any old wallpaper samples lying around? Containers lying around the house can be equally useful. Small gifts can be placed in glass jars or cigar boxes.

Use towels: Towels are the perfect wrapping material because they are huge, fairly inexpensive, and reusable after the gift is opened. Besides, who couldn't use an extra fluffy towel? For our first garbage-free Christmas, both of our parents wrapped our gifts in pretty towels tied with ribbon. It's best to use towels to wrap something square that's already in a box.

Make your own gift bags from fabric: You'll need a sewing machine to accomplish this, but if you have access to one, this is my favorite way to wrap gifts, hands down. Even those with rudimentary sewing skills can handle constructing a simple drawstring bag (instructions below). Before the holiday season gets under way, I head to my local fabric shop, usually with a 50-percent-off

HOW TO MAKE A SIMPLE DRAWSTRING BAG

1. Measure the item you plan to wrap to determine the size bag you'll need to make. The length of the box determines the length of the bag. Add an inch to the length to leave room for the drawstring. Combine the height plus depth to see how wide you'll want to make your bag. Cut two equal pieces of fabric to match your measurements. Alternatively you can cut one piece of fabric twice the length you need, fold it in half (right sides together), and sew up the two sides, leaving room for the drawstring.

2. Lay both pieces of fabric next to each other with the right sides down. Fold the top of the first piece of fabric down 1 inch, and iron. Repeat with the second fabric piece. Sew straight across the folded fabric 1/4 inch from the top to create a channel for your drawstring.

3. Place the right sides of the fabric together and line the two pieces up neatly with the drawstring channels on top. Sew around the left, bottom, and right side edges of the bag, starting just below the drawstring channel on one edge and ending in the same place on the opposite edge. Turn the bag right side out.

4. Cut a length of ribbon or yarn long enough to act as your drawstring. Attach a safety pin to one end. Using the safety pin to guide the ribbon through both pockets of the bag, string your drawstring through one side and then the other, creating a circle. Tie the ends together, and voila, your bag is finished.

coupon in my pocket, to peruse the holiday fabric selection. I pick out two or three patterns I like, then buy several yards of each along with some ribbon or yarn for the pull strings. I have found that recipients love to receive these drawstring bags with their gift, and experience has shown me that people are happy to reuse their new cloth gift bags for gifts they are giving.

Special Traditions

This section covers holiday-specific items that might create trash, with strategies for determining what is recyclable and how to work around what isn't. We all have our special holiday traditions—candy hearts on Valentine's Day, beer on St. Paddy's Day, and fireworks with the Fourth of July, to name a few—that we don't want to give up. This part of the chapter aims to help you celebrate a traditional holiday in a trash-free way.

Valentine's Day

Valentine's Day is filled with sweet treats—heart-shaped boxes filled with chocolates, a small army of conversation hearts, cookies, cupcakes, and more. Add to this the stuffed animals, greeting cards, and flowers, and suddenly one small holiday has the potential to make a lot of trash.

The bad news is that those ubiquitous heart-shaped boxes of chocolate are not really recyclable. They are usually wrapped in an outer layer of thin plastic that is always garbage. Inside the box, you'll find a plastic tray that holds the chocolates; if this plastic is stamped with a resin number, check to see whether it's recyclable, but for most people it won't be. The heart box itself may or may not be recyclable. If it is made purely from cardboard (subject it to the tear test), it is. Most boxes, however, are covered in velvet or sequins or fake flowers, which cannot be recycled. Do consider repurposing these lovely boxes into a Valentine's Day decoration you could use for future celebrations; search for "upcycling candy heart boxes" on the Internet, and many crafty ideas will pop up.

To avoid the heart boxes entirely, shop for your Valentine's Day candy at a local confectioner or try your hand at making your own chocolates. Nothing says "I love you" more than a homemade gift—this is certainly more thoughtful than grabbing a plastic-wrapped box off the shelf.

Boxes of conversation hearts, on the other hand, can be recycled. The plastic window will be filtered out and thrown away during the paper recycling process, but the box itself is recyclable. The same is true for all boxes with plastic windows, including boxes of pasta.

Valentine's Day is not complete without the valentines themselves, but luckily these are largely recyclable. Greeting cards can be sent to St. Jude's Children's Ranch (see page 250) for recycling. When purchasing valentines, look for ones made from recycled paper. Avoid all the fancy frills that render valentines nonrecyclable, such as sequins, fabric, plastic, or ribbon. Better yet, make your own valentines with materials found around the house for a special homemade card.

Bouquets of flowers pose their own environmental problem. Besides the packaging garbage created from the plastic sleeves the flowers come in, there is a significant environmental impact created from cutting and transporting exotic flowers halfway around the world to the coolers of our grocery stores. You can minimize this impact by seeking out a local flower shop or nursery. Try to find locally grown, in-season flowers—they will have a much smaller carbon footprint if they were grown close to home. I once received a lovely gift from my eco-conscious husband— a single rose wrapped in a sleeve made from a banana leaf and tied with twine. You can also consider gifting a potted plant, which is a much better investment for the planet.

St. Patrick's Day

Luckily St. Patrick's Day doesn't create much trash. The revelry of this holiday is mostly limited to food and libations. As long as you're recycling your beer cans or bottles, feel free to indulge in the luck o' the Irish with no environmental guilt at all. And if you need to decorate or give a St. Paddy's Day gift, consider purchasing a shamrock plant, which shows up in local flower shops and grocery stores in March in time for Ireland-themed celebrations.

Easter

Easter poses a trash problem only when it comes to Easter baskets filled with candy and plastic grass. Don't worry, though, because putting together a zero-waste Easter basket is easy and fun, starting at the bottom of the basket with those thin plastic strands of plastic "grass." How artificial! Consider one of several eco-options. In my family, we use paper from the paper shredder—even though it's not green, it's a good, cushy substitute for the basket's lining. You can also consider growing real grass in your Easter basket.

You have to start this a good three weeks before the holiday itself, but it makes a fun project to do together as a family. Instructions abound online; search for "growing real grass in an Easter basket" for tutorials using wheatgrass.

Candy, which often comes wrapped in garbage, will create another problem, but it's not insurmountable. (See a complete discussion about candy in the Halloween section later in this chapter.) For some reason, a lot of Easter candy comes wrapped in foil, which is recyclable. Opt for a chocolate bunny wrapped in foil versus the kind that comes in a box with a huge plastic window. Cadbury eggs come wrapped in foil, and malted milk balls usually come in a recyclable box. Try finding your favorite candy loose in a bulk candy store, which can then be placed in whatever recyclable/reusable container you wish. The only candy you might have to give up entirely is Peeps, though you could always recreate these chicken confections by making homemade marshmallows in your own kitchen.

As for Easter egg hunts, those brightly colored plastic eggs aren't particularly great for the environment, but because they are durable enough to last through many egg hunts, they aren't going to be the source of much garbage. Once they are broken, plastic eggs are not recyclable, but they can often be reused for craft projects. To forgo the plastic eggs entirely, you can also use real eggs for your egg hunts. If you go this route, try to avoid the commercial

HOMEMADE EASTER EGG DYES

Kitchen spices and fruits or vegetables can be used to dye Easter eggs naturally. Combine 2 cups mashed fruit or 2 tablespoons spices with 2 cups of water. Bring to a boil and simmer for 30 minutes; strain off the solids. The remaining liquid is your egg dye. You can use this dye like you would commercial egg dye, or you can drop your eggs into a saucepan and boil them in the dye for a few minutes. Homemade dye takes more time to work, so let your eggs sit in the liquid a little longer than you're used to.

Yellow: Lemon or orange peel, carrot tops, celery seed, ground cumin, ground turmeric, yellow onion skins

Orange: Chili powder

Red: Red onion skins, pomegranate juice

Pink: Red beets

Purple: Raspberries, blackberries, violet blossoms

Blue: Red cabbage, canned blueberries and their juices, purple grape juice

Green: Spinach

Brown: Black walnut shells

dye kits, which create garbage (plastic tablet wrappers, plastic egg wraps, stickers). Instead, pair real eggs with natural dyes, which are fairly easy to make with standard household ingredients.

Independence Day

The Fourth of July is one of my favorite holidays, and it's largely waste free. Independence Day is filled with picnics and barbeques, street fairs, parades, popsicles, and of course, fireworks. Any garbage you're likely to create on the Fourth of July will come from food or those fireworks.

Summer food is usually eaten outdoors, and this is where a lot of potential trash comes from. When planning your zero-waste picnic or barbeque, put the kibosh on disposable plates, glasses, or cutlery. Instead, serve your meal using real plates, glasses, and silverware, or consider using the type of serving ware you'd use on a camping trip. Using the real thing adds a touch of class to your celebration. It also evokes a sense of "simpler times" nostalgia to serve food in a way similar to how our founding fathers would have eaten it. Be creative and have fun with this! Consider serving lemonade from Ball canning jars, or use a watermelon as a punch bowl.

Fireworks are, unfortunately, not zero waste. There's no way around this— if you buy fireworks, they end up as garbage. If fireworks aren't something you can give up, please make sure you pick up the pieces after nighttime festivities—burned-out fireworks are a huge source of litter. If, however, you can forgo fireworks, this is the safer and more environmentally friendly option. Instead, take the whole family to a community fireworks show.

Halloween

A traditional Halloween involves children, costumes, and loads of candy. The garbage involved with a traditional Halloween celebration mostly involves mini-size candy wrappers, though with the growing popularity of this holiday, old costumes, disposable party supplies, and glow-in-the-dark plastic décor and knickknacks are making their way into the landfill, too.

Before we set out to eliminate all Halloween candy from the world, there are a couple of considerations. First comes the question of whether or not we want to eliminate the annual munchkin candy gathering. There are only a couple of options here: give trick-or-treaters something other than candy or give out nothing at all. We all know how most kids feel about the people on the block who give out things other than candy—you know, toothbrushes, raisins, or Jesus cards. And as for the other option of not giving out anything? I think that's way too Scroogey to consider.

Rose Brown has given the issue some thought, too. "I don't get trick-or-treaters where I live. However, I have thought about the fact that it would be hard to hand out candy or other goodies, because they inevitably create trash. If I move, or happen to start getting trick-or-treaters where I currently live, I will try some kind of alternative like pencils, crayons, or quarters." This is a great idea, because as much as most kids like candy, they love money even more!

Luckily there are a few alternative options to individually wrapped candy that are both earth-friendly and kid-friendly.

Buy candy in recyclable packaging: Most Halloween candy comes packaged in throwaway wrappers made from a composite of plastic and foil, like the ones you see on candy bars, gummi candies, peanut butter cups, and lollipops. However, some candy is still available packaged in paper wrappers or cardboard boxes. Your options here include Tootsie Rolls, Tootsie Roll pops, Nerds, Milk Duds, Dots, M&Ms, and Neccos. Try to pick out a bag of fun-size candy from this list so that children can recycle their Nerds boxes after they've finished eating. You might also consider attaching a little note that encourages trick-or-treaters to recycle when you hand out candy in recyclable packaging.

Participate in Books for Treats: Books for Treats is a small nonprofit organization that encourages people to give out new or gently used children's books to trick-or-treaters in lieu of candy. The organization's slogan is "Feed kids' minds, not their cavities." The simple idea behind Books for Treats is that Halloween candy contributes to obesity and diabetes while polluting the environment. The organization suggests that we instead spend time in October collecting children's books from our attics, garage sales, estate sales, and thrift stores. Then, when ghosts and goblins come knocking, they get to select a book of their choice instead of candy.

In addition to providing a healthy alternative to candy, Books for Treats allows participants to move up the waste hierarchy by reusing instead of buying something new, and it gives children a gift that lasts much longer than a piece of candy.

Although some participants worry that children will be disappointed to see books instead of candy, the organization reports that, overwhelmingly, kids are delighted with this new option. Visit www.booksfortreats.org to download a "how-to kit" and learn more.

Throw or attend a Halloween party: Chapter 6, "The Zero-Waste Kitchen," showed you how making homemade meals instead of buying prepackaged products leads to a healthier, simpler diet. The same logic applies to Halloween candy. Inviting over a group of friends and family to sample your own goodies is a way to control the ingredients you use—ensuring that there are no artificial colors or sweeteners and sourcing local ingredients—and control the packaging you use (that is, none). Throwing your own party gives neighborhood children a safe and healthy place to celebrate the holiday.

Participate in National Costume Swap Day: Brought to you by www.green halloween.org, National Costume Swap Day identifies costume waste as a major contributor to landfill contents. Because many children don't want to wear the same costume more than once, many costumes end up in landfills each year. Green Halloween estimates that if even half the children's costumes that wind up in the trash each year were swapped or reused, we would save 6,250 tons of waste from the landfill. Swapping costumes makes perfect sense because it embraces reuse and saves money.

Thanksgiving

Thanksgiving lends itself perfectly to the zero-waste lifestyle. Living zero-waste is about eating fresh, not prepared, foods; buying from local business owners; and generally living a simpler, more fulfilling lifestyle. Thanksgiving, the holiday of giving thanks for what we have, is the perfect time to practice these principles. A Thanksgiving feast made from locally grown and harvested food that directly supports your local community not only will create no waste but also will be more meaningful as it embraces the spirit of the holiday.

Thanksgiving food can be purchased using the guidelines earlier in this chapter about humanely raised meat (see page 212) as well as the information in chapter 6. Decorations for Thanksgiving can be simple if you use the natural bounty of the fall harvest. A cornucopia brimming with seasonal fruits and vegetables along with several floral arrangements featuring fall colors is all that is needed to brighten the Thanksgiving table.

Christmas

It's no secret that the winter holiday season has become an out-of-control orgy of excessive consumption and its byproduct, excessive landfill-bound waste. In fact, during the period between Thanksgiving and New Year's, Americans generate 25 percent more waste, which adds up to about a million extra tons of trash each year, according to the EPA. The majority of this waste is gift wrap or packaging, although some is from people throwing away old items like laptops and cell phones as soon as they unwrap the newest model.

Our first garbage-free holiday season forced me to examine my ingrained habits and beliefs surrounding my family's Christmas celebration. In fact, all of us on the zero-waste squad reported similar moments of soul-searching while navigating a garbage-free holiday in our consumer-driven society.

For her first zero-waste Christmas, April tried to instill some new values in her kids. "My kids are young enough that I can influence their experience of the holiday, focusing more on family time—the way it's supposed to be," she says. Her family spent time enjoying each other's company and avoiding the hype.

For me, it was important to ask myself why we celebrate our winter holiday of choice and to allow myself time to reflect on what I wanted to get out of the celebration. Even though gifts have long been an integral part of my extended family's Christmas Eve celebration, I realized that the family time, food, and memories being created are much more important than the actual gifts I received. Once I determined my own priorities for a holiday celebration, my Christmas season became much more relaxed and focused on the experiences I cherish. This allowed me to step back from the frenetic pace of the typical holiday experience and rework a number of our family traditions until they worked for me and the environment.

Christmas trees: I'm often asked whether I decorate with a real or artificial tree for the holiday season. To me, the choice is c lear—I patronize a local U-cut tree farm, give my business to a local family, and come home with a wonderfully fragrant grand fir. This is by far the greener option when choosing a Christmas tree. Christmas trees are a consumable crop, like anything else grown by farmers. When you're finished with a tree, it can easily be mulched and composted, returning nutrients to the earth. Artificial trees, on the other hand, end up as trash; they are made to last forever, and they pretty much do—doomed to stay intact inside a landfill.

New Year's Eve

New Year's Eve is brimming with opportunities for a zero-waste celebration. New Year's Eve parties are about food, alcohol, and glittering party favors. The first two—food and alcohol—are easy to make zero waste, but if you're attached to the party hats, confetti, and noise horns, you'll have to get creative in order to continue your traditions without creating trash.

What is a New Year's Eve celebration without champagne? Luckily the bubbly stuff is easy to consume without creating waste. The glass bottle is, of course, recyclable, and so is the foil seal around the bottle's neck. This leaves you with a handful of corks at the end of the evening. To learn how to recycle corks, see page 249.

New Year's Eve party favors are a different story. Generally the plastic favors you purchase from a party store are garbage after a single use. They are poorly made, which means they break easily. Additionally they are often made from several different materials that are difficult to separate, rendering them unrecyclable. You're better off making your own party favors (there are many viable alternatives) or forgoing the noisemakers and hats and focusing instead on music, dancing, and libations. If you opt for party hats, try to find ones made from cardboard without all the glitter and sequins. The only garbage you'll be left with is the chin string. Instead of noisemakers, try whistles, clappers made from durable (read: long-lasting) plastic, or old-fashioned cheering and wolf-whistling from guests. For crackers—the traditional tubes filled with confetti and a small gift—try making your own from toilet paper tubes and decorative paper (find instructions online by searching for "home-made party crackers"). Confetti can be easily reused, or you can make your confetti by cutting up pieces of colorful paper. After a night's revelry, clear the tables of all party paraphernalia, and then simply fold the tablecloth up, shaking confetti toward the center. This way, it's easy to gather for reuse or recycling. Crepe paper streamers are a good bet because they are inexpensive and compostable.

No matter what you're celebrating, there is a way to do so without creating so much waste. What is most important is the opportunity to gather with close family and friends to celebrate a special occasion. A party filled with decorations inspired by nature, good food, drinks, and company is sure to be a hit. Your guests will thank you for serving them from real plates instead of the flimsy paper variety, and you can feel good about sparing the planet while throwing a party to remember.

Meet Your Goal: Zero-Waste Holidays and Special Occasions

Easy

- Use paper plates instead of plastic or Styrofoam; compost when finished.
- Recycle valentines.
- Recycle wrapping paper.
- Send e-invitations.
- Compost crepe paper streamers.
- Make your own confetti from colorful paper.
- Give gifts that are homemade, benefit charity, or are antiques or experiences.

Moderate

- Save champagne corks for recycling.
- Buy humanely raised meat.
- Sew your own gift bags from fabric.
- Save gift bags and ribbon for future use.
- Use nature (plants, fruit, trees, veggies) to decorate for your next party.

Advanced

- Celebrate a meatless holiday.
- Make your own candy canes.
- Participate in Books for Treats at Halloween.

PART 3

Next Steps

Now that you've adopted a zero-waste lifestyle, you're probably wondering why everyone isn't doing the same thing. After spending some time integrating the strategies listed throughout this book, living without garbage is probably beginning to feel like second nature. If you're anything like me, you find it discouraging that more people aren't aware of what they throw in the trash. After we started living trash free, I sought out more ways to get involved in waste reduction not only in my own life but also on a societal level.

I found two promising movements that seek to re-imagine our country's waste landscape. One, called the Zero-Waste Movement, is a mindset being adopted by companies, nonprofits, and government organizations across the country. This movement aims to help these organizations restructure the way they do business and run events. In the same way that removing waste from your life required you to do a waste audit and creatively implement solutions, so too does the Zero-Waste Movement work to eliminate waste from organizations.

The other movement I discovered is called Extended Producer Responsibility. This fantastic initiative places the financial burden of trash disposal on companies that manufacture and overpackage their products. Instead of the consumer paying a heftier trash bill to deal with all this extra unnecessary waste, this second movement works to make producers pay for their trash.

In this final section of the book, I talk about the zero-waste movement on a global level and show you ways to get involved if you want to take your interest in living trash free up another notch.

Chapter 14

The Global Zero-Waste Movement

You are now part of a growing movement. You have taken the first big step toward removing excess waste and consumption from your life, focusing instead on what really matters to you and your family. Please don't stop here, because there's much more to be done. The term *zero waste* also has a larger, all-encompassing meaning, and this zero-waste movement, of which you are now a part, is the focus of this chapter. This movement arises from the fundamental idea that reducing garbage is not just an individual responsibility but also one in which governments, manufacturers, businesses, nonprofits, religious organizations, and schools need to take an active role. The first half of this chapter covers the ever-growing zero-waste movement, in which organizations set and achieve astounding waste-reduction goals on a company-wide scale. The second half looks at the concept of Extended Producer Responsibility—the belief that manufacturers are far more responsible for waste management than those of us purchasing their ridiculously overpackaged products.

Redefining Zero Waste

The term *zero waste* has only recently been expanded to include the lifestyle you are now living. Getting involved in the larger zero-waste movement, the one happening in the wider world, is critical to the success and expansion of the waste-free message.

So what else does the zero-waste movement entail? In 2004, the Zero Waste Alliance came up with what is the most widely referenced explanation:

"Zero Waste is a goal that is ethical, economical, efficient and visionary, to guide people in changing their lifestyles and practices to emulate sustainable natural cycles, where all discarded materials are designed to become resources for others to use. Zero Waste means designing and managing products and processes to systematically avoid and eliminate the volume and toxicity of waste and materials, conserve and recover all resources, and not burn or bury them. Implementing Zero Waste will eliminate all discharges to land, water or air that are a threat to planetary, human, animal or plant health."

In other words, the larger zero-waste movement looks at the manufacturing and disposal of a given product or industry in much the same way that you've begun to look at your own life. It's a ground-up approach, which means that how the philosophy is applied differs depending on the product or industry in question. The movement is catching on big-time in the corporate, industrial, and civic realms.

As the zero-waste movement is right now in the process of moving from theory to implementation, the current process of implementing a zero-waste plan is a bit ephemeral. There are a number of debates about what does or does not constitute zero waste. The fact is, each organization that sets forth a zero-waste mission will implement that mission in a different way simply because of the differences inherent in that specific entity. Let me give you some examples.

We know that zero waste means producing as little waste as possible, with an ultimate aim of no waste at all. We know, too, that the principles of reuse and reduce are more environmentally sound than just recycling. Consider for a moment a brewery that makes and bottles its own beer. The company might adopt two different zero-waste approaches. First, it could work to recycle all empty beer bottles, sending no glass bottles to the landfill. Some call this first approach "zero landfill" rather than "zero waste." On the other hand, brewery owners could opt to have all empty bottles returned to them to be washed, sterilized, and refilled indefinitely, thereby embracing the principle of reuse over recycling.

Single-use disposables that are recyclable or compostable are also at the forefront of the zero-waste debate. Consider a drink cup made from biodegradable plastic. To manufacture these cups, raw materials must be procured, the cup itself must be made (a process in which energy is used), the cup is shipped, a drink is consumed, and the cup is then (ideally) sent somewhere other than a landfill to biodegrade. Ultimately, if the cup biodegrades, there has been zero waste. However, detractors argue that a whole lot of time, money, energy, and resources were put into manufacturing a product designed for a single use. Maybe, they say, our time would be better spent producing a product that never needs to be disposed of.

Ultimately the zero-waste movement looks to nature as its model. Nature—that is to say, plants and animals—produces no waste. You never see deer landfills or raccoon garbage cans in the animal kingdom. This is because nature *never wastes anything.* Any excesses in nature get composted back into the ground, where nutrients join the soil and the life cycle begins again. The ultimate vision for all product design imagines the same thing: products built to last a human lifetime that create no waste during their manufacture and, once ready to be discarded, can be dismantled into reusable components.

Zero-waste supporters talk about manufacturing processes in terms of "cradle-to-cradle" (as opposed to "cradle-to-grave"). The cradle-to-cradle model is like the "circle of life" philosophy—manufacturing materials are returned to their raw form after use to be reformed and used again. This is pure recycling, as compared to the cradle-to-grave model, in which materials are doomed for the landfill after use.

The key aspect of the zero-waste movement is its customizability. A set of philosophies is in place to guide interested organizations through the process of implementing the shift required by zero-waste, but there is no one right or wrong way to do it.

Companies versus Individuals

If a company, community, or group is interested in adopting a zero-waste goal, here's what happens: that organization decides to adopt the zero-waste philosophy, making it their mission to generate as close to zero waste as humanly possible. Their first step, as yours was, is to take a look at the trash they generate on a regular basis. This will vary drastically. The Subaru car company, for example, will produce vastly different waste than the Mad River Brewery in California.

After the initial waste audit, the organization will have an understanding of their problem areas. Again, these differ depending on the specific group. Some might find that their shipping department produces excess waste;

another might find that food is being wasted in the cafeteria. The next step is usually to establish a zero-waste committee and a zero-waste goal. Just as with your zero-waste lifestyle, it is important for organizations to develop a long-term commitment to their zero-waste goal, because it won't happen overnight.

The real work begins after a zero-waste goal has been set. The next step is removing all the trash from the dumpster systematically. You're already familiar with how to personalize this lifestyle to your own circumstances; zero-waste organizations have to do the same thing. It becomes a challenge of innovation and creativity. They have a lot of legwork to do. Implementation could include everything from installing hand dryers in bathrooms instead of paper towel dispensers to ordering a dissolvable form of packing peanut to changing how an entire product is made.

The biggest step in implementing a zero-waste goal is communicating that goal to everybody—employees, volunteers, vendors, suppliers, manufacturers, and customers.

In the end, most organizations can achieve almost zero waste, but they are still left with some garbage to dispose of. Many turn to waste-to-energy incinerators as their solution. Although incinerating leftover garbage does

ORGANIZATIONS WITH ZERO-WASTE GOALS

Each organization on this list, as well as hundreds of other large and small organizations across the country, has worked in some way toward zero waste. Remember, each organization is unique, so how it has implemented the philosophy is also unique.

- Kimberly-Clarke
- The Body Shop
- Hewlett-Packard
- Epson
- Pillsbury
- Xerox
- Subaru
- City of San Francisco
- Walmart
- Yellowstone National Park
- Honda
- City of Boulder, Colorado
- City of Seattle
- Evergreen State College, Washington
- Anheuser-Busch
- Environmental Protection Agency

technically mean zero waste, this is still a controversial move, as the process of burning trash is laden with environmental pitfalls.

A couple of years ago, I was asked to speak about my zero-waste experience at Salem's Saturday Market. The organization Friends of Salem Saturday Market (FSSM) is a nonprofit staffed by dedicated volunteers who believe in the importance of shopping locally for sustainable products. Since 2010, the FSSM group has adopted a zero-waste goal for the Saturday market, and so far their efforts have been hugely successful.

At the Saturday Market, all food vendors now use compostable or reusable plates, cups, and utensils. Friendly volunteers help you properly sort your food paraphernalia after your local lunch at the farmers' market. All food and organic waste is composted. Recycling bins are also available for glass, paper, cans, and plastic. Only disposable items brought into the market from outside businesses end up as garbage. The compostable materials are then sent to a local composting facility, which sells compost back to the community that gave it its raw materials.

One unique element to the zero-waste Saturday Market is the availability of real metal utensils instead of plastic or compostable varieties. Customers can eat their meals with the real deal, then return used utensils to a station staffed by volunteers. The FSSM group has contracted with a food vendor that provides weekly washing in a commercial kitchen. So far, the utensils program has been a great success.

The zero-waste movement is all about taking responsibility for one's own trash, and this is a remarkable thing. In today's business climate, in which profit reigns supreme, it is admirable for these many companies to stand up and collectively say they will work to clean up their own mess. Ultimately there are many benefits to adopting zero waste. After an initial transition period, zero-waste companies tend to operate with fewer expenses. They discover new, innovative ways to do business, and there's the added PR benefit of promoting a company's environmental practices.

Not all companies have jumped on the zero-waste bandwagon, however, so the effort to clean up all the garbage being produced in the corporate world is now taking a two-pronged approach. Although participating in the zero-waste movement is voluntary, many people, including myself, are advocating for laws requiring that companies comply with waste-reduction measures. These efforts fall under the umbrella of Extended Producer Responsibility, a concept and a resulting movement that aims to place the financial burden of trash disposal on the producer, not the consumer.

Extended Producer Responsibility

Now that you've spent months achieving zero waste in your home, pondering each and every piece of would-be trash, I'm going to tell you that the real responsibility for weaning ourselves from our trash addiction does not rest on the shoulders of consumers. That's right, you're not solely responsible for the amount of trash you create. In fact, I'd argue you're not even mostly responsible for it.

So who is?

The answer is one of the greatest epiphanies I had during our first year of garbage-free living. Product manufacturers are responsible for the packaging they put around their goods. It's not your fault that a product you want or need comes wrapped in nonrecyclable materials. Although you can take steps to curb your consumerism, working to buy only things you need rather than simply desire, there's no getting around the fact that all of us ultimately must consume to live. We must have food, for example, and we may not have the luxury of growing our own, buying in bulk, or shopping at a farmers' market. This means we have to buy food to survive, whether or not it comes packaged in garbage.

The real rub comes when you consider that not only are we at the mercy of manufacturers when it comes to what they package their products in, but we are also responsible for paying to dispose of their waste. Yes, indeed, corporations can package their products in whatever they desire, and we bring home that product and pay to dispose of the overpackaging.

This is so backward it makes my eyes hurt. None of the onus of responsible packaging decisions rests on the shoulders of manufacturers because they have absolutely no incentive not to surround their products in layers of plastic. Instead, we take on the price of disposal in our garbage bills and we also take on the green guilt when we're stuck with a piece of packaging destined for the landfill.

Proponents of Extended Producer Responsibility (EPR) state that product manufacturers are responsible for the eventual fate of their packaging choices. EPR programs hold product manufacturers financially responsible for disposing of their products and packaging after use. The guiding principle of the EPR philosophy is that manufacturers are best suited to control the waste produced by their products because they are directly in charge of designing and marketing their products. It should be up to product manufacturers to design and market their products in a way that is environmentally responsible, rather than shifting the burden of responsibly disposing of poorly designed products to the consumer.

"We try to push EPR," says Chris Burger, a waste-buster and member of the Sierra Club's Zero Waste Task Force, "incentivizing makers of things to basically recover the materials that they put into their products. If you put it on them, that's an incentive to design for recovery."

Extended Producer Responsibility is also called *product stewardship*, because it encourages manufacturers to consider factors other than their bottom line. Where's the incentive to today's corporations to use less packaging when those corporations don't bear the burden of disposing of their mess? We dispose of corporate America's obscene packaging, and we assume the guilt for all this waste. Product stewardship suggests a spirit of manufacturer partnership with consumers and environmental advocates, as opposed to the current, "Here, you take care of our mess" attitude.

"What we're really trying to say is reduce consumption, reuse, make products such that they can be deconstructed," adds Robert Haley.

There are currently a number of EPR programs on the national and international level—some large-scale and others smaller, grassroots efforts. Just like zero-waste initiatives, EPR programs take a variety of forms. Some are small and voluntary, whereas others are government-mandated and all-encompassing. Let's take a look at a few.

The European Packaging Directive

In 1991, Germany passed legislation that mandated EPR for manufacturers across the country, basically recognizing that companies that design, distribute, and profit from a product should also be held financially responsible for the product's end-of-life. This legislation requires that companies pay a fee according to the type of packaging they use—an obvious incentive to reduce the amount of materials that go into a given product. In 1994, the European Union followed suit by passing what is now known as the European Packaging Directive, which mandated that product manufacturers assume responsibility for recovering, recycling, and disposing of their products and packaging. These groundbreaking pieces of legislation require exactly what EPR advocates push for—that manufacturers take back their packaging materials and deal with them themselves, as opposed to forcing the consumer to attempt to separate, sort, and recycle packaging materials.

The Green Dot program was created to help companies manage the logistics of this legislation. All companies are required to pay to manage all their packaging, and they have two options for doing so. They may opt to create and implement their own collection programs—though usually this is logistically sound only for smaller companies—or they may enroll in a nonprofit program like the Green Dot, which will manage packaging recovery for them.

Companies enrolled in the Green Dot program pay a fee according to the volume of their packaging material (creating an immediate incentive to use less packaging). They can then mark their packages with a circular green logo featuring two chasing arrows—a hybrid of the recycling symbol and a yin-yang. The Green Dot indicates a company's compliance with the packaging directive. Consumers then discard their green-dot-branded materials in a specified bin, from which the materials are hauled away and sorted for reuse or safe disposal.

American consumers may occasionally see the Green Dot on some of their products produced overseas. For awhile, before starting to live a zero-waste lifestyle, I bought a St. Ives face scrub that featured the Green Dot. Unfortunately we can't participate in the Green Dot program, though we can work to bring about such legislation in the United States.

Though not without its problems, the Green Dot program has proven to be highly successful in reducing packaging waste. In the first four years of the program, packaging waste decreased by 14 percent, while packaging waste in the United States rose by 13 percent during the same time period. The rate of decrease has since slowed, but the program has also had success in increasing recycling rates for materials like glass, cardboard, and metals.

Bottle Bills

Did you know that two-thirds of all beverage containers in the United States never get recycled? These cans and bottles wind up littering cities, towns, and natural areas, a problem that is both unsightly and harmful to wildlife.

My home state of Oregon passed the first bottle bill in 1971. Today nine other states have instituted their own form of container deposit laws, and although bottle bill legislation is always vehemently opposed by the beverage industry, these measures have proven to be an effective example of a producer take-back program in action.

For those not familiar with them, bottle bills mandate that a small deposit is charged when a customer purchases a beverage. That deposit, usually $0.05 to $0.10, is returned to the customer when he or she brings the beverage container back to the store or another drop-off center for recycling. Different states run their programs in different ways, but deposits are charged on everything from soda and bottled water to beer, juice, and sports drink containers—anything that comes in glass and plastic bottles or aluminum cans.

The rationale for implementing a bottle bill is the same as for Germany's Green Dot program—corporations and consumers pay to recycle their containers through a privately funded infrastructure instead of passing the burden along to taxpayers, who fund local recycling programs.

Beverage containers account for at least 40 percent of all litter, according to the Bottle Bill Resource Guide. Container deposit laws provide a simple and effective way to ensure that most of these bottles get recycled as opposed to ending up stagnating in the environment. Today states with bottle bills report a reduction in litter ranging from 70 to 83 percent, proving the effectiveness of the program.

Electronics Take-Back Programs

Twenty-five states, covering 65 percent of the US population, have implemented electronics take-back programs that require manufacturers to pay for recycling their old electronics. This means that in many states, consumers can drop off their old electronics for free at a designated recycling location. From there, manufacturers must figure out how to best recycle or safely dispose of the (sometimes hazardous) materials in their products.

Of course, electronics take-back laws vary from state to state, but may encompass materials such as TVs, keyboards, mice, computers and monitors, laptops, printers, fax machines, DVD/VHS players, digital picture frames, and video game consoles. To find out whether your state has an electronics take-back law (and to see what you can recycle), visit www.electronicstake back.com/wp-content/uploads/Compare_state_laws_chart.pdf.

Now that you've adopted the zero-waste lifestyle, you've probably become a little obsessed with trash. You wonder, having reduced your trash to next to nil, what else you can do to eliminate more trash from your neighbor's bin or the trash can in the park down the street. When you're ready to take your trash advocacy a step further, I encourage you to turn to the concept of Extended Producer Responsibility.

It's a plain and simple fact that not everyone is willing to adopt a zero-waste lifestyle, though many more are likely to when they see how easy and freeing it can be. Nevertheless, not everyone puts environmental activism at the top of their to-do list.

The beauty of EPR programs is that, when implemented, producers do much of the environmental work for the consumers—work that is rightfully theirs to do, as they package the products in the first place.

Producers hate EPR laws because right now they've got us exactly where they want us. We've been lulled into cooperating with a false paradigm. They know that, under the current system, they can manufacture a product any way they wish, overpackage it in obscene amounts of brightly colored plastic, and pawn it off on us. Remember that we're paying not just for the item inside all that packaging that we're bringing into our homes; we're also paying for the packaging and its disposal, too! And according to the EPA, containers and packaging made up the largest portion of MSW generated at about 30 percent (nearly 76 million tons) in 2010. Packaging is literally overflowing from our trash cans, and we're the ones paying to dispose of something we didn't want in the first place.

Of course it's our responsibility to carefully examine what we buy and communicate our displeasure with all that overpackaging to producers. But if companies truly care about the environment—as most of them claim to—it's time for them to step up and start producing responsible packaging.

Consider the infamous Keep America Beautiful example. Keep America Beautiful (kab.org) is an organization funded largely by companies that make and sell beverages in disposable containers (on its website, you can find PepsiCo and Nestlé Waters listed as corporate sponsors, having donated $500,000-plus to the organization). In a mission statement, written on the front page of its website, KAB states that the organization "believes that each of us holds an obligation to preserve and protect our environment. Through our everyday choices and actions, we collectively have a huge impact on our world." In practice, what this means is that KAB works diligently to make us see that litter is a problem that can be solved only through individual actions (as opposed to EPR programs). Two of KAB's three "focus issues" are on litter prevention and waste reduction and recycling programs (that is, our responsibility, not theirs).

The responsibility for protecting, not polluting, the environment rests on *all* our shoulders, not just the shoulders of the consumer. It is time that we consumers start rattling the cage of companies that insist on making nonsustainable products or packaging. You can help by taking the following steps:

- Learn as much as you can about EPR.
- Tell other people about EPR programs and laws.
- Call companies and tell them you will no longer stand for paying to dispose of their overpackaged goods and that you're working for legislative change.
- Call your senators and representatives, both local and national, and request that they start working on EPR legislation like Germany's Green Dot program.

The success of these two movements is critical to the future of our planet. I don't say this lightly. At the beginning of the book, I mentioned this statistic: for every can of trash each American hauls to the curb, corporate-industrial manufacturing produced an additional *forty to seventy cans* filled with trash generated during the manufacture of our products. You've found, as I have, that reducing your individual trash output is downright easy once you have a system in place. And although your efforts are going a long way toward reducing America's household trash, it's only fair that the people who manufacture our products take responsibility for their trash, too. As soon as you are ready to take the next step—from promoting zero waste in your life to promoting it in your community and beyond—I urge to you get involved in one of these two movements.

Epilogue

A couple of weeks after our garbage-free challenge officially ended, Adam and I set out for Olympic National Park in northwest Washington. We had spent the preceding winter planning a wilderness backpacking trip with my parents, and we were eager to spend some time immersed in nature, away from cell phones, computers, and other modern contrivances. The trip turned out to be the perfect segue between a year of zero-waste life and the period of "where do we go from here?" that followed.

Olympic National Park may be most famous (infamous?) for its role in the *Twilight* series, which takes place in the nearby community of Forks, though the teen vampire books don't do the park justice. Previously I had only ever set foot inside the park for a quick overnight camping trip—one that ended rather badly, after it poured rain so hard that we woke up in the early morning hours to find our belongings floating in the tent.

This time we had nearly two weeks to explore the rugged terrain of this lush temperate rainforest. We had planned two short backpacking trips into the wild lands, giving us ample time to steep ourselves in the natural beauty within the park. Olympic is unique among national parks in that it contains miles of the most isolated, desolate coastline I've ever seen, forests so saturated with green they rival Ireland, and pristine alpine meadows filled with grazing deer and roaming bear.

The real reason Adam and I entered into the Green Garbage Project was to do our part to protect the planet's wild places. As we backpacked through Olympic National Park, I felt more immersed in nature than I've ever felt before, namely because there were days when we didn't even see other humans.

I remember a moment when I felt particularly awestruck and frightened by the wilderness we were trekking through. We had decided to hike a stretch of the coastline that required a certain amount of skill—boulder-scrambling, squirming through kelp two feet thick, and dodging over and under fallen logs. Soon we had left behind the backcountry camp we had slept in, and all sights and sounds of people were gone. As if we were entering a temple—a

OOZING TRASH

Our trip to the Oregon Caves National Monument, a network of some of the only marble caves in the world, underscored the fact that trash is every-where. Visitors can enter the caves only with a tour guide, so we cooled our heels in the gift shop while waiting our turn. It wasn't long before I found an interesting display and called everybody over.

It was a Plexiglas box, about the size of dresser drawer, filled with trash. The interpretive sign above the box asked, "What is in your pockets?" Inside the box, we could see a Starburst wrapper, an empty paper coffee cup, a zip-locking bag, a juice bottle, and a string cheese wrapper. All were bits and pieces of trash visitors had—accidentally or purposefully—dropped inside the caves. The sign warned, "Oregon Caves has so many cracks and crevices that it can be quite hard and sometimes impossible to retrieve items acciden-tally dropped." Visitors are asked to "help keep the caves clean and healthy by removing lint, wrappers, extra pieces of paper, and other unneeded items from pockets" before entering the cave. I made Adam take a picture, and we threw our pocket lint into the nearest trash can, as there was no Green Garbage Project shoebox in sight.

The implications of this simple display are astounding. Our trash addiction is so severe that we literally walk around oozing trash. We are like Pigpen's character from *Peanuts*, except instead of a dirt cloud, we leave a cloud of trash in our wake. We stuff our pockets and bags and lives so full of trash that it just falls out as we walk around. We litter even when we don't mean to.

Inside the caves, we found an otherworldly environment that appeared pristine and untouched by humans, even though we knew otherwise. It was so cold inside the marble cave that we needed jackets. The eerie quiet was interrupted only by the steady dripping of water all around us. In places the caves narrowed into tight tunnels, forcing us to bend over and shimmy between the tight walls. Farther in we found ourselves in cavernous rooms the size of mansions, our whispers echoing behind us as we moved on. As we toured the caves, I kept looking for trash. I never did see any, though I must assume this was because some hapless bat had flown off with the lat-est candy bar wrapper left lying on the stone floor.

sacred space—we fell silent and allowed nature to wash over us. The ocean roared in our ears, and as we rounded a headland at low tide, we startled a coyote eating a fresh kill. A bald eagle that had been waiting nearby for its turn at the carcass took flight. The eeriness of the moment rolled over us as we realized we had forfeited any control we had to the power of nature.

Yet a little further down the beach, we came upon a disheartening sight— an old tire washed ashore, left to stagnate on the beach for eons into the future. Even here, in the dominion of nature, was evidence of humankind's trash addiction. Couldn't we escape this waste anywhere?

Sadly the answer was a resounding no.

The worst thing was, this moment of finding trash—a giant tire, no less— carelessly left behind in a wilderness area wasn't an isolated incident. Every single time we went into the wilderness during our garbage-free year, we found the same thing. Trash was—is—everywhere, even in nature's most pristine wild spaces.

In fact, ironically, the first real piece of trash we made in a year was a direct result of our backpacking trip. That's right: after a year of zero waste, while on a vacation to appreciate the very nature we are living trash free for, we bought a sponge. Yep, a sponge.

I know what you're thinking, because I thought it, too. In fact, I wanted to laugh like a loon in the cleaning aisle of the grocery store. Of all the things we'd done without, of all the things we'd missed, the first trashy thing we bought was a sponge in a plastic wrapper. Why in the world?

As it turns out, we'd forgotten to pack a sponge in our backpacks. Because we were traveling in bear country, where it's important to thoroughly wash away any traces of food, a sponge became a necessity, so we bought this one in a pinch. I don't regret it, because this one small purchase helped give us the chance to immerse ourselves in the beauty of nature.

Returning to the "real world" after a garbage-free year has been filled with similar moments of give-and-take. After a successful first year, we decided to shift the focus of our zero-waste project toward finding long-term, rather than short-term, solutions to our garbage dilemmas. During our first year, we just avoided anything packaged in garbage. Although we never felt deprived, we did miss out on some iconic American cultural experiences—like popsicles on the Fourth of July and Girl Scout cookies in February. We also put off a number of home improvement projects because we had yet to figure out how to do the repair work necessary without making garbage. Doing without some things or avoiding projects altogether are temporary, rather than permanent, zero-waste solutions. We decided to work toward adopting more changes we were comfortable making permanently, rather than just for a year.

During our first garbage-free year, we certainly struggled to find zero-waste versions of some everyday items we wanted or needed on a regular basis. I've mentioned junk food as problematic, though we did find ways to make our own healthier versions of sweet or salty treats. In the end, there were a number of other items that we struggled to find viable alternatives for, including dry pet food, specialty holiday foods, pet treats, toothpaste, and cheese.

I've come to recognize, as I'm sure you have, that it is not possible to buy every little thing you need without creating garbage. To that end, we've decided to allow ourselves one luxury item apiece each week. I get one, Adam gets one, and our pets get one. After a year of absolutely no splurges, this feels extravagant, though we usually create only three pieces of garbage a week.

When we do bring a luxury item into the house, we also continue to search for zero-waste alternatives. I've succeeded in finding a number of creative ways around garbage-y products. Most often I find the best way around a garbage-causing culprit is to figure out a way to make it from raw ingredients. My most notable successes to date have been sour cream, ricotta cheese, and bagels (see chapter 6 for the recipes).

The point is that, after much consideration, we've decided to make our zero-waste commitment permanent because we are as committed today as we were three years ago to doing our part to clean up the environment.

Throughout this book, I've mainly used the word *trash* as a noun, signifying a pile of unwanted junk that is headed to the nearest landfill. It's interesting to note that *trash* can also be used as a verb, as in "We are trashing our planet."

I really believe that's what we're doing to Mother Earth, and it's the reason I dreamed up this project in the first place. It can be disheartening to look around the planet and see or hear news of environmental destruction. It's everywhere. We're poisoning our water supply, polluting the skies, littering the ground, overfishing our oceans, all so we can have exactly what we want when we want it—pears from Chile in June, a long weekend in Cancun, sparkling water from a pristine spring in France.

Sometimes I get angry at my fellow humans because it can seem like too many of us don't care about this planet we live on. We can seem awfully selfish or lazy. Once I wrote the following on my blog:

> Dish soap has long been a pet peeve of mine, and it's a tiny example that encapsulates my entire frustration. Here's the scenario: You go to the grocery store because you're out of dish soap. You want a soap that costs a reasonable price, that smells good, and that cleans well. Why is it that when a majority of people get to the dish soap aisle, they buy a brand-name soap that contains phosphates, chemicals, and heavy fragrances when the green variety, which doesn't, costs the same amount, cleans just as well, and smells nice, too?
>
> There is no reason not to make this switch—not cost, not effectiveness, not smell, not hand-softness, nothing. So why aren't all the other brands out of business by now? Of course, it boils down to product loyalty and advertising budget, but that's just plain stupid. It shouldn't take an act of government to get chemicals out of our dish soap when we know they are bad for ourselves and the planet. Phosophates, which are found in dishwasher detergent, help soften water so it suds better and suspend food particles so they do not stick to dishes. Yet, phosphates, once they are washed down the drain, pose a threat to our waterways. They stimulate algae growth in lakes and rivers, which suffocates plants and fish. We as consumers should be making this happen.

I still believe this, and I still get disheartened sometimes. Yet during the past three years I have met amazing people doing truly amazing things for the environment. Most of these people volunteer their time, asking for and receiving no recognition. Some walk on the beach each day, picking up trash. Others work tirelessly to rescue and rehabilitate animals harmed by oil spills or litter. Several of my blogging colleagues live without using plastic, a feat I find incredible even after living trash free. Still others are average, ordinary men and women who lead busy lives and still find time to do the little things that count—recycle what they can, buy organic fruits and vegetables, shop locally, and bring their tote bags to the grocery store.

These people—you—give me hope. I have to believe that a single person can change the world through a series of small, seemingly insignificant actions. I shared with you early in the book how my decision to become a vegetarian influenced many other families to support the vegetarian lifestyle.

The zero-waste lifestyle is like that. This book you're holding in your hands is also the ability to start a movement. You've already taken the step to live with less trash. Please share this message with other people. There's no need to impose your lifestyle choices on them—simply make others aware of what you're doing. Create a blog or a Facebook page and then get in touch with me. I'll share your efforts with an already-growing network of like-minded people who believe in the power of small changes.

Before the end of our third zero-waste month, I was feeling particularly discouraged about the state of the world. Seeking the solace of nature, I found myself again trekking through the wilderness near dusk. Adam and I, along with my parents, decided to hike up to a fire lookout on Mount Rainier, hoping to see mountain goats. We were already chasing the daylight, and we weren't even halfway through our hike. Our return trip would be in the dark, by flashlight.

We lucked out when we spied a herd of goats in the distance. We passed the cameras and binoculars around, elated at a rare wildlife sighting. Though we had seen what we came to see, we boulder-scrambled the rest of the way up to the fire lookout tower and sat down for dinner.

I let out a sigh and relaxed like I can only when I'm surrounded by nature. We perched on a rocky ledge overlooking a green field. It could have been a scene out of *Heidi*, what with the goats and the high alpine meadow, except that when a breeze rustled through the trees, a candy bar wrapper came rustling up next to my feet.

What? Seeing garbage in the wilderness is like seeing someone pee in a public fountain—shocking and disgusting enough to shake you out of any reverie.

All hikers and backpackers are supposed to abide by the Leave No Trace principles. I spent a summer teaching these principles to middle-school day campers; we're not talking rocket science here. The Leave No Trace program says that you leave the wilderness exactly as you found it—you leave no trace of having been there. There are seven LNT principles, which include "dispose of waste properly," "respect wildlife," and "be considerate of other visitors."

Any time I find garbage in the wilderness, it's a violation of not only "dispose of waste properly" but also the "be considerate of other visitors" principle. Why? Because any time we head into the wilderness, we do so based on a wishful premise we all hold in common—namely, the idea that we are treading on untouched nature. Oh, logically we know we're not the first nor will we be the last to walk here, but we are allowed this act of self-deception. I head into the wilderness to forget about civilization, and when a candy bar wrapper comes scuttling across my path, my fantasy that I'm alone out here with just land and sky for company is rudely interrupted.

Am I not even allowed my daydreams anymore because we are such litterbugs?

There are people who find our attempts at trash-free living a bit of a joke or a waste of time. There are people who can't be bothered to recycle anything, because they don't see the point. Here's the point: if for no other reason than that your mother taught you to, you should pick up after yourself. I clean up the environment for the same reason I make the bed or do the dishes each night—I want to keep my home clean because I take pride in it. The earth is home to all of us, and we don't have the right to trash it out. I want to be proud of my home, not ashamed to show others what a mess we've made.

Maybe that simple reason explains why we started the Green Garbage Project in the first place—to leave the world a little cleaner than we found it.

Get in touch with me by visiting my blog at www.greengarbageproject .com or emailing me at amy@greengarbageproject.com.

An A-to-Z Guide to Recycling (Just About) Anything

Backpacks: Donate to the American Birding Association, aba.org/bex/items.

Batteries: Rechargeable battery recycling locations can be found at call2recycle.org/faqs. For single-use batteries, recycling options are more limited; these can be found at earth911.com.

Blue jeans and other denim: If you have denim scraps lying around that are too worn to be donated to a thrift store, send them to Cotton from Blue to Green, a nonprofit organization that turns used denim into housing insulation. You'll have to pay for shipping. Find out more and download a shipping label at cottonfrombluetogreen.org/Mail-in-Program.

Bras: Used bras with functioning straps and clasps can be donated to The Bra Recyclers: brarecycling.com.

CDs, DVDs, and jewel cases: The CD Recycling Center of America (cdrecyclingcenter.org) will connect you with the nearest facility that will accept, confidentially destroy, and recycle discs and all related packaging. They ask that you separate materials by category when you ship: the discs in one pile, jewel cases in another.

Cell phones: There are many places that accept cell phones for recycling. The EPA maintains a list at epa.gov/epawaste/partnerships/plugin/cellphone/index.htm, or you can consider donating your phone to a nonprofit like Cell Phones for Soldiers (cellphonesforsoldiers.com), which donates gently used phones to American servicemen and women. A number of domestic violence nonprofits also accept cell phone donations; try the National Coalition of Domestic Violence (ncadv.org/takeaction/DonateaPhone.php).

Compact fluorescent lightbulbs: CFLs contain trace amounts of mercury, so they should not be thrown into the trash. Instead, bring them to a facility that is able to process them safely. For a list, check out epa.gov/cfl/cflrecycling.html#retailers.

Cooking oil: Household cooking oil recycling facilities are popping up all over. Visit earth911.com to find a location near you. If all else fails, talk with local restaurants and see whether you can add your oil to their recycling vats.

Corks: Used wine corks (made of real cork from trees) are important to recycle, because they give a valuable natural resource a second life. Try recork.org for more information. All Whole Foods locations also accept corks for recycling.

Crayons: Donate used crayons to Crazy Crayons, which takes your unwanted colors and turns them into recycled crayons. Check out crazycrayons.com/recycle_program.html for more information.

Crocs: Donate your gently used Crocs to Soles4Souls, an organization that gives shoes to impoverished people worldwide. Learn more at crocscares.com/donate-your-crocs.

Electronics: The National Center for Electronics Recycling is a clearinghouse of information. See the "Recycling Basics" section of the NCER website (electronicsrecycling.org) to find out where to recycle the specific electronics you have on hand.

Eyeglasses: Old prescription eyeglasses and sunglasses (both plastic and metal frames) can be donated to the Lions Club International, to be worn by those who can't afford glasses. For more information, see lionsclubs.org/EN/our-work/sight-programs/eyeglass-recycling/the-need-for-eyeglasses.php.

Formal dresses: Visit donatemydress.org for a directory of locations accepting formal dresses for girls who can't afford their own.

Gift cards: earthworkssystem.com will take all your old wallet waste—any cards made from plastic, including gift cards, library cards, expired licenses, and the like. Fill out the contact form on their site for more information.

Golf balls: Dixon Golf retailers will accept old golf balls for recycling; if you recycle a dozen balls, they'll give you $6 toward a new golf ball purchase. For more information, see dixongolf.com/Recycle/tabid/208/Default.aspx.

Greeting cards: St. Jude's Ranch for Children accepts used greeting cards as part of their Recycled Card Program. The organization is able to recycle the fronts of used greeting cards by detaching them from the original card and gluing them to a new blank card. For more information, see stjudesranch.org/shop/recycled-card-program.

Halloween costumes: Participate in the greenhalloween.org National Costume Swap Day, which puts you in contact with families in your area. Because many Halloween costumes are worn only once, you can save money by trading your gently used costume for a new-to-you one.

Holiday lights: Holidayleds.com opens its incandescent bulb recycling program each fall, encouraging consumers to make the switch to the more energy-efficient LEDs. You will still pay shipping, but you'll also get 25 percent off your purchase of a single LED light purchase. If you'd rather not pay for shipping, try your local Home Depot.

Ink cartridges: Lots of places recycle printer ink cartridges, but the best program I've found is through Staples. Bring your used cartridges to any store location, where Staples will recycle them and give you $2 for every cartridge you return. Learn more at staples.com.

Makeup: Origins retail stores or cosmetic counters will accept all brands of cosmetic packaging for recycling. As a bonus, you'll get a free sample of an Origins product for being a good steward.

Packing peanuts: Don't ever throw away those foam packing peanuts. They can be reused over and over again. Visit loosefillpackaging.com, which has a list of drop-off locations and a "peanut hotline" so you can find a shipping store willing to take those peanuts off your hands.

Pens: Send your empty pens to the Pen Guy, an artist in the San Francisco area who is trying to collect one million pens. He's already covered a car entirely in pens, the Mercedes Pens art car, but he's not stopping there. Check out thepenguy.com or mail your pens to The Pen Guy, PO Box 994, Forestville, CA 95436.

Plastic bottle caps: Recyclable at Whole Foods locations through the Preserve Gimme 5 program.

Plastic number 5: Through the Preserve Gimme 5 program, Whole Foods stores have drop-off boxes for number 5 plastic (like yogurt and margarine tubs).

Produce stickers: Barry "Wildman" Snyder, an artist in Colorado, wants your produce stickers for his artwork (it's neat stuff—check it out!). Simply peel your produce stickers off your fruit and place them sticky-side down on a piece of paper, then mail to Barry "Wildman" Snyder, PO Box 301, Erie, CO 80516. Learn more at stickermanproduceart.wordpress.com.

Rags: A little-known secret is that Goodwill locations will accept rags (cloth items that are no longer wearable). When you drop off your rags, let an employee know your rags are for salvage, not sale.

Scrap metal: Anything that is made completely from metal can be taken to a scrap metal dealer. Try to save up a good-sized load and bring it all in at once. Metal items you may not think of include metal keys, coat hangers, BBQ grills, empty aerosol cans, foil, chains and chain-link fencing, bottle caps, jar lids, and metal nail clippers.

Six-pack rings: Join the Ring Leader Recycling Program in one of two ways. You can either hook up with a local school or group that is already enrolled in the program or start your own collection program. For more information, go to ringleader.com.

Smoke detectors: Smoke detectors contain trace amounts of radioactive material, so they should not be thrown into the trash. Many smoke detector manufacturers participate in take-back programs. To find one near you, type "smoke detectors" into the earth911.com search function.

Sneakers and Livestrong bracelets: Donate your worn-out athletic shoes (and Livestrong bracelets) to Nike's ReUse a Shoe program. Nike takes old sneakers and grinds them up, turning them into a raw material that can be used as a new athletic surface like a track or gym tiles. Find out more at nikereuseashoe.com/get-involved/individual-shoe-recycling.

Ski equipment: You'll have to pay a hefty shipping fee, but the Green Mountain Ski Furniture company will turn your obsolete equipment into decorative furniture. Learn more at recycledskis.com/got_old_skis.

Tyvek envelopes: The Tyvek company (dupont.com) posts the following recycling instructions on its website: "Turn any Tyvek envelope inside out, so the unprinted white surface shows on the outside. Stuff the inside-out Tyvek envelope with other used Tyvek envelopes for recycling."

Trophies: Lamb Awards and Engraving will accept used trophies, medals, and plaques for recycling. You pay shipping, and the company requests that you email them before mailing them equipment. Find more information at lambawards.com/recycle.html

Further Reading

If you would like to discover more about the issues and ideas discussed in the book, I recommend the following:

Books

The Story of Stuff by Annie Leonard (New York: Free Press, 2010)

Garbage Land: On the Secret Trail of Trash by Elizabeth Royte (New York: Bay Back Books, 2006)

Waste and Want: A Social History of Trash by Susan Strasser (New York: Holt Paperbacks, 2000)

Gone Tomorrow: The Hidden Life of Trash by Heather Rogers (New York: The New Press, 2006)

Confessions of an Eco-Sinner by Fred Pearce (Boston: Beacon Press, 2009)

Documentaries

Garbage! The Revolution Starts at Home (Andrew Nisker, garbagerevolution .com)

The Clean Bin Project (cleanbinmovie.com)

Websites/Blogs

Greengarbageproject.com (my blog)

Myplasticfreelife.com

http://noimpactman.typepad.com

Royte.com

Thecrunchychicken.com

Trashfreeliving.blogspot.com (April Luebbert's blog)

Treehugger.com

Zerogarbagechallenge.info (Rose Brown's blog)

Zerowastehome.blogspot.com

Bibliography

"About Green Dot and Europe's Packaging Waste Recovery Efforts," Emergo Europe, greendotcompliance.eu/en/about-green-dot.php.

"About Pro Europe," Pro Europe, http://pro-e.org/About.html.

Atkin, Peter, "Trash Landings: How Airlines and Airports Can Clean Up Their Recycling Programs," Natural Resources Defense Council, 2006, nrdc.org/cities/recycling/airline/airline.pdf.

"European Packaging Waste Directive and Green Dot Consulting," Emergo Europe, emergogroup.com/services/europe/green-dot-consulting.

"Facts about Pollution from Livestock Farms," Natural Resources Defense Council, last modified January 13, 2011, nrdc.org/water/pollution/ffarms.asp.

Heimbuch, Jaymi, "Why Recycling Plastic Bottles Doesn't Help the Problem," *Treehugger*, June 8, 2011, treehugger.com/clean-technology/why-recycling-plastic-bottles-doesnt-help-the-problem-video.html.

Johnson, Ruthanne. "The Deadly Truth About Trash: HSUS Animal Caretakers See Litter's Lethal Danger," *All Animals*, July/August 2009, Humane Society of the United States.

Jordan, Chris, "Midway: Message From the Gyre," Chris Jordan Photographic Arts, chrisjordan.com/gallery/midway/.

"Landfills: Hazardous to the Environment," Zero Waste America, last modified March 14, 2010, zerowasteamerica.org/Landfills.htm.

Leonard, Annie. *The Story of Stuff: How Our Obsession with Stuff Is Trashing the Planet, Our Communities, and Our Health—and a Vision for Change*. New York: Free Press, 2010.

"Methane," Environmental Protection Agency, last modified April 1, 2011, epa.gov/methane.

Miljo, Ardea, "Marine Trash: Litter That Kills," Environmental Protection Agency, last modified November 2001, epa.gov/owow/oceans/debris/toolkit/files/trash_that_kills508.pdf.

Mitchell, Stacy, "Key Studies on Big-Box Business and Independent Business," Institute for Local Self-Reliance, last modified December 22, 2011, ilsr.org/key-studies-walmart-and-bigbox-retail/.

"Municipal Solid Waste Generation, Recycling," Environmental Protection Agency, epa.gov/osw/nonhaz/municipal/pubs/msw_2010_rev_factsheet.pdf.

Pearce, Fred. *Confessions of an Eco-Sinner: Tracking Down the Sources of My Stuff*. Boston: Beacon Press, 2009.

"Plastic Marine Debris: An In-Depth Look," NOAA Marine Debris Program, last modified September 21, 2011, marinedebris.noaa.gov/info/plasticdet.html.

Rathje, William, and Cullen Murphy. *Rubbish: The Archaeology of Garbage*. Tucson: University of Arizona Press, 2001.

"Recycling and Reuse: Packaging Material: European Union Directive," Environmental Protection Agency, last modified April 2007, epa.gov/oswer/international/factsheets/200610-packaging-directives.htm.

Royte, Elizabeth. *Garbage Land: On the Secret Trail of Trash*. New York: Back Bay Books, 2006.

"Sources and Emissions," Environmental Protection Agency, last modified April 18, 2011, epa.gov/outreach/sources.html.

Sutton, Rebecca, "Don't Get Slimed: Skip the Fabric Softener," *Enviroblog*, last modified November 1, 2011, enviroblog.org/2011/11/dont-get-slimed-skip-the-fabric-softener.html.

"TCDD-Dioxin is Listed as 'Known Human Carcinogen,'" National Institutes of Health press release, January 19, 2001, nih.gov/news/pr/jan2001/niehs-19.htm.

Weisman, Alan, "Polymers Are Forever," *Orion Magazine*, May/June 2007, orionmagazine.org/index.php/articles/article/270/.

Whelan, Carolyn, "Blooms Away: The Real Price of Flowers," *Scientific American*, February 12, 2009, scientificamerican.com/article.cfm?id=environmental-price-of-flowers&page=2.

"The Yellow Bin for Recyclables: Option for the Future?," The Green Dot (*Der Grüne Punkt*), www.gruener-punkt.de/en/corporate/sustainability/the-yellow-bin-for-recyclables.html.

"Zero Waste Zone: New Volunteer Information Sheet," Friends of Salem Saturday Market, friendsofsalemsaturdaymarket.files.wordpress.com/2011/05/volunteercheatsheet2011.pdf.

About the Author

Amy Korst lives on the scenic Oregon Coast with her husband and a small zoo of shelter animals. She is the creator of the Green Garbage Project (www.greengarbageproject.com), which has been featured nationally and internationally on CNN, MSNBC, London's *The Guardian*, and *USA Today*. She is a certified master recycler through the City of Salem, and spends most of her spare time reading or writing about environmental issues. When she's not busy teaching high school English, she practices heritage hobbies such as soapmaking, baking, canning, and sewing. Amy can also be found jogging on the beach at sunset most evenings.

Index

A

Advertisements, 173–74
Aerosol cans, 146, 151
Aftershave, 149
Air travel, 187–88
Alima Pure, 144
Animal shelters, donating
    to, 59
Antique stores, 59–60,
    209, 216
Art projects, 56–58, 60
Ashes, 101
Athletic equipment,
    158–59
Audits
    home-waste, 23–31
    workplace-waste, 201
Auto batteries, 20

B

Babies, 175–77
Backpacks, 248
Bagels, 129–30
Bags
    cellophane, 100
    drawstring, 219–20
    garbage, 53, 89
    paper, 53, 100
    plastic, 53, 79–80
    produce, 53, 116
    reusable, 53, 54, 116
Baking soda, 147, 168
Balloons, 101
Bamboo skewers, 100

Bathroom
    tracking waste from,
        23–25
    zero-waste, 132–54
Batteries, 20, 248
Bedroom
    tracking waste from,
        25–26
    zero-waste, 155–61
Berry stains, removing, 160
Bioaccumulation, 17
Birth control, 142–43
Blood stains, removing, 160
Books for Treats, 224–25
Borrowing, 56
Bottle bills, 83, 237–38
Bottle caps, plastic, 77, 251
Bottles
    plastic, 20, 53
    prescription, 138
    spray, 77, 152
Boy Scouts, donating to, 59
Bras, 248
Bread, basic sandwich,
    124–25
Brita water filters, 76
Broken items, 61
Brushes, 152
Bubble wrap, 3
Bulk shopping, 54, 114–15,
    117–21
Burnable materials, 82–83
Business cards, 101
Butcher paper, 101
Butter, 126–27

C

Cabins, 189
CAFOs (Concentrated Animal
    Feeding Operations),
        122–23, 213
Camping, 190
Candy
    canes, 211, 212–13
    packaging for, 220, 222,
        223–24
Cans, 20, 151
Car
    kits, 42–43
    traveling by, 185–86
Cardboard, 79
Cards
    business, 101
    electronic, 208
    greeting, 250
    plastic, 249
Carpets
    cleaning, 165
    deodorizing, 164–65
Cats. *See* Pets
CDs, 248
Celebrations, planning,
    207–8
Cellophane bags, 100
Cell phones, 84, 181, 248
Charitable gifts, 217
Checks, carbon copies of, 77
Cheese
    crackers, 127–28
    ricotta, 126

Chemicals, toxic, 16, 85, 160, 170, 175–76, 245
Children
    donating to organizations for, 59
    zero-waste living with, 171–82
Chocolate
    packaging for, 220
    stains, removing, 160
Chopsticks, 53
Christmas, 226–27
Cleaning, 162–70
Clothing, 100, 101, 155–58, 180–81
Coffee stains, removing, 160
Combs, 152
Commercials, 173–74
Community connections, making, 33–37
Compact fluorescent lightbulbs, 249
Compost, uses for, 99–100
Composting
    bin, 80–81, 91
    city-operated curbside, 91–92
    determining suitability for, 99, 100–101
    fears about, 90
    in a hot pile, 94–96
    lazy, 93–94
    as recycling, 89–90
    travel and, 190
    worm bin, 96–99
Computers. *See* Electronics
Conditioners, 151
Condoms, 100, 142
Condos, 189
Consumerism, 49–51, 173–74
Cooking oil, 249
Corks, 100, 249
Costumes, Halloween, 225, 250
Cotton
    balls, 53, 100
    clothing, 100
    swabs, 100

Crackers, 127–28
Crayons, 84, 249
Crepe paper streamers, 101
Criticism, dealing with, 37–39
Crocs, 249
Cups, paper, 77, 79

D
Dairy products, 122–24
Decorating, 208–10
Denim, 248
Dental appointments, 136
Dental products, 133–36
Deodorant, 77, 145–47
Depilatories, 149
Diapers, 175–76
Difference, making a, 39–40, 246
Dining out, 191–95
Dish soap, 245
Disinfectant spray, 166
Disposable products
    average usage of, 40
    avoiding, 53, 132–33, 205
Diva Cup, 139–41
Dogs. *See* Pets
Donating, 59–60
Downcycling, 65–66, 84
Drains, clogged, 166
Drawstring bags, 219–20
Dresses, formal, 249
Dryer lint, 100, 160
Dryer sheets, 159–60
DVDs, 248

E
Easter, 221–23
E-cards, 208
Egg cartons, 100, 124
Electronics, 181, 238, 249
English muffins, 130
Envelopes, 77, 101, 252
Environmental issues, 5, 14–18, 82–83, 85, 244–45
European Packaging Directive, 236–37

Extended Producer Responsibility (EPR) programs, 235–40
Eyeglasses, 83, 249

F
Fabric softener, 159–60
Family
    members, support of, 21–22
    staying with, 189
    values, defining, 172–74
Fanaticism, avoiding, 22
Feathers, 101
Feminine hygiene, 139–41
Fireworks, 223
Fish food, 101
Floss, 135–36
Flowers, 101, 221
Flower vases, 79
Food
    baby, 177
    bioaccumulation and, 17
    decorating with, 210
    healthier, 5
    for the holidays, 210–13
    as percent of waste, 19, 20
    recipes, 124–31
    shopping for, 106–24
    traveling and, 185–86, 187, 190, 191–95
Food scraps. *See* Composting
Fourth of July, 223
Freecycle, 60–61
Friends
    reactions of, to zero-waste lifestyle, 37–39
    staying with, 189
Friends of Salem Saturday Market (FSSM), 234
Frozen food boxes, 79
Fur, 100
Furniture polish, 166–67

G
Garage sales, 60
Garbage. *See* Trash
Garbage bags, 53, 89
Garbage Project, 15–16

Gas stations, 185
Gift cards, 249
Gifts
    ideas for, 215–17
    packaging and, 214
    receiving, 34
    wrapping, 217–20
Girl Scouts, donating to, 59
Glad Rags, 141
Glass
    cleaning, 167
    recycling, 66, 78, 79,
        81–82
Global warming, 15
Gloves, 53
Goals, setting, 31–32
Golf balls, 250
Goodwill, 157
Green Dot program, 237
Green Garbage Project, 2–3,
    34–35, 241, 247
Greeting cards, 250
Grout, cleaning, 168

H
Hair, 35, 100, 153
    accessories, 152
    care products, 151–52
Halloween, 223–25, 250
Hand wipes, 53
HDPE (high density
    polyethylene), 86
Herb crackers, 127–28
Herbs, 100
Heritage Turkey
    Foundation, 214
Highlighters, 202–3
Hobbies, 180
Holidays
    decorating for, 208–10
    food for, 210–13
    lights, 250
    planning celebration of,
        207–8
    special traditions for,
        220–28
Home-waste audit,
    conducting, 23–31
Hotels, 188

I
Incinerators, 82–83
Independence Day, 223
Ink cartridges, 203–4, 250
Instant gratification,
    combating, 50
Invitations, 208

J
Jack-o'-lanterns, 101
Jeans, 248
Jewel cases, 248
Jordan, Chris, 18

K
Keep America Beautiful,
    239–40
Kitchen
    tracking waste from,
        26–27
    zero-waste, 106–31

L
Landfills, 14–16
Laundry detergent, 159
Laundry room
    tracking waste from,
        29–30
    zero-waste, 159–60
LDPE (low density
    polyethylene), 87
Leachate, 14–15, 16
Leather, 100
Leave No Trace principles,
    246–47
Leaves, 101
Leelyn, Lou, 57–58
Lemon juice, 168
Leonard, Annie, 47
Life cycle, of products,
    47–49
Lightbulbs, 79, 249
Linen spray, 167
Lint brushes, 53
Litter, 5, 17–18, 242, 243,
    246–47
Livestrong bracelets, 251
Local businesses, supporting,
    5, 33–37

Local Harvest, 214
Locks of Love, 153
Loofah sponges, 100, 150
Lou's Upcycles, 57–58
Lunapads, 141
Lunch baggies, 53
Lush.com, 143

M
Makeup, 143–44, 250
Manufacturers, responsibility
    of, 235–40
Marine litter, 17–18
Masking tape, 101
Matches, used, 101
Meat, 34, 99, 102, 122–24,
    212–14
Medical appointments, 136
Medical products, 34, 137–39
Menstrual pads, 139, 141
Mesh produce bags, 53, 116
Metal, recycling, 66, 78,
    79, 251
Methane, 15, 16
Microplastics, 17, 85
Milk cartons, 77
Mirrors, 79
MRFs (Materials Recovery
    Facilities), 65
MSW (municipal solid
    waste), 14, 18–19
Mulch, 99

N
Nail clippings, 100
Napkins, paper, 53, 77, 100
National Costume Swap
    Day, 225
Newspapers, 20, 78, 101
New Year's Eve, 227
Nut shells, 100

O
Obsolete items, 61
Oceans, trash in, 17–18, 85
Office supplies, 202–4
Oils
    cooking, 249
    removing stains of, 160

Olympic National Park,
241–43
Oregon Caves National
Monument, 242
Organizations, with zero-
waste goals, 232–34
Origins.com, 144
Outdoor spaces, tracking
waste from, 28–29
Oven cleaner, 166

P
Packaging
composite materials as, 75
as percent of waste, 20
recycling, 41–42, 77
responsibility of
manufacturers for,
235–40
Paper
bags, 53, 100
butcher, 101
composting, 100–101
cups, 79
egg cartons, 100
napkins, 53, 77, 100
plates, 100
recycling, 65–66, 78, 79
shredded, 77, 101
tablecloths, 101
tissue, 66, 79
towels, 79
waxed, 79, 101
in the workplace, 202
Paper clips, 203
Parkinson's Law of
Garbage, 44
Parties
Halloween, 225
New Year's Eve, 227
at work, 43, 204
Pawn shops, 59–60
Peanuts, packing, 250
Pencils, 203
Pencil shavings, 101, 203
Pens, 53, 202–3, 250
PET/PETE (polyethylene
terephthalate), 86

Pets
food and treats for, 101,
121–22
toys for, 179
waste from, 34–35, 99,
102–3
Pizza boxes, 100
Plane, traveling by, 187–88
Plants, 101, 209–10
Plastic
bags, 53, 79–80
bottle caps, 251
cards, 249
compostable, 77
containers, reheating food
in, 85
recycling, 65–66, 76,
78–80, 84–87, 251
silverware, 53
straws, 53, 77
stretchy, 78–80
trash, 17–18
Plates, paper, 100
POPs (persistent organic
pollutants), 17
Potpourri, 101
PP (polypropylene), 87
Precycling, 49
Prescription bottles, 138
Preserve Gimme 5, 76, 87, 251
Produce bags, 53, 116
Produce stickers, 83, 251
Product stewardship, 236
PS (polystyrene), 87
PVC (polyvinyl chloride), 79,
86–87, 214

R
Raffia, 101
Rags, 251
Rathje, William, 15–16,
44, 92
Rawhide dog chews, 101
Razors, 148
Receipts, 101
Recipes, 124–31
Recycling
commingled, 65, 73–75
composting as, 89–90

determining suitability for,
40–42, 74, 77, 79, 80
guide to, 248–52
of "hand-carry" items, 67,
72, 76
local requirements for, 66,
72–73
plastics, 84–87
process of, 65–66
rates of, 18, 19, 20
setting up system for,
73–84
strategies for, 66–67,
72–73
transportation costs and,
76–77, 78
traveling and, 192–95
waste hierarchy and,
46–47, 64, 66
Reducing, 49, 51–55, 61–63
Resorts, 188
Restaurants, 191–95
Restrooms, public, 185
Reusing, 55–61, 62–63
Rhythm method, 142–43
Ribbon, 218
Ricotta cheese, 126
Rope, 100

S
St. Patrick's Day, 221
Salt, 169
School projects, 180
Schools, donating to, 59
Scrap metal, 251
Shampoos, 151
Shaving, 148–49
Shoes, 158, 251
Shopping
bulk, 54, 114–15, 117–21
for clothes, 156
consumerism and, 49–51
at local businesses, 33–37
master checklist for, 67,
68–71
for meat and dairy,
122–24
researching zero-waste
options for, 106–15

Shopping, *continued*
   reusable containers for,
     115–17
   traveling and, 195–98
Silverware, plastic, 53
Single-serve products, 52, 62
Six-pack rings, 251
Ski equipment, 252
Skin care, 144–45
Smoke detectors, 251
Sneakers, 158, 251
Snyder, Barry "Wildman,"
   83, 251
Soap
   dish, 245
   laundry, 159
   scraps, 101
Soil, enriching, 100
Sour cream, 125–26
Spices, 100
Sponges, 53, 150
Spray bottles, 77, 152
Stain removal, 160
Staples, 203
Sterilization, 143
Sticky notes, 77, 101
Straws, 53, 77
Streamers, crepe paper, 101
String, 100
Styrofoam, 87
Subscription cards, 101
Sunglasses, 249
Swiffer sheets, 77

T
Tablecloths, paper, 101
Tags, 218
Tampons, 100, 139–40
Teenagers, 181
TerraCycle, 58
Thanksgiving, 225
Thrift stores, 59–60, 209
Tires, 19, 20
Tissue paper, 66, 79
Tissues, 53, 100, 150
Toilet paper, 47–49, 100, 150
Tomato stains, removing, 160
Tom's of Maine, 112, 135, 146

Toner cartridges, 203–4
Toothbrushes, 134
Toothpaste, 135
Toothpicks, 100
Towels, paper, 53, 79
Toys, 177, 178–79
Trash
   average amounts of, per
     person, 1, 2, 18, 23,
     30, 40
   composition of, 18–20
   consumption and, 49–50
   from corporate-industrial
     manufacturing, 51
   impact of, 1, 14–18
   in landfills, 14–16
   plastic, 17–18
   ubiquity of, 242, 243,
     246–47
Trash cans, removing, 44–45
Trash-free living. *See* Zero-
   waste lifestyle
Travel
   accommodations, 188–90
   entertainment, 198–99
   food, 185–86, 187, 190,
     191–95
   kits, 42–43
   packing, 199
   planning, 184–85
   shopping, 195–98
   transportation, 185–88
Trophies, 252
Turkey, 214

U
Upcycling, 56–58, 83

V
Vacations. *See* Travel
Vacuum cleaner waste,
   35, 101
Valentine's Day, 220–21
Vermicomposting, 96–99
Video games, 179
Vinegar, 168
Vinyl, 86
Vodka, 169

W
Waste hierarchy, 46–47
Waxing, 148–49
Wet wipes, 177
Whole Foods, 58, 76, 87, 123,
   194, 251
Window panes, 79
Wood
   ashes, 101
   burning, 82–83
   treated, 99
Wool clothing, 101
Workplace
   ground rules for, 35, 201
   kit at, 42–43
   occupational supplies for,
     204–6
   office supplies for, 202–4
   social activities at, 43, 204
   waste audit for, 201
Worm bin composting,
   96–99
Wrapping paper, 101, 217

Y
Yard trimmings, 19, 20
Yogurt, 128–29

Z
Zero Waste Alliance, 230–31
Zero-waste lifestyle
   benefits of, 3–6
   establishing ground rules
     for, 33, 34–35
   examples of, 4, 6–9
   first month of, 32–45
   gathering family support
     for, 21–22
   as global movement,
     230–34, 239–40
   impact of, 39–40
   meaning of, 3
   planning, 23–32
   setting goals for, 31–32